THE CANDIDATE

THE CANDIDATE

FEAR AND LOATHING ON THE CAMPAIGN TRAIL

NOAH RICHLER

DOUBLEDAY CANADA

Doubleday Canada and colophon are registered trademarks of Penguin Random House Canada Limited

Library and Archives Canada Cataloguing in Publication

Richler, Noah, author
   The candidate : fear and loathing on the campaign trail / Noah Richler.

Issued in print and electronic formats.

ISBN 978-0-385-68727-0 (hardback).--ISBN 978-0-385-68728-7 (epub)

   1. Richler, Noah. 2. New Democratic Party. 3. Canada. Parliament—Elections, 2015. 4. Political candidates—Canada—Biography. 5. Political campaigns—Canada. I. Title.

JL193.R52 2016   324.971   C2016-902273-0
                                                 C2016-902274-9

Book design: CS Richardson
Printed and bound in the USA

Published in Canada by Doubleday Canada,
a division of Penguin Random House Canada Limited

www.penguinrandomhouse.ca

10 9 8 7 6 5 4 3 2 1

To the memory of Terry Wall,
to Doug Bell,
and Sarah, of course.

. . .

"Buy the ticket, take the ride."

—Hunter S. Thompson

I didn't run in the October 2015 general election to write about it, but neither did I win the MP's seat I was campaigning for, so here I am back in the old one. To be honest, it took some time to recover from the delightful frenzy and then exhaustion of an electoral campaign and a part of that process was mitigating the worry I had that I'd not write again. For several months the old ways seemed pointless and done. I'm sure that many fellow candidates, no matter the party they were running for, felt similarly redundant after dedicating heart, soul and foot soles to the invigorating hard work of running for office; MPs that lost their seats, all the more so.

And yet the abiding sensation I took away from my brief political adventure was not one of disappointment but of being immensely moved by men and women of all ages and backgrounds giving of their time, resources and money to a cause that was never, in their estimation, without hope. I loved Canada already; the even greater affection for my country that the experience of being a candidate left me with is inextricably mixed up with admiration for all the folk that help make campaigns possible, so many of them strangers and some new friends.

The dates, names and streets of this account belong to a particular campaign fought on behalf of a particular party, but this book is intended neither as a platform for that party nor as a history of a specific election. We have a surfeit of political memoirs by folk operating from on high—prime ministers,

ministers, party leaders—which this book is not. If it is successful, then it will please Canadians across the barriers of belief we erect for a time and remind people of the tremendous and invaluable work that is done come election time by people at the base.

We Canadians are such a lucky bunch. As I have said before, at our best we are aware of our good fortune and do what we can to share it. This book is a part of that enterprise.

December 3, 2015, the House of Commons.

"You're a drug addict!" hollered Chris Alexander across the floor of the House of Commons. "Shame!"

The Conservative critic for public safety was brandishing, high above his head (and hard to come by), a copy of an anthology about fatherhood to which I'd contributed some twenty years earlier.

"Order!" called the Speaker.

Raged Alexander, "How are we to trust a low-rent back alley criminal—a man who harms himself—with the task of keeping Canadians safe?"

The CPC minions, all seventy-four of them, pounded on their desks and jeered and harrumphed.

"Mr. Speaker," I started, making a deliberately half-hearted effort to stand. "May I congratulate our honourable friend for bothering to read when our publishing industry is so out on a limb. If he's billed himself and not the taxpayer for the book, I'd be delighted to sign it."

A thunderous roar of laughter erupted from the NDP benches on both sides of the floor. I sat down and Tom Mulcair, the country's

twenty-third prime minister, winked at me as he rose. I dropped
back into my seat and made a show of checking my government-
issued BlackBerry, this small gesture the finishing touch to my
excellent performance of effortless dismissal. I scrolled through my
inbox: some kid at Ryerson wanted to chat for his end-of-term
paper about the party's landslide win. An ex at the CBC who'd
been adamant that our distant, ill-fated liaison prohibited any
coverage of me during the campaign was, now that I was
comfortably in office, suddenly of the mind that historical
circumstances permitted an interview. A woman in Nigeria
needed help with the $785 million USD in her account and was
offering half the sum if she could deposit it with me, the sweet-
heart. (Delete.) Ezra Levant had obviously been browsing porn
again, some Russian scammer using the URL of his The Rebel
site as a proxy:

> Oops my dearie :-S
>
> I found your pics on instagram. you are pretty boy.
>
> i need cOck right now ! don't tell my hubby.

(Delete.) And—well, that's interesting, the same junk mail had
reached me via the Toronto Star's editor-in-chief, Michael
Cooke. (Delete.) Quickly typed the Ryerson student's name into
Google Images: nice. Cleared my browser and made a note to
have a word with the Hill guys about our firewall. Then I cast
an ear, if only for appearance's sake, to House proceedings,
banging my desk on cue with the rest. Mulcair had completed his
announcement of the return of the long-form census and was on
to the details of the "nation to nation" relationship with
Indigenous peoples, a policy that we'd made a cornerstone of our
campaign and the Liberals a callow attempt to pinch. He'd be
some time yet, opposition having imposed a discipline that was
somewhat wanting in our new prime minister, very pleased with

himself, so I took the opportunity to email my assistant, Ethan Farquharson, the political science grad who'd worked so hard on my campaign:

> Say yes to the kid from Ryerson but tell those CBC fucks at Power & Politics *thanks for nothing and they can wait.*

Whoops! Thought better of it, the litany of my wife's admonishments coming to mind. I wrote, instead:

> Hi Ethan
> Say yes to the Ryerson student and tell Power & Politics I'd be thrilled and that we'll work out some convenient times when I'm back at the office. Give my best to Rosemary Barton and tell her I think she's doing splendidly and what a treat it is to be invited to join her panel. Our new government is committed to transparency and the CBC's hard work is essential to the task.

Then I pulled out the iPhone I kept for personal business and texted home to say I'd booked a flight for Thursday evening and, punctuality of Porter permitting, a table for two at F'Amelia under the name of "Lifeline Syria," the better for anonymity and handy for expense claims afterwards. As my attention drifted back to business, Mulcair belittling the opposition with aplomb, I noticed the Conservative rookie member from somewhere out on the prairie was still staring at me as she'd done for most of Question Period and I wondered at what point this might constitute a flirt. Alexander, seething in the seat next to her, was, I thought, a very strange man and not at all attractive when he was pissed. The blond hair across the brow, so Teutonic, had always made me feel uneasy. I looked up from the floor and saw that Carolyn Bennett, now a consultant with Turtle Island Fracking, was taking notes in the Gallery and looking especially sour, lips tightly pursed. Even *from this distance I could see she was gripping her eagle feather quill so tightly that she was fraying the barbs.*

I waved. Gave her the thumbs up. She frowned some more, put her head down, and a text from her popped up on my BlackBerry:

"Miigwetch, boy wonder. You're a traitor to your class. See you in 2019 or before."

Okay. So none of this happened. Not a bit of it. But the candidate's a liar who pretends he does no such looking forward.

"WILL YOU

CHAPTER ONE

N AGAIN?"

Most of the time, I think back to May 7, 2015, as the start of it all.

Justice Myra Bielby had granted bail to Omar Khadr, who'd been found guilty of throwing the grenade that killed U.S. Sergeant First Class Christopher Speer during the 2002 fire-fight of which he was the lone Afghan survivor. Fifteen years old at the time, Khadr had been pulled from the rubble with a volleyball-sized hole in his chest. It had all seemed outrageous and absurd—to have charged a child, to have considered the act of self-defence in battle a crime, to have passed judgment about the terrifying intensity of such a scene. Now Khadr was twenty-nine and about to have his first taste of freedom after the thir-teen years of incarceration, in both Guantanamo and Canada, that followed his dubious conviction as a terrorist by a U.S. military tribunal with which not just Stephen Harper's Conservative government but also Paul Martin's Liberals had been in cahoots.

On the steps of the Edmonton courthouse, Khadr's Scottish-born lawyer, Dennis Edney, addressed a scrum of reporters.

"My view is very clear: Mr. Harper's a bigot. Mr. Harper doesn't like Muslims," said Edney. "He wants to show he's tough on crime and who does he pick on? A fifteen-year-old boy who's been put through hell in Guantanamo. We left a Canadian child in Guantanamo Bay to suffer torture and we, Canada, participated in this torture. So today's a wonderful day for justice."

The moment was, for anyone clinging to progressive ideas of Canada so long in abeyance it was not certain they still held, riveting. It felt like the Canadian equivalent of another that brought at least a moral end to the Senate Permanent Subcommittee on Investigations' communist witch hunt, when, on June 9, 1954, Joseph N. Welch asked Senator Joseph McCarthy, "Have you no sense of decency, sir?"

I waited, as I'm sure many others were doing, for blowback from the "Harper Government" (as the prime minister had ordered it be called). But there was none. Harper did not sue, Edney remained vocal and Khadr, who'd proved so appealing in what must have been a terribly difficult first encounter with the media, remained free.

The silence was telling; it said *enough is enough.* There was a welling, and I felt a part of it. I'd been feeling, as a former Yugoslavian might, that the country in which I'd been raised did not exist anymore, but realized, during this late stage of Khadr's odyssey, this was not the case. My Canada was not dead, not a fiction to which I'd been writing misguidedly for a decade, but dormant and impatient: impatient for change, impatient to rouse itself. Impatient for a new government.

. . .

But the true beginning came earlier.

I'd been journeying around the idea of a life in Ottawa for a while. I'd intimated—not more than that—to Liberal MP Scott Brison, Green Party leader Elizabeth May and New Democratic Party MPs Craig Scott and Megan Leslie that I was open to running for office or helping with policy. And in the autumn of 2013, I'd arranged to meet Chrystia Freeland, freshly installed as a Liberal MP, for a coffee at Terroni, an Italian restaurant in the east end of her Toronto Centre riding. At the time, the forty-second general election, which law stipulated would happen no later than October 19, 2015, was on the minds of only a few: Ottawa's backroom machinators, media pundits, incumbent MPs, a new slate of candidates already in place and, late to the game, a few vacillators such as myself. I'd been thinking of running, though without any real application, for a couple of years already. What with the steady degradation of Canadian parliamentary democracy under Harper's Conservatives—the omnibus bills, the bullying of bureaucrats, the muzzling of scientists and the contempt shown to so many parts of the franchise—I was feeling with increasing desperation that it was time to pitch in by doing more than writing about the situation.

And yet I'd arranged my chat with Freeland, whom I knew by reputation but had never met, for reasons not entirely clear even to myself. I liked what I knew of Freeland, liked her trajectory—*The Globe and Mail*, the *Financial Times*, Thomson Reuters and a couple of books behind her. We were loosely of the same generation and our social circles intersected on occasion. She knew my sister, Martha, and we had journalist friends in common. But really, I think I wanted to have a word to see if there was more to her than the entitlement to power and clubby self-regard that experience taught me was the characteristic of so many Liberals: MPs and operatives who spoke of theirs as "the natural governing party" in the same off-putting way some journalists describe their newspaper or television or radio platform as the one "of record," or diminish the New Democratic Party's historic contribution to Canadian political evolution as no more than the actions of Parliament's "party of conscience." I deplored these pat phrases and the arrogance they excused. They spoke, even in Canada—a country without an obvious class system (it exists, but typically between the urban and the rural)—to structures of privilege of which I wanted no part.

As Freeland sat down, it occurred to me that, not for the first time, I had booked an appointment with my inner resentment of folk with whom I had a lot more in common than I cared to admit. I did not much like *Plutocrats: The Rise of the New Global Super-Rich and the Fall of Everyone Else*, a book that struck me, despite itself, as an apology for the status quo. One day, I thought, I really must get to the bottom of what may simply be my indisposition to people having made more of their good fortune than perhaps I have done. Or at least I should fathom why I believe that they have, and how it is I have cast myself as the righteous underdog. Me, the anodyne Canadian equivalent of the Saudi Arabian turning to *jihad* after doing so well by the family: wealthy, Oxford-educated and imagining some better idea of the social good—a parody, surely.

Actually, I was surprised that Freeland showed at all. The invite I'd emailed, explaining that I'd voted for the NDP's Linda McQuaig and not her, had hardly been charming but here she was anyway. She smiled. We ordered. Freeland talked about meeting Trudeau and her decision to run for the Liberal Party.

"Justin has the brand," she said.

I felt my hackles rise. Was that, I wondered, a good enough reason to sign up? I told Freeland how, after the 2011 election that had reduced the Liberal Party to thirty-four seats, I'd visited the Parliamentary Dining Room of the House of Commons, in Ottawa, for an article I was writing for the United Kingdom's current affairs weekly, the *New Statesman*, and had watched as Justin Trudeau, who might as well have been wearing his father Pierre's cape, swanned into the room with a gaggle of advisors as if onto the set of a film of which he was the star. I'd introduced myself (we knew of each other) and asked if we might find a few minutes to converse for the piece I was writing. Trudeau, not yet party leader, pointed me towards one of his assistants, a fella who pulled out his BlackBerry and thumb-typed my email address into it before providing me with a cell number at which to call the Papineau MP for the series of interview requests to which neither would respond—until, that is, I'd emailed,

> Justin
>
> You apparently earned a reputation for not behaving like an old-fashioned Liberal, and working the hustings well. So let's get together and have that chat. I've sent several emails and made the calls.
>
> Best
> Noah

One of those calls, maybe the third or fourth, had been a little chippy. Something along the lines of "Justin, you're the third party. I don't even *need* to speak to you." An email from Trudeau arrived the next day, suggesting lunch at the Parliament Pub on Sparks Street, but I'd left Ottawa and it never happened. Some time later, I met a young and attractive blond woman in smart and unimpeachable business attire, who said she was working for him. There was, of course, far more to the person than her looks, but she *did* have the looks and she *did* have the clothing—and appearances, I would soon learn, count for a lot in politics. Some part of me, the resenting part, was irritated by this—hated the immaculate lawyer-cool suaveness of, well, *the brand*. Like a eugenicist's world was upon us.

"You're jealous," said Sarah, my wife. "You resent them for not choosing you."

No, I didn't think so, though I'd been doing a measure of prospecting during my coffee with Freeland, that's for sure. But I knew even then the Liberal Party would not be the fit—that I was turning up my nose at "the brand" as if politics were the province of higher principles and somehow I had claim to these.

. . .

And, besides, I'd already been talking to Craig Scott, the NDP MP who'd succeeded Jack Layton in Toronto—Danforth in 2011. We'd met in the riding in April 2012, when I'd handed over a copy of a book of mine, recently published, as a way of broaching the subject of running. There had been sporadic phone calls over the ensuing months and a failed attempt at dinner with a couple of sitting NDP MPs in the Greater Toronto Area—pokes to gauge whether or not I was serious—before, on a hot day in July 2014, I sat with him, pastry and coffee in hand, on the steps of a small café on Parliament Street in Toronto's Cabbagetown district. We talked about the phenomenon, in Quebec, of the "Orange Crush" that had seen the province turn away from the Bloc Québécois and to the NDP, carrying it to the status of Official Opposition for the first time, and I suggested that the party make a virtue of the extraordinary youth and diversity of its members in the House.

"Take a shot of Harper and the CPC's Nixonian front bench of overweight male white thugs—Fantino, Kenney, Moore, Van Loan—and put another of the NDP's diverse bunch beneath it with the slogan *WE ARE YOU, CANADA*," I said. "And, while you're at it, change the name of the New Democratic Party to the *National* Democratic Party, because you're the only one that is. Look on the upside. You won't need new stationery."

Craig, Nova Scotia–born and not given to histrionics of any kind, simply nodded. Barely. I talked about how it was important to any democracy that not just the "career politician" enters into the fray, and then we discussed, overtly this time, the feasibility of my candidacy either in Nova Scotia, where initially I had been imagining I might run, or in Toronto, as he'd intuited the party would prefer.

"Would you run to lose?" Craig asked.

Well, I thought, he would say that. Craig, damn it, had been my captain on the Oxford University hockey team for the all-important Blues match with Cambridge, thirty years before, when he'd benched me for the first two periods and nearly all of the third before putting me on ice for less than the final minute of a game already lost. The memory was an amusement more than a grudge (I was a lousy player), but I understood the point my friend was making. He'd been through several major life transformations—the Nova Scotian turned Rhodes Scholar at Oxford, the Osgoode Hall professor of law turned art gallery proprietor and now member of Parliament and democratic reform critic for the Official Opposition—and wanted to make sure I grasped the bigger picture; that I understood the magnitude of the life changes that just might occur despite the almost insurmountable odds of victory facing any NDP first-timer.

Since Jack Layton's death, Craig told me, the party had been slipping steadily in the polls.

"Not an issue," I said. "I'd be running so that Canadians would see that a fella whose own family has likely always voted Liberal thinks the NDP is the right choice. I want us to show that ours is more than a two-party system, and there's an alternative to what we've known forever. Real choice is vital to the country. The idea that the NDP is able to lead is a good one across the board."

"So, would you?" Craig asked again.

"Would I what?"

"Run to lose."

"Sure," I said. "Sure. I'll run to lose."

A month later, Thomas Mulcair, the New Democratic Party leader, called me at the house my family keeps on the Digby Neck, in southwestern Nova Scotia. Mulcair and I had met once before, when Craig brought him by the stand in Riverdale Park at which I'd been flipping burgers and steaks for the Canada Day fair of the Chinatown community of nearby Gerrard and Broadview, a bit of holiday volunteering I'd enjoyed doing for a couple of years for Judy Ouk, a businesswoman and tremendous community advocate. Mulcair had been friendly then, and over the telephone was just as congenial. He spoke about the party's plan for fifteen-dollar-a-day child care spaces—a subject I'd not spent much time thinking about as my wife's two daughters were already of university age—but the pitch made sense. The man credited with having brought Quebec so dramatically into the fold sounded impressive and the call was flattering.

"I don't know that I can do this," I said. "I'm worried about raising money—I've never had to do that—but, more so, that my past may get the party in trouble. You see, I was a heroin user in my late teens. Most of all, I don't think my family is behind me."

We talked some more, the NDP leader upbeat all the while and, as I listened, I thought the press really needed to stop resorting to what seemed like the only photograph in their possession, of Mulcair on the floor of the House remonstrating angrily. Mulcair suggested that Sarah and I have dinner with him and his wife, Catherine Pinhas, but I'd made the point of my family's recalcitrance well—likely too well. I did not hear from Mulcair again and in our house the subject of my running was as good as dead.

Then, on October 20, 2014, Warrant Officer Patrice Vincent was run down and murdered in Quebec in what was being described as "a possible terror attack." Two days later, the deranged Michael Zehaf-Bibeau, a petty criminal and drug addict from Montreal, killed Corporal Nathan Cirillo while the reservist was on ceremonial guard duty at the National War Memorial. Zehaf-Bibeau went on to storm Parliament with his rifle, and died in the Hall of Honour after being shot thirty-one times. Ottawa was under lockdown and Sergeant-at-Arms Kevin Vickers, a figure of lethal calm at the scene, became the hero of the moment—though consternation at killing a man seemed writ deeply into his face when, the next day, Parliament accorded him a standing ovation. MPs had tweeted the terrible goings-on and yet despite the hyper-excited, even manic, responses of members of all parties finding themselves at the centre of the maelstrom—and, too, the zealous embrace of the drama by media stimulated by the new and made-at-home nature of the incident—the terrorist element of the narrative did not categorically hold. Many raised the issue of the perpetrator's mental health. This aspect was less inflammatory and therefore less exciting a subject of discussion than the incident being one of "terror," the latter interpretation providing an un-proclaimed dry run for the election slated to occur almost exactly a year afterwards. The major parties' leaders all paid tribute to Corporal Cirillo and Warrant Officer Vincent. Harper described the Ottawa shooting as a "brutal and violent attack on our soil" and Zehaf-Bibeau as a terrorist, no surprise. Mulcair, to his credit, refrained from rushed judgment and called the act "criminal" and "cowardly," referencing the shooter's "attempts to get help, even to be in prison to get help" that, had they substance, meant Ottawa had not been "in the presence of a terrorist act in the sense that we would understand it." Trudeau appeared more impassioned—certainly it was the first time I'd found him convincing—exhorting Canadians not to let "anger and perhaps confusion" win the moment. "Losing ourselves to fear and speculation is the intention of those who commit these heinous acts," said Trudeau. And yet, within the week, Trudeau would side with Harper, describing the shooting as "motivated by political ideology." "The RCMP was clear," said Trudeau on October 29, "these were acts of terrorism."

Less than three months later, after the indubitable terrorist attack on the Paris offices of the magazine *Charlie Hebdo* that killed twelve people on January 7, 2015, Harper made another speech true to form.

"We are looking at additional powers to make sure that our security agencies have the range of tools available to them to identify potential terror threats and to [undertake] detentions and arrests and other actions where necessary," said Harper. "The fact of the matter is this, ladies and gentlemen: the international *jihadist* movement has declared war. They have declared war on anybody who does not think and act exactly as they wish they would think and act. They have declared war and are already executing it on a massive scale on a whole range of countries with which they are in contact."

And yet, despite the gravity of the incidents in Paris and Ottawa, the unceasing Conservative rhetoric felt tired and hollow. The stern admonitions, so trumped up and ominous, were devices the government was repeatedly turning to because these were all they knew how to deploy—"Is it clear people?" tweeted Conservative MP Michelle Rempel during the House of Commons lockdown—but the fear mongering seemed the last tool of an atrophied arsenal. For a decade it had been used by Harper's Conservatives as the barometer of anything and everything of political worth: as a gauge of party loyalty; of *Canadian* loyalty; as a rationale for domestic fossil fuel development; as a grant-deciding measure of the merit of artistic endeavour—even as a litmus test of allegiance and good conduct in business. By the end of the month, the Conservatives would initiate the passage into law of Bill C-51, a highly contentious set of provisions of power for police and security forces that would prompt responses in all the parties' unofficial and then official campaigns—most of all, if not immediately, the NDP's.

On February 2, three days after the government introduced Bill C-51, Green Party leader Elizabeth May said she would oppose it. May pointed out there were already sufficient permissions and safeguards in existing laws to oppose crimes that the bill was designed to quash ham-fistedly, and warned the powers it allotted the Canadian Security Intelligence Service would make of CSIS a "secret police force" and could be "applied to anything." A particular concern was that the proposed laws would be used to curtail demonstrations against pipelines and energy projects by First Nations and environmental "activists" (a term that, under Harper's government, was a softer way of saying "terrorist").

When the bill came up for its second reading on February 18, Mulcair and the NDP followed May's lead. Trudeau, however, prevaricated, speaking of the proposed law's "concrete measures"—such as strengthening the no-fly list, improving coordination between national security agencies and loosening rules around preventative arrest—as steps of which he approved. Trudeau also spoke of the necessity for "oversight and a review process," which his party was committed to bringing in "after the next election" were they not approved by the committee in the interim. But then, on March 4, Trudeau told an assembly of University of British Columbia students his party was planning to support Bill C-51 because he didn't want the Conservatives to "bash people on security" or to make "political hay" of the issue. An overwhelming number of Canadians reacted negatively to what was widely regarded as a weak stance of appeasement and opportunism, and support for the Liberals and their young leader dropped. Progressives were worried another violent incident at home or abroad would shore up Conservative support, but there was significant opposition to Bill C-51's potential curtailing of civil liberties and what Trudeau himself had described as the government's "fear narrative." The store of vaguely focused Canadian anxieties about security, on which Harper's expedient stoking of fear relied, was being exhausted.

. . .

This was encouraging. In an op-ed column for the *Toronto Star* in the wake of the Ottawa attack, I'd challenged the description of Vincent's and Cirillo's murderers as terrorists ("Were they financed? Were they part of a cell? With whom were they in communication?"). I'd written that "the 'heart of our democracy' is to be found in the spirit with which we imbue it—in the fair-mindedness that, not to be confused with 'innocence,' is the result of Canadians' awareness of their good fortune and wanting to share it." The article garnered kudos, enough to keep the idea of running in mind despite my family's being opposed, and occasionally, in its wake, others would ask if I'd ever considered politics, typically no more than a gambit of conversation, but fanning the embers of an idea I'd not quite abandoned. At a downtown Toronto bookstore, I ran into the author John Ralston Saul, whose ideas about Canadian inclusivity, derived from the country's experiences of First Nations, I shared. He was congratulatory about the piece and told me outright to make something more of it. Then, a few weeks later, I found myself at dim sum with a group that included the writer Margaret Atwood. She'd been supportive of my first book, which we both knew to be in a line with *Survival*, her groundbreaking consideration of Canadian literary identity. I said outright I was thinking of running, and now here she was nudging me on again, if cautiously.

"Don't be too clever," said Atwood, leaning in to me close enough that I had no choice but to confront her intent, affixing gaze. "*Keep your message simple.* You use far too many words when you speak. And take a look at Leadnow—do you know what they're doing, Leadnow?"

"Yes," I said. "They're polling ridings and instructing voters which is the candidate most likely to turf the Conservative."

"That's the most important thing," said Atwood. "We have to get Harper out."

APRIL 8

CPC	NDP	LPC	BQ	GRN	OTH
32.3%	21.5%	31.0%	4.8%	7.0%	2.6%

. . .

April 8, 2015, 8:40 a.m.

It used to be that I played squash to stay in shape, but come my late forties the habit was, as much as anything, a way to get out of the house for games in which the banter was more important than the ball. My partner was Doug Bell, author of *Run Over: A Boy, His Mother and An Accident* (Doug had been the unfortunate boy) and subsequently a political blogger for *The Globe and Mail.* He'd covered the 2008 and 2011 federal elections and the better sparring came during the coffees, lunches and drinks post-match. Our talk, however impassioned, was not going to lead to one iota of the country's problems being solved, but that did not stop the flow of outrage, complaint and gossip, the two of us harping on like Statler and Waldorf, the curmudgeonly pair of old men in the balcony of *The Muppet Show*. The previous afternoon, I'd lost as usual. I always lost, unable my whole life to put away the last points of a game, as if there was something gauche about winning. Or I just wasn't good enough and lacked the killer instinct. For someone else to judge.

Now it was morning, and Doug and I were having the usual: the *Toronto Star*, the *National Post* and the CBC's *Metro Morning* with coffee and toast—Sarah mildly entertained, maybe relieved that her stay-at-home fella was not rendered so eccentric by writing that he was entirely without friends. The Toronto Blue Jays' season had started, news of Senator Mike Duffy's trial for corruption was on the papers' front pages, and Doug was repeating the case for my running that he'd made the night before over a couple too many whiskies "for the road." Except there had been no road, only a train that he was not taking, and we'd known already he was staying the night. I was frying bacon and ignoring Doug urging me to think again, or that he was carrying the argument to Sarah, as was his habit: *once more unto the breach*, inevitably to be stonewalled with a "Noah's not suited."

Never assume.

"Okay," said Sarah. "Run. You should. You need to."

. . .

Sarah, the spouse:

Noah wakes up in the morning and before he's even had a coffee he's thought of some way to save the world, some innovation that will revolutionize our lives and make things better. I'm so used to this that mostly I tune out. I'm forever saying, "Great idea, but who will implement it?" Be careful what you ask for.

Over the period of about a year, I took note the idea of running for politics was looming large in his mind. My guy was making more and more comments that indicated to me that he was considering a career change—he was going to be the one to implement. He was serious, and the only thing keeping him from throwing his hat in the ring was my agreement, but I was dead set against it. We already had a busy life, my job was more than full-time running House of Anansi Press and, while it was true that we were empty nesters—both the girls off and following their own paths—we still had pets to care for, and plans to set up a not-for-profit arts centre in Nova Scotia. Also, I truly believed Noah was more effective writing about politics than participating in the game, but he continued to agitate—aided and abetted in this game of persuasion by his major domo, Douglas Bell.

I'm not exactly sure what made me change my mind, but it happened sometime in the winter of 2015. Maybe the two of them just wore me down, though actually I think I came round to the idea that if he felt he could sacrifice his time and income to fight for his idea of a better Canada, then who was I to stand in his way? Why should he not put himself forward? It felt like I was being selfish to hold back my endorsement. So, reluctantly, I agreed.

. . .

April 8, 2015, 9:48 a.m.

Sarah is at work. Doug has departed. I am in my office with three numbers for Tom Mulcair and I try his cellphone first.

"Please stand by while we complete your long-distance call. To avoid this message, please dial one before a ten-digit long-distance number."

I try the number for Mulcair's Ottawa office.

"Votre appêl à été acheminé à un système de traîtement de la voix. Chantale Turgeon, chef de cabinet adjoint au bureau de Thomas Mulcair n'est pas disponible. Au signal veuillez laisser un message."

"Bonjour Chantale, ç'est Noah Richler qui appelle pour Thomas. Hi Tom. I wanted you to know that the discussions about your party and the upcoming elections have been ongoing with my wife and a couple of close friends and I now have the home endorsement that I need to be able to run—if you still think that there's, umm, a possibility of that. That's what I want to talk about, being a candidate of yours—about contesting the *nomination* to be a candidate of yours, I suppose. And I'd like to do it in West Nova. Give us a call when you have a moment. All the best, bye."

April 8, 2015, 9:51 a.m.

I try again.

"Hello," says the speaker at the other end of the line (an actual voice!), "Leader of the Opposition. *Bonjour.*"

"Hello," I say. "Is that Chantale Turgeon?"

"I can transfer you if you like."

"Sure."

"Votre appêl à été acheminé à un système de traîtement de la voix. Chantale Turgeon, chef de cabinet adjoint au bureau de Thomas Mulcair n'est pas disponible. Au signal veuillez laisser un message."

"Salut, Chantale, ç'est Noah Richler qui appelle pour Thomas. J'ai laissé un message sur votre cellulaire. Si ç'est encore d'interêt à monsieur Mulcair, j'aimerai bien lui parler car j'ai maintenant la permission de participer in this very important election that's coming up. I'm taking nothing for granted but perhaps Mr. Mulcair would be kind enough to call me, mon numéro je le laisse. All the best, bye."

April 8, 2015, 9:56 a.m.

I try the leader of the Official Opposition at his constituency office in Outremont, Quebec.

"Bureau de Thomas Mulcair, hello."

"Hello, is that Chantale?"

"No. C'est Miriam."

"Okay. Miriam. Hi. Monsieur Mulcair me connâit. On a parlé, il y'a peut-être six mois, au sujet des elections qui approchent and I wanted to tell him that after a long discussion with my wife, I have the go-ahead. So, umm, he may not want me anymore but perhaps he'd be kind enough to give me a call, or, maybe you can tell me what to do."

"Okay, so what level was he talking about?"

"He was suggesting that I be prime minister—"

"Ahh-ha!"

"Just kidding. No, my name's Noah Richler. I live in Nova Scotia and Toronto and we spoke, as I did with Megan Leslie and Craig Scott, about my seeking the NDP nomination in Toronto or West Nova—which would be the riding of preference."

"Wonderful," said Miriam. "Someone will get back to you. Mr. Mulcair's out of the country at the moment, but possibly whoever's in charge of the campaign will be in touch. They're going to be the ones on the ground knowing what the state of play is."

. . .

That afternoon, James Pratt, the NDP director of organization, called.

"I got a message from the leader indicating that you would like to run for us," said Pratt. It was the first time I had heard his voice and I could sense the big grin he was putting on. I said yes, and told Pratt Sarah had not been keen but had given me the go-ahead at eight-thirty that morning. But, I added, I was worried that whatever authority I might have as a writer would be affected by being visibly partisan, and that the last thing I wanted to do was get the party into trouble.

"I have dodgy moments in my past," I said. "I've written about these, though I'm sure they could be worked to my advantage. I was very involved with drugs for a while but am also proof of why one should have a lenient policy."

"It's great to know the negative stuff," said Pratt, explaining that the better part of his job was overseeing the vetting of candidates.

"There isn't a person who doesn't have something potentially hazardous," said Pratt. "Offering yourself up for public office isn't like entering a court of law. It isn't about what's right or wrong—it's not about what's *just*. This is politics, and time and again our opponents will throw whatever they can at us, so you just need to be prepared. Potentially they could say some nasty things."

Pratt told me I needed to join the party—I was not officially a member yet—and that he'd be sending me the candidate's package that prospective nominees need to complete.

"We can't do anything till you're vetted. With authors, these things tend to take a little bit longer."

"For sure."

"In rare instances, and I can't imagine this happening in a million years, the national director, Anne McGrath, says something is just too grave, we can't let it go. That's the process."

"I'm a fairly on-the-record guy," I said, "and in a way I relish some of this stuff coming up because it could serve us well."

"I agree with you," said Pratt. "There's a good story we can tell—you know, *boy done good*. I'd be excited about that."

"And I have two dogs," I said. "That probably works in my favour."

"Sure. People love dogs. Dogs and babies."

I was enjoying the talk. This political life, yet in its infancy, felt like a wide-open avenue.

"So tell me about West Nova," said Pratt. "How much time do you spend there?"

"Oh, I get out about five times a year," I said. "I've worked on a friend's lobster boat and that's something that would give me a bit of cred. I'm from away, but I don't mind that either. It's not like I'd be facing a guy who's really entrenched. The Conservative, Greg Kerr, is no great shakes—and wasn't it a Liberal riding before Kerr won it?"

"It was."

"So the riding is shaped like a tuning fork and if I did run there, I'd like to walk, not take a car, from the very southwestern tip of Brier Island to Digby, up a bit into the Annapolis Valley, and then back down the French Shore along the other side of St. Mary's Bay to Yarmouth. I'd visit every house in the riding along the way."

"Okayyy," said Pratt, like he was talking to a kid in nursery school proclaiming he was going to be an astronaut, and as the teacher his job was to nurture impossible dreams that life would crush soon enough. "While being a little hokey, your dream of walking the riding is the sort of thing that plays and I'm not opposed. Visiting every house is certainly how you win."

"Nova Scotia is a place where the old ways still matter," I said.

"I'm assuming you've looked at the results?"

"Has the NDP ever won it?"

"No."

"Well," I said, "when Craig Scott spoke to me, he was suggesting I should be prepared to run in Toronto 'to lose.' I'm very happy to do that as well. I mean the real reason I'd run is to get certain ideas across, if that's allowed. We'd all love to win, but that may be less important than having someone come out and say, 'Look, this is the party of principle.' It's shocking to me, as it must be to you guys, to pick up a paper in which some mandarin has written a piece in which the Liberals are placed ahead of the

NDP in the text as if it's their choice and not the NDP's to cooperate. It's so ingrained, this idea that there are only two options. I'd like to do something about that."

"It's frustrating to me on a daily basis," said Pratt, "and if you were to announce that you were to run for us it would be a sign of momentum and generate some media. As for where you run, what is most important is that you are comfortable—and I hear you, that stuff in West Nova all sounds good."

"Thank you."

"But for what Craig mentioned to you, I'd have put it a little differently. Toronto is a battleground—it's *the* battleground for us. If you were to run in Toronto, certainly we would have more attention, and if we hold our seats in the GTA and pick up a couple more, then my gut says that something would be happening across the country. If I can't hold those seats, then that will have ramifications as well."

"Got it."

"Now these are tough seats—as tough as West Nova."

"If I run in Toronto my identity in Nova Scotia is left alone and there's something to be said for that. But look, I'm offering myself up to you guys. If you want me to run in Calgary, I'll run in Calgary."

Pratt laughed.

"I don't think we have to decide this today, but just to finish my thought, there is a riding that's not held by us, though it was until very recently, and that's Olivia Chow's old riding."

"Spadina—Fort York?"

"Just wanted to put it in your head."

"Listen, I have plans to be in Nova Scotia for a bit of August. Is that an issue?"

"No. I don't believe the campaign will be in full force until September. Great to talk to you, Noah. We'll be in touch."

Pratt emailed the link to the candidate's package. "I'll work on keeping a couple of seats warm for you," said the note.

The conversation had been invigorating—who doesn't want to feel sought out—but the path ahead felt like a one-way street with no possibility of a U-turn, and in truth I was still uncertain about running. But Luminato Festival, where I was literary curator, was in high production mode, and I had plenty of other work to do. I would use the time as a last opportunity to take stock.

APRIL 29

CPC	NDP	LPC	BQ	GRN	OTH
32.6%	22.9%	30.3%	4.5%	7.6%	2.2%

· · ·

A month passed before I heard from the party again, enough time to wonder if the vetting was going badly. Then, on May 4, Pratt called with a view to meeting. The next day, Rachel Notley led Alberta's NDP to a historic win, ending the nearly forty-four-year run of the province's Progressive Conservative Party—the longest-serving government in Canadian history.

"We are bouncing off the walls," emailed Pratt. "This could be a real game changer."

NDP supporters across the country were giddy with the victory of the "Notley Crew," though the elated sense that such a triumph might be duplicated nationally left me wary. In Ontario, what with the party's blemished history at both the federal and provincial tiers of government (though because of former premier Bob Rae's financial blunders more than Andrea Horwath's failed 2014 campaign)—not to mention the province's tendency to want to leave its own mark and cut "tall poppy" pretenders down to size—such misgivings were especially warranted. But Pratt was not so distracted that he did not have the good sense to suggest other parties would be scouring my posts on social media for stuff that could be used against me—"oppo research," it's called in the trade. "I'll follow you on Twitter now," he wrote. "We will vet you but you should be taking down anything that you think may be a bit controversial." We arranged to meet in Toronto on the Thursday, outside the Artscape building on Shaw Street, where Luminato Festival of Arts & Creativity has its offices.

. . .

The afternoon of May 7 was sunny and hot and I was thrilled with the news of Khadr's bail when I stepped out to meet Pratt, who was waiting in front of the Penny Café across the street and so obviously a political operative. There was something theatrical but also marvellously incongruous about the man pacing in front of the corner store's street-side trays of farm-fresh asparagus and strawberries. The pallid skin, white beard and head of thick hair pushed back (white, though he was certainly younger than me), the dark suit ill-chosen for the temperature, the collar of his white shirt unbuttoned and the frown of consternation as he spoke into his BlackBerry: here was a man who'd traded in salubrious sunlight for the sake of his political ambitions.

We bought coffees and sat by the window as well-to-do children and their young moms with state-of-the-art strollers and the latest running gear came into the store to buy sweets and kale salads. When did walking kids become a competitive sport, I wondered.

Again I pushed the possibility of running in West Nova. "I think I could get Antonine Maillet to support me," I said. In the tight-knit Acadian community along Nova Scotia's French

Shore—united by a lively oral tradition, summer festivals and the interrelationships of perhaps sixty founding families—it was not a stretch to imagine that the endorsement of the great writer, whose leonine character I greatly admired, would make a difference.

Pratt shrugged. I'm not sure he knew who Maillet was, but it wasn't important.

"We want you to run in Spadina—Fort York, where Adam Vaughan is. We need an attack dog like you in there. He's got money and resources and we need the Liberals to have to spend those resources in the riding."

"I don't know if that's me."

"West Nova has nothing. But if you run in Spadina—Fort York, we've a significant amount of money and a crew of good volunteers ready to go. It's not even about winning. If we lift just a few points, it could mean thirty seats. Get the forms in. That's the most important thing."

MAY 20

CPC	NDP	LPC	BQ	GRN	OTH
32.0%	24.3%	30.3%	4.1%	7.1%	2.2%

. . .

Still I was slow to commit, and Sarah aghast that I might have to run against Vaughan, who was regarded as having run a particularly nasty campaign against the NDP candidate Joe Cressy in the 2014 by-election following Olivia Chow's resignation (so that she could run for the Toronto mayoralty). Sarah and I absconded to Nova Scotia for a week, and on May 23, the Saturday of our return, I'd arranged for us to meet Megan Leslie at Il Mercato, an Italian restaurant at the Sunnyside Mall in Bedford, en route to

Halifax Stanfield International Airport. I'd first met the NDP's charismatic member for Halifax at the Writers' Trust Politics and the Pen dinner in Ottawa in March 2013, when Mulcair had been the politician assigned to my table at the gala at which I was a nominee. The NDP leader had not lingered—the House was in session at the time and MPs typically arrive late or leave early during the evening—and it ended up being Leslie with whom I'd chatted afterwards at Zoe's, the bar of the Château Laurier raucous with heavily drinking journalists and politicians by night's end. Leslie, liked across the spectrum of political parties and media (in a fashion I figured I'd never be), struck me as smart, vivacious and savvy. After that first encounter, she wrote:

> Don't worry about disappointing anyone. This is a personal decision, it takes a lot of thought, and the decision is ultimately yours, either way. I've listened to people going through this process that have ended up with such a range of final outcomes! But in the ruminating, it can be helpful to bounce ideas off of someone.

We'd talked again at the same gala the following year—Leslie's turn, this time, to host the evening, with the Conservative minister of transport, Lisa Raitt. But it wasn't until our meeting at Il Mercato that we managed to speak at all substantially, Leslie interrupting a day of events in the riding to do so. Busy days and the compulsory attendance at umpteen local functions were other factors I would need to consider—I, who had always enjoyed working at home and alone—but I spoke to her instead of my more general anxiety. She told me I was right to be nervous and, performing in the House, she was still; I told her how compelling I had found the experience of listening to the party's 2012 leadership contest that, in the wake of the former leader Jack Layton's death from cancer, Mulcair eventually won. That campaign had been criticized for being protracted, but I'd found it fascinating and impressive, replete with the voices of contenders from B.C., Ontario, Quebec and the Atlantic provinces. The NDP, I said, possessed a pan-Canadian pedigree none of the other parties could match. I told her just how capable she seemed as the NDP's deputy leader, said I'd admired her work as the NDP's environment critic and suggested she might try for the top job one day—it was certainly time for a woman to have it.

"I can't," said Leslie.

"Why not?"

"Because there are better and worse places in Canada and I think New Brunswick's a useless province."

I could see from the Trickster smile that Leslie was having a tease and we talked more specifically about my running in West Nova.

"Don't," said Leslie. "I'd be thrilled to have you for a colleague here, but the NDP here killed the Yarmouth Ferry and the situation is such a mess that I don't think you'd win in West Nova."

We discussed the "McGill Four"—the students Charmaine Borg, Matthew Dubé, Mylène Freeman and Laurin Liu, all in their early twenties when they'd been elected—and I said how much I'd been impressed by Ruth Ellen Brosseau, nicknamed the "Phantom Politician" and, more cruelly, "Vegas Girl" by national media because the hard-working single mom travelled to the Nevada city to celebrate her birthday during the 2011 campaign she'd never expected to win. When I'd met Brosseau for my *New Statesman* piece about the 2011 election and the NDP's astonishing rise, I told Leslie, she'd seemed shy but extraordinarily resolute.

"She's a great MP," said Leslie. "If the tsunami comes and we're wiped out, Ruth Ellen will be the one left standing."

. . .

The next day I sent the completed Prospective Candidate Information Package to Pratt with a cornucopia of my published material I figured needed to be scrutinized. Among the many inclusions was "How Stephen Harper is using paranoia to win in 2015," an article for the *New Statesman* that had been printed only the week before. In it, I'd suggested that should sufficient Conservatives and Québécois *souveraintistes* behave as an unlikely alliance of Christian, Jewish and Muslim religious leaders had done in Jerusalem a decade before—homophobes united across the usually antipathetic triad of faiths in their fulmination against the prospect of a Gay Pride parade planned for the city—then the 2015 election would likely go Harper's way. I'd also included "Canada and its Peacekeepers," a piece of satirical fiction I'd contributed to *Canada in 2020*, an anthology of speculative political essays edited by Rudyard Griffiths, co-founder of the Dominion Institute (the Canadian think tank that would later merge with the Historica Foundation to become Historica Canada) and afterwards the mastermind of the Munk Debates and Chair of the Aurea Foundation backing it. In the piece, a Métis MP rises to become prime minister after recordings of a party thrown by an Albertan petroleum company reveal the scandal of a Conservative minister of defence delighted at the occurrence of a terrorist attack on Canadian soil because of the political advantage he imagines his party will accrue as a result. A real-life reiteration of this dark assessment would—*mea culpa*—get me in trouble soon enough, as would a couple of tweets espousing positions concerning Quebec nationalism in the *New Statesman* article I'd submitted. However, at the time I was not so much oblivious to the political toxicity of these ideas as I was overestimating the rigour of NDP scrutineers and the time they had on their hands to vet yet another prospective candidate. I actually felt a little guilty about all the stuff they'd have to pore through and didn't want to pile it on.

"I have not deleted my Facebook or Twitter accounts," I wrote, saying that I would do so "either partially or completely after you and your team have perused my occasional moments of pissed-offedness."

A week later I emailed to ask just how much longer the vetting process was going to take—if I was going to run there was a lot of work to be done in a very short time—and asked what I should be doing in the meantime. But when Pratt returned the call, it was to tell me that there was a "possible complication": Olivia Chow was contemplating another go at the Spadina—Fort York seat previously hers. Chow's candidacy appeared to me to be of dubious benefit, but I was not yet a player and it was not my place to pass judgment. Clearly the party thought her return to the fold a coup.

"Is there another Toronto riding that's open?" I asked.

Pratt was silent for a moment.

"Well," he said, "there's Toronto—St. Paul's."

"Fine," I said. "I'll run there."

"Really?"

Toronto—St. Paul's was a fat wedge of a riding that might be thought of as the keystone of the city. Just north of downtown, it houses some of the city's most prosperous neighbourhoods: Cedarvale, Forest Hill, Poplar Plains, Rathnelly and Wychwood, as well as parts of Leaside and Summerhill. It is also home to a plethora of "middle-class" streets, though its working-class districts were inevitably being gentrified. The riding was well connected by public transport soon to be augmented by the Eglinton Crosstown LRT line, a work-in-progress that will fundamentally alter the character of "Little Jamaica," the poor neighbourhood in the northwest corner of the riding populated in large part by Caribbean Canadians who arrived in the sixties when Pierre Elliott Trudeau was prime minister. At least here, as well as between the diagonally travelling Vaughan Road and the western limits of the riding along north–south axes of Dufferin, Winona Drive and Ossington Avenue, was a fair amount of community housing and an NDP-inclined core.

But Toronto—St. Paul's had never elected a federal NDP MP. The riding was reconfigured for the provincial election in 1999 and was marginally adjusted again for the 2015 federal election. A previous incarnation of a part of the electoral district—the provincial riding of St. Andrew—St. Patrick, did elect an NDP member in 1990 for one term but, then having incorporated more densely populated lower and middle-class portions of the Annex, Kensington Market and Spadina Avenue neighbourhoods, its demographics were so different as to bear little meaningful resemblance. The previous federal NDP candidate in Toronto—St. Paul's, the twenty-three-year-old Ryerson University graduate William Molls, polled 22.6 percent of the vote, a historical high. But the seat had been Liberal since 1993, and Carolyn Bennett, the incumbent, had occupied it for eighteen years.

JUNE 12

CPC	NDP	LPC	BQ	GRN	OTH
29.9%	30.4%	26.7%	4.8%	6.4%	1.8%

. . .

A couple more weeks of no contact with HQ followed. The silence was discomfiting, even my friends within the party unable to explain it, but I attributed it to the Alberta NDP victory causing all sorts of pleasant upheavals and a party playing catch-up to the demands of its relative success. Then, on June 14, Craig emailed to ask "How go discussions re running for us?" I mentioned that Chow might be running, to which he replied:

> I have been assuming that, as long as we keep the nomination open until end of summer, she could jump back in.
>
> As for St. Paul's, different folks had expressed interest, I understand, but a) you would be great for it though it would be a bully-pulpit race (and hard to beat Bennett even if Liberals tank further) and b) it would signal NDP seriousness of purpose.
>
> Have you actually submitted papers that are being vetted in the green-light process?

I answered that I had, and decided to needle Pratt a little.

From: Noah Richler
Date: Monday, June 15, 2015 at 12:42 PM
To: James Pratt
Subject: Fred Checkers has been in touch . . .

> Hi James
> You may or may not have seen the op-ed of mine in the *Toronto Star* yesterday re Truth and Reconciliation Commission and the likely suicide of an aboriginal writer friend of mine. I'm aware that education is a provincial, not federal responsibility, but it's a position.
>
> By the way, I remembered that I ran a very successful shoplifting ring in my UK school when I was nine, complete with guides to which stores to rob of confectionery, and how Robin Hood notions ascertained which neighbourhood stores it was not cool to steal from because their owners were too poor.
>
> I'm sure it's out in the open somewhere, though likely not in the letter from Harry Jones, the principal, to my parents, touting how

successful an entrepreneur I was on the path to being later in life. Still, should come clean.

Best

Noah R.

"Fred Checkers," I'd assumed correctly, was the avatar of an NDP scrutineer signalling the review of my social network posts was well underway, though really I wanted Pratt to see "The Hard, Important Truths about Indigenous Literature," an op-ed piece I'd written for the *Toronto Star* that spoke of the death of the Gwich'in novelist Robert Arthur Alexie, who'd been a friend of mine and a survivor of the residential school system though not of the psychological tumult it brought on. I'd not written the piece for NDP bona fides, but Aboriginal issues were close to my heart and, I'd long argued, constituted the most serious (and unacknowledged) challenges the country faced. A little naively, I was imagining that somewhere in Ottawa the vetting of my writing was also taking place because the *positive* was being discussed—is Richler the best way forward, are his ideas up to scratch, are they consonant with our own?—and I wanted Pratt to know that in a possible contest against Bennett, the Liberal Party critic for Aboriginal Affairs and Northern Development (as the ministry was called under the Harper government)—I had credentials.

But it was another ten days, and altogether a month since I'd submitted my material, before Pratt emailed, "I've got your vet back and things look pretty good." Another week went by and then he called to say Chow was running, so Spadina—Fort York was definitely out.

. . .

James, the Ottawa correspondent:

Sarah.

Noah, is he really going to do this?

Does he know what he's getting into?

This is an election, not an argument—I know, I know, politics is all about ideas, so why shouldn't he do it?

Well, because that's bullshit. Politics is not about ideas. It's about winning. Power. Kicking the other guy's ass. And winning and winning and winning.

It's not a debate, it's pugilism—no, not pugilism. It's street fighting.

It's fucking tough out there. His strengths are ideas, right? Thoughts! Not the calculated algebra of poll-by-poll analyses.

But winning an election is not like writing a magazine article, or a book. It's not about being understood, not at all, does he know that, Sarah? It's about making voters THINK they've been understood and then converting that into votes.

Ideas are pure. Politics is grubby.

Politics is a transaction.

Politics is grunt work. Dirty, boring, disciplined grunt work. There's no room for thinking, no room for argument.

By the time Election Day rolls around, all the thoughts have been thought, all the ideas idealized. An election is not the time for big thoughts. Tell him to have those later, if he must— after he's elected, in the caucus room with his colleagues. That's where an MP can help make policy.

But St. Paul's?

Ouch.

JUNE 30

CPC	NDP	LPC	BQ	GRN	OTH
29.1%	31.6%	27.2%	5.3%	5.5%	1.3%

. . .

A few days passed and Pratt emailed to say that Julian Heller, president of the Toronto—St. Paul's riding association was "very interested in your potential candidacy." I said that was good news and let him know I'd officially joined the party. "We're in this together," wrote Pratt. "Welcome to the family." An hour later, I heard from Stéphanie Lévesque, the NDP's candidate search director, and we discussed the possibility of my representing the riding.

"It's very important to me not to feel parachuted in or less than welcome," I said.

Heller, said Lévesque, had spent six months courting a lawyer to be the NDP's candidate, but unsuccessfully. "When one door is closed," said Lévesque, "maybe the second person is the one that's meant to be."

Lévesque explained that Toronto—St. Paul's was one of those ridings "with a lot of richer New Democrats," deftly hinting at the task of fundraising, to which I'd not yet paid much attention. It was also she said, a community with many artists who, despite the "legend" of Bennett, previously a doctor, having delivered half the babies in the riding, could help swing the riding the NDP's way. It was not so much a safe seat as a bellwether one.

"One question, Stéphanie," I said, thinking of the diversity of the NDP benches that I'd wished for so long the party had advertised. "I heard James rattle off his Toronto front line, and I'm worried about being just another white guy. Do you have any black people fronting ridings in Toronto?"

"Yes, we do," said Lévesque. "Not in downtown Toronto, but yes we do."

The party, said Lévesque, had affirmative action goals, and the target, though they had not reached it, was fifty percent. We talked a little more about the vetting and arranged to meet with Heller the next day—July 1, Canada Day.

. . .

Heller, a tall Montreal-born Jewish lawyer in his mid-fifties and a McGill graduate, had been an NDP member since 1980. He'd also been a candidate for the provincial party three times. The three of us sat in my backyard and Heller reminded me that Toronto—St. Paul's was one of the wealthiest ridings in the country—a fact I'd hear a lot—and one of the best educated. It had, said Heller, a strong activist core but also the highest percentage of tenants in the province. No other prospective candidates had put themselves forward, so my acclamation was a near certainty, he said. But I was aware of the country's history of tension between the grassroots and national parties operating from on high and was eager that my nomination be rolled out with minimal antagonizing. A recent but by no means singular lesson, Justin Trudeau had been embarrassed by his ill-thought-out welcome of the floor-crossing Conservative Eve Adams earlier in the year. Trudeau's announcement of her conversion at a televised news conference had been a performance described by the *National Post* columnist Andrew Coyne as "crawlingly demeaning." Adams had been dropped in as the candidate for the Eglinton—Lawrence riding despite the Liberal Party leader's promises not to interfere with nomination processes. The local favourite, Marco Mendicino, would come to defeat Adams, no doubt given a boost by Trudeau's maladroit interference. It was interesting to me, this tension. It reflected a greater national one of deep-seated wariness evident in the attitudes of smaller communities within the Canadian fabric towards the powerful centre that seemed an indication of just how far away from the seat of power most Canadians imagined themselves to be situated. The power in question has been held for almost all of Canada's history by indifferent, distant authorities: London, Washington and now Ottawa—a town insignificant other than to the small coterie of bureaucrats, journalists, MPs and drive-through senators who have fashioned their own little Brasilia out of it. Now here was this resentment of the distant authority, such a quintessentially Canadian dynamic, being played out in numerous ridings in advance of the upcoming election, and not just in Eglinton—Lawrence. In March, twenty-two-year-old Zach Paikin had withdrawn from the contest to represent the Liberals in Hamilton West—Ancaster—Dundas, protesting what he claimed to be obstruction from above, and, in Toronto—Spadina, Christine Innes had cited interference with open nomination processes when her candidacy was blocked. I was adamant that mine would not be another theatre mounting this familiar show.

The friction between ridings and the centre that is a commonplace of Canadian parliamentary politics reflects a similar dynamic between the provincial and national wings of parties. This, too, being played out across the country in different ways. In Alberta, it was fast becoming evident that Notley, while being respectful of Mulcair and the federal NDP, was nevertheless keeping an adroit distance at least until her surprising victory was entrenched somewhat. And, in Ontario, provincial leader Andrea Horwath's loss of the 2014 election exacerbated an already fractious relationship because of what appeared to many party stalwarts to have been her abandonment of traditional NDP principles for a more rightist platform of budgetary restraint. Just a year had passed since the Ontario NDP's defeat, and now, with sound prospects of a national win for the first time in the party's history, the federal push was going to be managed in large part by veterans of the provincial scene. After decades of NDP candidates and their supporters having toiled in the trenches, many—perhaps Heller, too—were probably wondering why 2015 was not their time. This uneasy relationship was already being demonstrated to me in myriad small ways, such as the habit of one influential player in the first stages of my approach prefacing any useful bit of knowledge with the remark, "I don't know what they do in Ottawa about [*fill in the blank*], but this is how we do things in the provincial party. . . ." Eager to put the ogre to rest, I asked Heller right away why he was not running. He said that he'd had his turn and that was that; I would not hear mention of his having been a candidate again. The early lesson was that every campaign is its own invention—though of course there are constant features. The need to fundraise is the first of these, finding free labour the next. I'd need to raise fifty thousand dollars for a decent campaign, said Heller, and secure fifteen to twenty core staff and a couple of hundred volunteers. We discussed essential jobs to fill—none of the positions were familiar, everything was new—but I did know something about negotiating and that now was the time to be making demands of the party's central office.

Heller said to ask for a campaign manager and a pre-election organizer. "If the federal party finances these positions," said Heller, "that would solve a lot of 'what ifs.'"

"Pratt said there's a possibility of the party putting resources in," said Lévesque. "Nothing's in writing, but there's a possibility."

. . .

The next afternoon, the NDP Director of Search and Nominations Jordan Reid emailed. "We've completed the vetting process and you are officially approved to seek the NDP nomination in Toronto—St. Paul's," he wrote. "It's great to have you on board!" Then Greta Levy, the party's senior press secretary, contacted me to say she wanted to arrange an interview with the *Toronto Star*, the timing of which would coincide with the riding's confirmation of my candidacy. I was due to meet Heller again—this time with Penny Marno, a veteran of several provincial campaigns—and was still unsure when my effort to become the candidate would receive the riding's imprimatur. It may have been no more than formal process, but I was adamant that the riding not be allowed to feel that it had been circumvented in any way. The *Toronto Star*, Levy assured me, would respect an embargo at least until the riding executive committee meeting scheduled for July 8, the deadline for anyone else contesting the nomination and therefore the date determining whether or not I was to be the presumptive or a competing candidate, "because the party can't be seen to be meddling in a nomination race." There were still no signals anyone else was planning to run, wrote Levy. "We're taking a bit of a risk but not a great one."

The cogs had ratcheted up a gear and I was having a hard time respecting the embargo myself. I decided the time had come to share the not-quite-news and that my good friend Raymond Perkins, one of Toronto's most entertaining fixers, would be the first to know. Well, no, the second. On my way, I visited my mother, who lived just a few blocks away. Her summer custom, we sat in the small, high-walled front garden of her Cabbagetown home, the statue of a Thai Buddha resting beneath a miniature arbour a serene presence by my side. The day was balmy and still and the only sound other than our talking was of water trickling into a tiny pond surrounded by impatiens and roses, all the blooms white.

"Why not the Liberals?" she asked.

I said that I found the Liberals hopelessly and chronically entitled, and that three times in recent months that party had demonstrated—in its compliance with Bill C-51 and in its acceptance of the Conservative MP Eve Adams and the former Toronto police chief Bill Blair as prospective candidates—the puruit of power trumped principle. By contrast, I thought the youth and diversity of the NDP terrifically exciting.

My mother, who is legally blind, turned her gaze to the ground and then skyward in the direction of a singing cardinal.

"Did you tell them what ministry you'd like?"

No, I said, impressed by my mother's inordinate confidence in her children's destiny. I never get excited about the place I'm headed, I said—never believe I'm there till I'm in it—and left it at that. Then I went to see Ray at Oxley's, the pub my U.K.-born pal favoured near the Bloor Street flagship store of Roots Canada. He'd been working for the company for the better part of three decades—arranging, among other things, for film, sports and music celebrities to visit and be feted and bolster the brand. This, I suspected, would be handy. But, above all, I wanted to raise a glass—it was summer. Patio season.

Ray, originally a Londoner, was another with a political bent. Before Ray made Canada home, in 1968, he'd canvassed with his father for Shirley Williams in the 1964 U.K. general election that brought Harold Wilson to power. Williams won her seat and became one of the most redoubtable of British Labour Party members (and a baroness). In Canada, Ray had worked at age fifteen for the NDP and campaigned for his brother, who'd run as the Ontario NDP's candidate in Orangeville. We belonged to the same generation, shared similar political memories and, much to my relief, Ray was ebullient. We toasted the prospect of a political adventure and, a few rounds the stronger, I decided to follow up with Pratt, my go-to man, whom I'd already emailed with a shopping list of sorts. I'd asked that Mulcair visit Toronto—St. Paul's during the campaign, for the party to commit to paying for a campaign manager and pre-election organizer and—what the hell, I'd been on a roll—for Pratt to tell me "what is reasonable to expect vis-à-vis my future with the party in the scenario that (a) I lose (b) I win."

"Your initial conversations have some Party heavyweights rattling the chains," wrote Pratt. But then, unnervingly: "The message I usually give to candidates asking for party resources is that we invest in those who invest in themselves. If we can raise a little money off your nomination and you'll continue to make that a priority, I'll see about a manager/organizer for you. Better to discuss on the phone."

"We invest in those who invest in themselves," I knew, was Pratt's dig at my still planning to take an albeit significantly truncated portion of the holiday I'd booked with my family for August. The put-down was a first glimpse of the hard truth of being one of the many—one of the 338, in fact. (There had been 308 federal electoral ridings in 2011. In 2015, thirty more were added.) I stepped out onto the sidewalk to make the call, a greenhorn due for another experience of the director of organization's whip.

"About that email," I said to Pratt. "I'd asked in the spring if plans to be with my family were permissible and now you're holding them against me. Wouldn't the proper thing to have said been, 'It's 110 percent from the time you commit'?"

"Let's see how you do," said Pratt.

In truth, I was angry with myself for failing to have anticipated the obvious but tried my poor hand anyway.

"So, if it works out, how about Fisheries and Oceans?" (I figured Heritage was taken—and, besides, too predictable a fit.)

"Lots of people want Fisheries and Oceans," said Pratt.

Well, this wasn't going very well, I thought. Instead of learning the name of the lucrative portfolio that would be handed me (a minister's top-up of $80,100 plus my MP's base salary of $167,400 equalling $247,500 per annum and the chance finally to recompense my family for the diminishing returns of my writer's profession), I listened to Pratt tell me that $90,000, not $50,000, was a good fundraising target, and he couldn't promise the party would chip in.

"But I'll look into it," he said.

. . .

Then, on Saturday, July 4, I met with Heller and Marno at Bar Espresso, the Bloor Street café popular with University of Toronto academics and students, and Doug's and my post-squash haunt. I learned there was still no other contender and, if all went as anticipated, riding members would be alerted and my nomination approved at an open meeting on July 29 (which also happened to be my birthday). The first and most crucial step, said Marno, was to find an official agent, the functionary necessary to have in place before donations towards a campaign can be accepted or expenses incurred. This is the notoriously thankless post of the person who oversees fiscal aspects of the campaign, ensuring these are handled properly. "If not, the candidate goes to jail," said Marno, bringing to mind images of convicted Conservative MP Dean Del Mastro in handcuffs. Marno suggested I find someone thorough but, critically, said the official agent needed to be someone I trust, and Heller, that whomever I convinced to take on the unpaid position needed to be "in tune with banking, financial statements and the crushing specificity of government forms." We discussed the need for a speaker and someone other than me to do a fundraising ask at the July 29 nomination meeting, an event that would double as an opportunity to revitalize the riding's lagging membership. I suggested we might have a musician play. Marno was not so keen, but I made plans to do so anyway. Marno was clearly an asset—I worried that the relatively recent Ontario election had exhausted her. Already, I was relying on her expertise and I thought about what I could do to assure her and Heller I'd not be a party mistake.

. . .

Julian, Riding Association President:

I'd been pursuing a candidate for Toronto—St. Paul's for some months but couldn't get the person to commit, and so we were starting anew when the Central Party set me up on a blind date on short notice. Noah Richler had been discussing his prospective candidacy for a while, and HQ thought we might be a match.

Still bruised by the previous experience, I was nonetheless hopeful. Our chat in his backyard with a chaperone Ontario candidate search organizer in attendance was good, but I wasn't wowed. There was no doubting his commitment to social justice and to the values of the party, but how would the clipped, vaguely British speech play out on the doorsteps? I called him out on some British pronunciation of a word—that probably annoyed him—but he countered with a funny story about ridiculous British dinner party snobs. The man did have a sense of humour, even if he seemed to have a hard time smiling.

My sense of it? An excellent match for the riding and the party, but it would be up to him and us to draw in loads of enthusiastic volunteers, donors and attention. I asked him if he would run again, and started to think about how to get more smiles, handshakes out of him—get our candidate wading into crowds of strangers at the local latte emporiums like he enjoys it!

. . .

On the Sunday, Levy called again, this time to say she'd been through the vetters' files and there were "just a couple of things we think we have to be careful about—the ayahuasca and Quebec."

"What about the ayahuasca?" I asked. I'd written for *Maclean's* magazine about taking the brew, the three major ingredients of which are listed in Canada as Schedule III drugs and therefore criminally prohibited, at a retreat in Ontario.

"You paid for it."

"Research. I may even have a receipt."

"Quebec could be a more difficult subject," said Levy.

"I have my own relationship with Quebeckers that's independent of my father's," I said, a defence I was used to providing. "Both my books are published in French by Québécois publishers and having them translated is very important to me. Quebec has always been a fundamental part of my Canada. But, I forget, what did I write?"

"You wrote in the *New Statesman* in 2011 that the NDP 'was unable to drop the socialism from its constitutional lexicon, or to amend its troublesome resolution that, in any Quebec referendum on sovereignty, a mere 50 per cent plus one would constitute victory.'"

"Well, that's true, no? But if anyone brings it up, I'll say it's our job to keep Canadians happy in Confederation,

Quebeckers or otherwise. I believe that—and that doing so won't be an issue."

"I can see I'm not going to be having problems with you," said Levy. "But understand, I have three hundred candidates, so I have to do this."

"And I have no intentions of being a problem."

Famous last words.

. . .

Things I was told when I started:

This will end.

The days can be unbelievably long.

You will move through a carousel of moods.

Politics is everybody else believing they know better than you.

Politics is other people telling you what happened after the fact.

Some days, the last thing you will want to do is canvass, and then you'll go out and canvass because that's what will make you feel better.

Ninety percent of your vote will depend upon the performance of the leader in the last three weeks of the campaign.

The Liberals start slow and then come on strong.

. . .

The week of the all-important Executive Committee meeting started and, in advance of my interview with the *Toronto Star* reporter, there was no shortage of advice from both party and riding.

Say you want "federal support ('sustainable funding') for subways, or (in my wildest dreams) high-speed rail Windsor–Quebec," wrote Heller and I liked that. We'd both come of age in *la belle province* and I liked that for Heller the train to Montreal was simply the logical extension of the St. Clair streetcar line.

"God save me from Liberals," said Debbie Parent, another experienced provincial NDP operative who telephoned to provide encouragement prior to the *Toronto Star* interview. "The Liberal Party isn't really a progressive party in the sense that they're not willing to change the paradigms and to take radical steps on core issues like fifteen-dollar-a-day child care. Justin's response to Bill C-51—that I have serious problems with it but I'm prepared to vote for it—sums it up."

"You're looking to identify projects in the riding that matter," wrote Levy. "You'll say, 'I know people are concerned about Project X and, after years of PM Harper leaving our infrastructure crumbling, they're excited that Tom has an urban agenda.'"

I asked Levy what the *Toronto Star*, a paper to which I had contributed political and cultural op-ed articles for years, was saying about my running.

"That if political candidates who wrote for the *Star* can't be covered, they'd be out of business."

I suggested placing an op-ed about my candidacy, but Levy was lukewarm about the idea.

"What's okay for me to do?" I asked.

"Look, I'm not here to shut things down," said Levy. "I just need to know they're happening. If I see something that raises a red flag, it allows me to say, 'Keep such and such in mind.'"

"I asked for the party to fund a campaign manager, a pre-election organizer and for Tom to visit," I said. "If I go ahead with the *Star* interview, then I've basically signed on. I want Pratt to respond."

"As soon as I get off the phone I'll go and talk to him," said Levy, "though it's outside my purview."

"Sure. I just want you to understand. I'm not trying to make you my advocate, but if he says, 'You're on your own, swim,' it's a different ball game."

The day of the interview, Levy called again. Sure that every prospective candidate was doing the same, I told her that I'd been going through Hansard (the official transcripts of parliamentary proceedings available online) and listing all the instances in which Carolyn Bennett had voted with the government and against the NDP. "Bill S-7, whatever that was, and the Act to Amend the Citizenship Act, Bill C-26 was it?"

"C-24."

"Right. And the omnibus Bill C-59. There's also something technical that seems to be an affirmation—the word 'concur' is used—for the Senate budget that I presume the NDP voted against and she voted for?"

Levy was silent. I was babbling and felt like a schoolboy cramming for exams. Did I really know so terribly little about parliamentary procedure? Yet I was running exactly because I was not the career politician type: Parliament should be open to all—and novices.

"She'd have voted for Bill C-51," said Levy.

"Right."

"In terms of what you should be telling the *Star*," said Levy, cutting gently to the chase, "one of the strengths we have right now is how dissatisfied a lot of people are with the way the Liberals have handled the Bill C-51 anti-terror law."

"I'm aware of that," I said.

"And the other thing I was going to suggest to you is that Bennett has a good reputation as the Liberal critic for Aboriginal affairs—"

"For sure," I said. "I noticed that she was the one who proposed the inquiry into murdered and missing Aboriginal girls and women—"

"—and it can be a strength for you to have one nice thing to say about her. But deliver it with a little bit of an attack on the brand."

That word again.

"A widespread view of the press is that, as the Aboriginal affairs spokesperson, Bennett knows what she's doing but her leader does not. Obviously, given the Liberals' top-down approach to things, the leader's ability in this area is important, so journalists will perk up if you say something unexpected. Like, for instance, the work she's done on the Aboriginal affairs file has been of credit to her party—Trudeau must have to rely on her quite a bit—and that's something you would look to carry forward."

"What I worry about the most is how to talk about Israel and Palestine. And I feel I need to go once more through Quebec and ISIL."

"The chorus to my life," said Levy. "I'm sending you a message guide. It's not a script, but it's been incredibly tested over and over again through focus groups. It's essentially a frame and argument to our narrative for why we are able to form a government."

That afternoon, Levy sent the NDP document, *What This Election Is About*. It started:

This election is about change.

After 10 years of Stephen Harper, middle class families are working harder but can't get ahead. Stephen Harper's plan just isn't working.

That's why Canadians are looking for a change.

Tom has the experience to replace Stephen Harper.

Tom has a concrete plan to help middle class families get ahead.

Tom's ready to bring change to Ottawa.

KEY MESSAGES

Tom's a principled, trustworthy leader with the experience needed to replace Stephen Harper.

Here are some points to help reinforce this message with voters and grow our support.

- Tom's a <u>former cabinet minister</u> and has the <u>experience to make difficult decisions</u>.
- Tom <u>knows where he stands</u>—and backs it up with action.
- Tom is the second oldest of ten kids. He <u>knows what it means to work hard</u> and <u>live within your means</u>.

This was it? This was all a candidate was meant to say? I flipped through the scant pages.

Tom was raised on middle class values and gets the things that are going on in your life.

Here are some points to help reinforce this message with voters and grow our support.

- Families are working harder than ever to build a good life for their family, but can't get ahead.
- Too many Canadians are unemployed and the jobs being created are part-time and precarious.
- More and more Canadians are struggling to retire with security.

· · ·

I showed the banal document to Doug.

"When you run, you sign off on the party platform. Period. Now make it your own."

"But what's with all this talk of the 'middle class'? We never talk about class in Canada. The rural–urban divide, sure, but *class*?"

"The Liberals are doing it too," said Doug. "Big time."

"It feels too much like exclusion—frankly, even at the top end. What *is* the 'middle class' anyway?"

"Eighty-five percent of Canadians used to identify themselves as 'middle class.' Now only half do."

"So thirty-five percent are up for grabs?"

"You could say that."

"Still. It bothers me. We're here for the poor. We're not here for the rich. I want to talk about 'working families and families that would like to be working.'"

KEY MESSAGES

After 10 years, middle class families are working harder but can't get ahead. Stephen Harper's plan just isn't working.

Instead of focusing on the things that matter to you and your family, Stephen Harper has the wrong priorities for Canada.

He's the reason they want change in Ottawa.

Fair enough.

Then, on page four, "Us on Trudeau and the Liberals."

Being Prime Minister isn't an entry level job and on issue after issue, Justin Trudeau's inexperience is showing.

It's no wonder that when it comes to taking on Stephen Harper and winning, many Canadians have decided Justin Trudeau isn't up to the job.

KEY MESSAGES

Canadians gave Justin Trudeau a chance, but he hasn't lived up to expectations.

Here are some points to help reinforce this message with voters and grow our support.

- Trudeau promised to do things differently—like open nominations—but hasn't.
- Trudeau said he'd stand up to Stephen Harper on key issues—like C-51—but didn't.
- And he's still not sure where he stands on the serious issues facing Canada. Justin Trudeau's inexperience is showing.

"Politics isn't about being clever," Levy said in our first telephone call. "Any time you talk to the media, imagine the story you'd like to see."

Right, then. Forward.

. . .

It was raining the next morning when, at the Rushton, I met with Alex Boutilier, the *Toronto Star* Ottawa correspondent whom Levy had described as "a good guy and a fair reporter, young but old-school." The restaurant, on St. Clair Avenue West, was where Ray and I had watched England in the World Cup a couple of tourneys back, and in the heart of a riding I was a day away from being able to call mine. ISIL, Israel and Palestine, oil, the environment—none of this came up. We talked about child care, urban infrastructure and transit, precarious work, and the fact of my living outside the riding. I tried responses I'd rehearsed: the issues that mattered to Toronto—St. Paul's were true across the GTA, and in such an economically diverse riding, a fella from Cabbagetown had no more or less of a connection to residents in the streets of the district in which we found ourselves than did someone from Forest Hill, such an exclusively wealthy corner, or

Cedarvale, a little less ostentatiously so. I volunteered information about my past drug use, wanting to be the source rather than to be sideswiped by it. Taking Levy's instruction, I was imagining the story I wanted to see and suggested, in good faith, that I had no connection, anymore, with the heroin user that had been me more than thirty years before. Acknowledging my drug use had always been, for me, a minor political act. It was, I believed, a question of integrity that, rather than refraining from mentioning it, I should own this moment of past experience so that merely, in this instance, participating in an election might serve as an example to people having trouble with the drug. There are other courses I have known: you can pretend to your best friend you're free of it, as mine did with me, and then ride stoned and have a motorcycle accident and crush your voice box and forever speak with a rasp. Or you can die, as a couple of other friends of mine did (though they did so not from heroin but from teenage angst augmented by the drugs of their choosing). But there are other outcomes. My friend who crashed his bike subsequently became a very successful medical equipment salesperson. The addict daughter of a friend was now the owner of a prospering boutique. I'd stopped using and gone on to Oxford University and successfully pursued a rewarding career path and would relish the chance to say as much in Parliament. I was proof, I told Boutilier, that Draconian policies of the sort that Harper and his ministers of justice favoured did not work.

JULY 8

CPC	NDP	LPC	BQ	GRN	OTH
28.4%	27.2%	32.1%	5.3%	5.0%	1.3%

. . .

Then, at five o'clock the next day, I locked my bike to a railing outside the tower on Adelaide Street that housed the offices of Heller and Associates, an hour and a half before the riding executive was due to meet. Inside, I sat with Heller, Penny Marno and her spouse, Rob Milling, and Erinn Somerville in a cramped meeting room just big enough for our roundtable of five. Erinn, who had been a lawyer until, twelve years prior, brain cancer cut that career short, had agreed to be the campaign's official agent. (A true survivor, she had already outlived her prognosis by more than a decade.) She also had the NDP and its precursor, the Co-operative Commonwealth Federation, in her blood. Her father's uncle, Edward Bigelow Jolliffe, had known David Lewis as a Rhodes Scholar at Oxford. He had co-founded the CCF's international wing before becoming an Ontario MLA and, from 1942 to 1953, was the provincial leader of the party. We sat together awkwardly, and Marno handed me the meagre members' list for the riding and explained the difference between active and non-active members, listed as "A" and "B," and suggested I start calling to introduce myself ahead of the general meeting called for July 29.

"And ask for money?"

"Yes."

"Should I call them all?"

"If you can start we'll get help," said Marno.

"Happy to do so."

Marno followed Heller into the boardroom, where the executive was discussing my nomination, but Milling remained.

"I'm not allowed in there," Milling explained. "I work for Greenpeace, and if I go in then the organization is breaking rules about its activism. So I'll just stay in here."

Milling watched as I perused the list for names I might recognize.

"It's not very up to date," he said.

"I can see."

"But it will put you in touch with NDP people who were active twenty years ago and still breathing."

I flipped the page.

"There aren't many," he said.

. . .

Just ten people were in the boardroom when, that afternoon, my bid for the nomination was approved. The ten applauded as I entered, and immediately, the certainty came over me that had this been a Conservative gathering the room would have been filled with portly men all seeming in their fifties, whether they were that old or thirty years younger. They would have been wearing heavily starched white shirts with broad ties under the vests of their double-breasted suits, a couple of equally fierce-looking women dressed for power in the wings. And had it been a Liberal enclave, then dashing men a decade or two the Conservatives' junior would have had their narrower ties loose, if they were wearing ties at all, their slim jackets off, and the women would have been just as stylish and dismayingly beauti-ful, not a blemish or a ripple of fat on anyone. Our NDP room, though, was like a scene from some Bill Murray comedy in which the softball team full of misfits and perennial losers needs to win the championship to save the clubhouse. The pitcher can't pitch, the base-stealer's overweight and the outfield—well, they don't have an outfield, but there's a blind guy who'll play on the right and a fella in a wheelchair who can roam centrefield at speed—and I felt immediately at home. You could see right away we had only a slim chance in hell of winning anything, but this was the team of my choosing and I loved them already.

. . .

Kristian, the guy sitting to my left, was small and lean and athletic and his eyes darted as keenly as a lizard's. The women numbered more than the men, and two at one end of the table had bicycle helmets plonked down in front of them where the Conservatives would have had ledgers and the Liberals multiple electronic devices. Joyce Rankin, whose brother was the NDP MP for Victoria, asked me about "social justice."

"All politics begins from principle," I said, "and the first of mine is that government exists to lend a hand to those that need help."

"Don't say *help*," said Joyce. "Say support. Help suggests dependency."

"Of course."

She stared slightly disapprovingly. The answer had not been quite enough, but it demonstrated goodwill. "I work in social housing," she said. "Perhaps we should talk."

I made a mental note of it. *See Joyce about social housing. Make her your friend.*

Kristian asked me about Bill C-51.

"It's a terrible law," I said. "One of the things that makes my running so easy is that I am so wholly in agreement with the party's platform."

He nodded.

Opposite me, slouched in his chair and scrutinizing the new candidate, was the riding treasurer Bernard Ross Ashley, a thin, wiry man with a grey beard who looked like a ZZ Top band member on month three of a detox. He asked me for my views on the Gaza blockade, a test I had been expecting.

"I'm not about to reduce such an exasperating and complicated issue to a one-word answer, yes or no," I said. "But I can tell you I believe in the right of the State of Israel to exist, though concomitantly, we must recognize conditions in Gaza make it indiscernible at times from an internment camp. I believe, as the party does, in a two-state solution, but feel sadness even as I say it because, of course, one state would be ideal. But we're not there, and likely won't be for a long time. It's the job of the NDP—of the Canada I believe in—to build bridges, not walls, and to do whatever we can to promote conditions in which co-existence is possible."

Ross smiled, shook his head, stroked his beard. The answer would do for now. At the end of the table to my right was Sean Caragata, a lawyer in his early forties with a thoughtful air. He asked me for my views on the fifteen-dollar minimum wage.

"I'm not sure why it's limited to government workers," I said.

"That and federally regulated industries are all we can legislate," he said.

"I'm all for the example," I said, "but as you see, I have some homework to do."

Marno took up the conch, alerting the executive that I would be out of town for a part of August and declared there would be a follow-up meeting to lay plans for the night of the nomination on the twenty-ninth.

Heller asked how much money was in the riding account.

"Three hundred and fifty dollars," said Ross. "Or thereabouts."

Not to worry, said Marno, wanting to cushion the blow, the riding would come through. I endeavoured to be upbeat and outlined plans I had for "funky town halls." These would be gatekeeping but also fundraising events held at bars and cafés around the riding, each to be paired with a musician and a theme—sports, arts, Bill C-51—that would be debated over the course of the evening. It would be a way of introducing the party and our concerns to constituents—and encouraging youth, in particular, to be interested in the election and vote.

"What about having Rocco Galati speak to Bill C-51?" asked Kristian. "We've been talking a lot."

"And he is?"

"A lawyer and activist. He challenged Harper's choice of Marc Nadon for the Supreme Court, and won. Now he's taking on Bill C-51—and how the Bank of Canada operates."

"Great idea," I said.

A couple more suggestions followed before Marno asked who was able to work on the campaign. As she made the circuit of the room, most of the dozen apologized and said they were already committed to work in other ridings: in Toronto—Danforth for Craig Scott; in Davenport, with Andrew Cash. Elizabeth Glor-Bell, one of the cyclists at the table, said that she would love to join the campaign but was committed to her role as organizer of the Scarborough chapter of NoJetsTO (a citizens' group advocating against jet traffic at the city's island airport).

Which was about the time that Rebecca Elming, on staff with Ontario's provincial NDP, looked up from her smartphone and announced that the *Toronto Star* had posted Alex Boutilier's story online.

"Nice," she said.

It was perfect timing, the story having come after the executive's endorsement, and others read the article approvingly. At just before seven, Marno dissolved the meeting and Heller left the boardroom to email the letter we had prepared for NDP members that announced July 29 as the date for the nomination meeting and explained why I, who lived outside the riding, was putting myself forward. The conversation around the table was light-hearted and animated. I shook a few hands (better get used to this) and then Kristian, who had unsuccessfully run as a candidate in the 2014 Toronto District School Board election, leaned his head in towards mine and spoke quietly and confidentially.

"A word of warning," he said. "The woman I ran against was a trustee for nearly seventeen years, and when I started I thought if I win, that's fantastic. If I don't, well, that's a great experience, too."

"Sure. That's how I feel."

"But a friend of mine told me that's totally the wrong way to look at it. He said that when he'd been an athlete, the only way he could get through a playoff series was by hating the other team. He told me what you're going to do is you're going to go home and grab a picture of that woman and write her name on it, stick it on your bathroom mirror, and every morning take a look at it and remind yourself how much you have to hate her.

"So I did. I wrote KILL ME across the picture and every morning I'd look at it and it saved me on days I didn't want to canvass."

I thanked Kristian for the tip.

Outside, the rush hour traffic that had greeted me on the way in was ebbing and the street was bathed in a soft ochre light. In a matter of just the few hours between my arriving at the Adelaide Street tower and leaving it, my world had been fundamentally altered. I was The Candidate. I had the sense that my life would be affected in ways I did not yet know how to gauge.

. . .

"My whole life, I've avoided Ottawa," said Sarah when I arrived home. "As a teenager, I went to dance camp there. In high school I won a scholarship to Ottawa U., and then I went to Carleton. I was happy to leave. Now you're going to take me back? My life is over."

AVERAGE DONATION TO ST. PAUL'S RIDING ASSOCIATIONS, 2011–2014

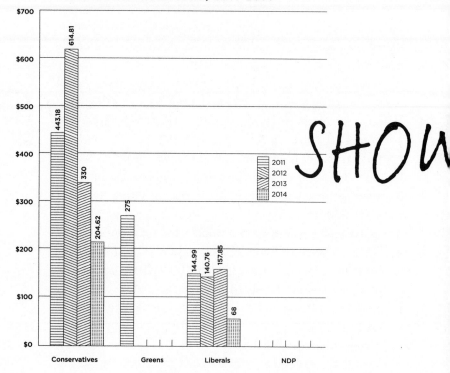

SHOU

Legend:
- 2011
- 2012
- 2013
- 2014

Conservatives: 443.18, 614.81, 330, 204.62
Greens: 275
Liberals: 144.99, 140.76, 157.85, 68
NDP:

TOTAL AMOUNT OF CONTRIBUTIONS AND TRANSFERS TO ST. PAUL'S RIDING ASSOCIATIONS, 2011–2014

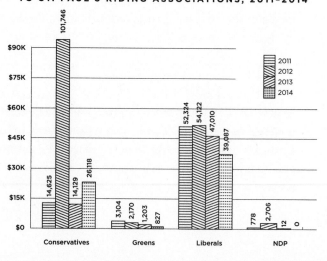

Legend:
- 2011
- 2012
- 2013
- 2014

Conservatives: 14,625, 101,746, 14,129, 26,118
Greens: 3,104, 2,170, 1,203, 827
Liberals: 52,324, 54,122, 47,010, 39,087
NDP: 778, 2,706, 12, 0

ᴍE THE MONEY

I was reading tweets in the wake of Boutilier's *Toronto Star* reveal—

@LadyBlerd: this is great news. congrats

@RabNew: hoping it doesn't lead to CPC coming up the middle and snatching the riding

@Joyce504941: what counts is his ability to represent the issues not his postal code

@ColdandMean: "Noah Way" could be as successful as "Notley Crew"

—when Chrystia Freeland called.

"I wish you well," she said. "Not so well that you beat Carolyn, of course, but best of luck. It's a good thing that you're doing."

"Thanks, Chrystia," I said, thinking how much good graces are in short supply. "You're the first MP of any of the parties to call."

. . .

Then a pal from the Ottawa press circuit called.

"Don't use my cell and absolutely don't use my work email," she said. She sounded frantic. But always did. "We can't speak on this line anymore, do you get it?"

"Sure. Any tips?"

"Oh God. I'll call you later."

And then another:

"If you have to call me, call me at home, okay?"

"Absolutely."

"This won't be easy. The Conservatives are brutal and disciplined and you just can't count the Liberals out. And, are you sure about the NDP? I've always sensed you had that affliction, but Mulcair won't take kindly to some author in the corner wonking on about arts policy. Don't get me wrong. Of course Canada needs authors in the corner wonking on but elections are *not* about that. Elections are about getting behind the leader and sticking to media lines delivered by HQ—and dear God, *please*: don't freelance a single thought!"

"Okay."

"And you want to win?"

"That's the plan."

"Then be seen in the riding. Eat in the riding. Drink in the riding. Walk your dogs in the riding. You're going to have to shake every hand in the riding. Three times. And listen, while I have you, do you really know what an MP does? Shit, it's a terrible job. You're away from the family, you'll have to do committee work with people you don't like, there's too much booze, too much arrogance, not enough sleep and so many assholes every which way you'll want to spit. I wish it were better, brighter, I wish it were more—well, worth it. But, it's not. Really."

"Noted."

"Noah. I love that you're doing this and I'm proud as heck to be your friend but I'm terrified for you. You'll want to win this and, well, you might not."

"It's okay. The party knows that. I'd say they were pretty surprised when I said I'd run in Toronto—St. Paul's."

"People lose elections. Smart people do. Good people do—*fuck*, the wrong people do! You're okay with that?"

. . .

Then it was Elizabeth May's turn.

"Noah, I don't want to upset you. I know how much the Digby Neck means to you."

Such a smart woman: ever the lawyer, now sowing insidious seeds of reasonable doubt. May's voice was piercing, agitated—and familiar; she was not a person to make a call without purpose. She knew that, years back, I'd written about an environmental dispute in the part of Nova Scotia in which I spend a good part of the year. Bilcon, a New Jersey company, had seen a mega-quarry project it was planning on the Neck overturned on environmental grounds by a federal–provincial joint review panel of the sort that had ceased to exist under the Harper government. Bilcon sued the Government of Canada under the North American Free Trade Agreement's Chapter 11 "investor-state" clause (by which a company is able to sue for lost profits if it is deemed that domestic laws have altered the conditions of its investment). Bilcon won, the company awarded three hundred million dollars because the "community core values" that had provided grounds for the project's rejection by the panel were ruled inadmissible. Feigning incredulity, May told me Murray Rankin, the member for Victoria and the NDP Opposition's critic for health, had appeared as an "expert witness" on behalf of the U.S. corporation.

"MPs swear an oath 'bearing true allegiance' to Her Majesty—it's understood to mean allegiance to Canada—and it may be unprecedented for an MP to serve as an expert witness against Canada in an arbitration in which a foreign corporation is seeking three hundred million dollars in damages," said May. "What am I meant to think of the NDP's green policies? Does Tom even understand the implications of what Murray has done?"

I admired the Green Party leader, had profiled her glowingly some time back, and was impressed that she'd not even waited for me to be confirmed as a candidate before using the situation to advance the environmental agenda she held paramount. I knew she was manipulating me, but it felt like a privilege, being the object of her resolve. This, I told myself, was what Ottawa would be like.

. . .

"No one from the NDP called," I said to Sarah.

"You're always expecting gratitude," said Sarah. "Not going to happen. Besides, Levy told you that it's all about Twitter these days. You had plenty of congratulations there."

"It's not gratitude I want." I could hear my own petulance. "I just wasn't expecting this to be a story I could tell."

"Then don't tell it," said Sarah. "It's not like you don't have enough to think about. Have you called Rocco Galati yet? That was a good idea."

"No."

"Have you been through your Facebook?"

"No."

"Twitter?"

"No."

"Do you have an office?"

"No."

"Have you arranged for a PA system for your nomination?"

"No."

"Refreshments?"

"No."

"A candidate's event page? Have you looked at Jennifer Hollett's? Hers is good."

"No. I haven't. The answer to every question you have is 'No, I haven't done that yet.'"

. . .

We asked the candidate to list the eight crazy things he knew about politics so far and you won't believe what he told us.

1. MONTREAL, 1974, AGED FOURTEEN: ELECTIONS ARE MADE OF TEDIOUS WORK.

It is the eve of Canada's thirtieth federal election and my father, having noticed my marijuana habit, has volunteered me for the Montreal NDP candidate Nick Auf der Maur's campaign. I am to distribute leaflets on "postal walks" for his Crescent Street drinking buddy. Most of the twice-folded photocopied yellow pages get only as far as the litter bins along de Maisonneuve because I am stoned a lot of the time, see no favour or point in it and resent being the prop for conversations full of hearty chortles at bars I am too young to drink at. Or so the begrudging teenager sees it. Come July, Pierre Trudeau turns the Liberals' 1972 minority into a comfortable majority. The NDP, down from a historical high of thirty-one, drops to sixteen members and the party leader, David Lewis, loses his seat.

"Third parties do well against a minority government," says my father, unperturbed. "The next time around, voters squeeze them out."

2. MONTREAL, 1976-77, AGED SIXTEEN: REAL POWER LIES BEHIND THE SCENES.

I am the vice-president of Westmount High School's student council. My neighbour across the boulevard is the student council president. The future Harvard Law School student rats on my friend Donald after he has a car accident between his house and mine. This upsets me, as does the incontrovertible fact that my girlfriend, Jennifer, is more impressed by the president than me. But I have abandoned petty jealousies in favour of wielding the clandestine power that comes from the judicious application of quid pro quo. Steve, Frank, Rick and his buddies, who have given up attending classes because they have no chance of passing them, scalp Habs tickets for extra income. They provide these to me gratis as—an early proponent of lending a hand to those who need it—I am the fella who understands root causes better than the Harvard guy and passes math answers up the aisle during exams, and who makes the trip across to Outremont for better drugs on Friday afternoons. After a couple of months, I am no longer bothering with student council meetings at all as the meaningful deals are made outside of them.

3. CANMORE, 1983, AGED TWENTY-TWO: THERE ARE SAFE SEATS AND ONES TO HAVE FUN IN.

I am the stage manager, fundraiser and producer of the musical *100 Times Better*, written by Terry Wall, a bard of Irish-Montreal stock who works at the Canmore Radio Shack. *100 Times Better* celebrates the centenary of this former mining town and small sleeper community east of Banff National Park on the Trans-Canada Highway. Wall is in-your-face and brilliant and a trickster, but also lyrical and romantic. He's a talented nutcase. We become fast friends. One of the characters played by Terry, who stands over six feet tall, is Gaetan Feuille D'érable, an Albertan francophone separatist who sings,

> *It's da Wes', build a wall around it*
> *It's the best, help preserve it*
> *And I'll bet Ev'ryone can help*
> *Tell your relative' to put OFF coming out*
> *To da Wes', oh they wan' it*
> *It's da East, those Centralistes!*
> *They Want our Heritage Fund*
> *TO SPEND ON U.I.C.*

. . . which is what EI (Employment Insurance) used to be called. The following autumn, after the show came and went, a piece of Canmore folklore, Terry drove in the school bus he'd adorned with his stage character Gaetan Feuille D'érable's pink maple leaf livery to Vancouver Quadra to run against the Liberal Party leader John Turner as an independent candidate. It was Canada's thirty-third general election. Brian Mulroney's Conservatives won 211 of 282 seats, still a record, and the Liberals' tally dipped to 40. Turner won Vancouver Quadra, a safe Liberal seat ever since, with 21,794 votes; Gaetan Feuille D'érable, representing the Party for the Commonwealth of Canada, earned 20, slightly fewer votes than there were members of his singing troupe but who's counting? Later, he became a councillor for Canmore. His last political act was to stand and sing the new "Democracy Song" he'd written for fellow palliative care cancer patients in a Calgary hospital as news of Rachel Notley's provincial NDP victory came in before midnight on May 5, 2015. Terry died eleven weeks later.

4. MONTREAL, 1983, AGED TWENTY-THREE:
STAYING IN POWER IS THE PREOCCUPATION.

Soon to be a classics and archaeology graduate from McGill, I have applied for a Rhodes Scholarship and undergo an interview at the Mount Royal Club on Sherbrooke Street. Jeanne Sauvé, Speaker of the House and the governor general designate, is in the chair. Several other members of a Liberal government that will lose to Brian Mulroney and his record majority are on the committee. That won't happen until the following September, but already they seem to know what's coming at them. I am asked about Operation Opera, Israel's 1981 bombing of an Iraqi nuclear reactor and how this will affect electoral outcomes. But I have just finished the English writer Margaret Drabble's novel *The Realms of Gold*, in which a historian, an archaeologist and a geologist offer differing views of events shaped by the scales of time their professions demand. "An archaeologist," I declare, "is compelled by empire more than the rise and fall of governments." I am very impressed by my answer—as impressed as my jury is not. Sauvé and the Liberal members of the panel look at me stone-faced and I realize that I have blown it. My father asks me how it went but is not distressed when I say not well at all. "We're not the prize-winning type," he says.

5. OXFORD, ENGLAND, 1984, AGED TWENTY-FOUR:
A SENSE OF SELF-IMPORTANCE IS KEY.

I get to Oxford anyway, though on my own steam. Once there, I am invited to socials by the successful Canadian Rhodes

Scholars. I am baffled at colleagues whose kind I knew back home suddenly dressing in tuxedos and toting delicate glasses of sherry in hockey-playing hands that previously held brown stubbies. Often there is not an Englishman in the room, as they're not much interested in being members of the British North America Society. The Canadians are busily playing pretend to each other and talk openly about their future careers "on the Hill." I drink a lot, it's all I can do, and at one of the last such meetings I can abide, a dinner at the graduate residence, Holywell Manor, a group of Canadians in the M.Phil programs developed specifically to garner cash from North Americans not content with the initials B.A. are discussing a prospective trip to Israel. I'd worked in the Negev for a time and say, jestingly, that maybe I'll come along. There is a long, awkward silence. "I don't think that can happen," says one, not sure quite how to cope with un-credentialled, on-the-make me. "You see," he says, "we'll be *talking* to people." The group of eminent Canadian Rhodes Scholars travels, yet somehow the crisis in Israel and Palestine remains unsolved.

6. BERLIN, 1994, AGED THIRTY-FOUR: BEING TRUE TO ONESELF IS A LOUSY CAREER CHOICE.

A BBC Radio documentary maker, I am representing my employer—and England—at the Prix Futura, an international competition held, disconcertingly, at the Haus des Rundfunks, in which Joseph Goebbels housed the Nazi Ministry of Public Enlightenment and Propaganda and the network that disseminated it. A curiosity of Europe's eminent and multilingual radio competition is that anyone whose work is entered is also a de facto member of the jury. The contestants are from many European countries but also Australia, Canada, Japan and the

United States, and the deliberations last for three days. The Serbian steps up and begins with "I just want to say one thing!" and then speaks for forty excruciating, hectoring minutes. The Parisian holds a man-purse and, ignoring the lingua franca of English, perorates in French before his pretty interpreter—he is the only contestant with one—stands and translates. (At the bar, of course, the Frenchman speaks English freely.) The man I am watching with the most interest, though, is the American contestant, Gregory Whitehead. When he steps up, it is to say only praiseworthy things—a policy of expedient kindness that he will pursue categorically and charmingly for the whole of the proceedings. He will even find nice things to say about a two-hour Swiss radio documentary on being deaf that is surely well intentioned but punishingly dull. It occurs to me that there is a lesson here about the strategic choice to be made between seeking to be liked and speaking one's mind—one, I see in retrospect, to be especially instructive vis-à-vis social media. But who knew what a tweet was, back in 1994? The Norwegian's show comes up, is on par with the Swiss, and it is my turn to speak. "It is heartwarming," I say, "that in at least one country of the world public radio can count on folk with nothing better to do than to gather around the wireless. . . ." When my show is debated, no surprise, it is excoriated. Even the French and Germans have united in its condemnation, while the American stays seated. I also learn that historical ties matter; ever friends to Canada, the Dutch take me out and get me very drunk to prove the point.

7. TORONTO, 2012, AGED FIFTY-ONE: SUCCESS IN POLITICS AFFECTS LIVES.

After Canada's forty-first federal election, I meet with one of the NDP's winners at a coffee shop in Toronto. We've known each other for decades, and when the bill for our meagre breakfast arrives, I move to pick it up but my friend, now a parliamentarian, stops me. "Sorry," he says. "Can't do that. It's against the rules." I am stunned that he imagines he could be done in for the favours an eight-dollar tab might bring. I've not seen this sort of adjustment since the fella I used to do heroin with thought he could lie to me. I decide that if politics is changing old friends' conduct in this way, then I want nothing to do with it.

8. OTTAWA, 2012, AGED FIFTY-TWO: THE MEDIA ARE NOT YOUR FRIENDS.

Twenty-six years after trading exam answers for Habs tickets in what remains the best-ever season of any NHL team (132 points, 8 losses in 80 games, 387 goals scored and just 171 against, a sweep of Boston in the Stanley Cup Final), I learn that the quid pro quo comes to naught if the quo you're trading for demands extra-curricular effort. The quid are drinks and oysters at Ottawa's Metropolitan Brasserie, occasional hangout of politicians and journalists rather than the more expensive bar of the Château Laurier, up the steps and one street over. The quo is maybe a review or just a mention but at least looking at my new book, an overtly political one, and talking about it—a little brokering on behalf of a colleague. But I overestimate the interest of my Ottawa press corps pals, who drink the booze and eat the oysters anyway, some five hundred dollars leading to zero coverage from the thirsty bunch. Uplifting (not), but the lesson is media cannot be bought, damn it—or at least not with the paltry payola that was Noah's Happy Hour. I try not to nurse a grudge along with my whiskey, but I am a writer and Old Testament and this is hard.

. . .

Heller has emailed suggestions for the appointment of the EPC and "Strategic Direction" Committees, and the barebones list of a campaign team with names of members he thought might fill the posts of:

1. Campaign Manager
2. Canvass Organizer/Deputy Manager
3. Phone Bank Organizer
4. Outreach, Media and Press Scheduler
5. Social Media
6. Data/Analytics
7. Sign Captain
8. Official Agent/CFO
9. Volunteer/Canvasser Recruitment Organizer
10. Events Organizer
11. Videographer
12. Election Day Organizer
13. Office Manager

"Hope this helps you get a grasp on what is involved."

I had no grasp at all, of course, though I did have the beginnings of a bunch for 5, 10 and 11. Item 1, campaign manager, was the most important job to be filled, that much I did know, and if I was feeling anxious, it was because I'd no idea where to look. I was not part of a long-established political circle. I did not have the contacts. I did not know the name of a single person with the experience of such a job. I was in the peculiar position of needing to hire my own boss but without knowing what qualifications that person should have.

"Ask Penny what she thinks," said Sarah. "You're going to need to learn to let go if your campaign is to be at all effective."

"Better to ride the horse than to pull it," said Doug.

And if I needed to raise money—which Heller was already on at me about—it was not only to make the campaign viable but also to be able to craft it to my liking. The less money there was, the less choice I'd have about staff and strategies and the more off-the-shelf the whole campaign would be. Money bought freedom—freedom from the template. Such a mundane lesson, really.

. . .

Sarah arranged for us to see a member of her publishing board whose wife, like mine, was singular and a dynamo. Michael Tamblyn was the CEO of a major tablet developer marketing its Canadian product internationally. He liked to write speeches, identify problems and solve them, and had a particular affinity for Excel spreadsheets. His partner, Laura Watts, a past national director of the Canadian Centre for Elder Law and internationally recognized expert in matters of law reform and issues related to aging, liked to laugh and to project information onto a screen—the kitchen wall would do. She liked *action*, even if this meant press-ganging friends of hers or staff of Michael's into my incipient adventure. At The Ace, a bistro diner on Roncesvalles where we celebrated afterwards, it occurred to me that even the owner needed to keep Laura's attention on the menu or he might have ended up a part of my team with no idea of how he'd been roped into it. It was very affecting. The evening was the first of several moments in which I'd see the party I had chosen was less important than my having put myself forward; Michael and Laura were helping me because they were my friends, not because I was NDP or Liberal or Conservative, and because the privilege of a freely contested election was never to be taken for granted, even in

Canada. They were contributing, as so many other friends and then strangers would come to do, to this most basic of democratic acts being replicated in hundreds of campaigns across the country led by businesspeople, lawyers and career politicians, but also by artists, carpenters, doctors, educators, farmers, health care providers, journalists, mechanics, soldiers and students; by Aboriginals, Asians, blacks, Christians, Hindus, Jews, Sikhs, Muslims and Tamils—this but a portion of the country's participating, peaceable diversity and a consensus worth upholding. *Elections mattered.* It was really very moving, enough so that, sitting in Michael and Laura's kitchen, I felt a wash of sentiment coming over me. And it was getting in the way of my having a proper grasp of the PowerPoint SWOT chart Michael had conjured up in a matter of minutes. For the other truth was that this was a very competitive pair and they relished the *contest* of politics—its tactics and strategies.

"What's a SWOT?" I asked.

"*Strength, Weakness, Opportunities, Threats,*" said Laura.

Barely was I coming to terms with that bit of homework before Michael projected a map of the St. Paul's riding (subsequently adjusted to become Toronto—St. Paul's), and then a list showing the paltry 27 of 257 individual polls that, in 2011, the NDP had won. Michael typed in new formulae, quickly recalibrating the numbers to identify very exactly the NDP margins of victory or loss in every one of the riding's polls.

"You can see now where your strengths are," said Michael.

So this is what politicos do, I thought: they scramble the numbers, they churn the data, they make lists. Now it was Laura's turn:

THINGS TO MAP OUT

- religious communities
- ethnic communities

- long-term care facilities/seniors facilities
- gated communities
- demography
- poll-by-poll returns

CONSTITUENCIES
- Holy Blossom Temple
- Unitarian Church
- Private schools (BSS/UCC/St. Clements/York/Greenwood/De La Salle)
- Oakwood/Northwood/North Toronto
- Rathnelly/Trains

The formidable wealth of the riding was apparent. It was there in the list of private schools, some of the most exclusive in the country; and in the Holy Blossom synagogue, its reform congregation the most powerful in the city (and that included, in its number, the former provincial NDP and then federal Liberal Party leader Bob Rae, and the CPC minister of finance Joe Oliver); it was there in districts such as Rathnelly and gated communities such as historic Wychwood Park, with its arts and crafts architecture; though, also, north of St. Clair, in the Lower Village Gate condominiums offering "gatehouse security" as attractive as you'd find on a Middle Eastern U.S. embassy compound. Would these "communities" of the rich and the anxious even let me in, I wondered?

We left and at midnight, Laura emailed a PS: "Consider downloading the free app Viber. Great messaging service and doesn't keep any messages. You know, *for the cautious.*"

. . .

As soon as the prospect of my nomination was plausible, I'd contacted Stephen Lewis, Ontario NDP leader from 1971 to 1978.

Lewis was Canada's ambassador to the United Nations from 1984 to 1988, the UN special envoy for HIV/AIDS from 2001 to 2006 and, afterwards, the co-director of AIDS-Free World, the international advocacy organization founded in 2007. I'd called him—one of the most impassioned and able orators in the country and immensely popular for that reason on university campuses—out of the blue, and somewhat hesitantly, to ask if he'd speak at the riding association's meeting planned for the end of the month. Lewis had been a delightfully eloquent thorn in Stephen Harper's side, and he and his wife—the former journalist and author Michele Landsberg—were principals in that core of "Dipper" activists I'd been told several times would be a source of strength in the riding. I'd interviewed Lewis when, in 2005, he'd delivered the CBC Massey Lecture "Race Against Time, Searching for Hope in AIDS-Ravaged Africa," but still I was astonished when he'd said, "Yes, absolutely"—and then, playfully (a master of words, he is also beholden to them), that he was at my "call and beck." I was so excited I did a little dance in the street.

"What happened?" asked Sarah, alarmed. Sarah, who cannot dance with me without suppressing giggles at my unorthodox form, was walking ahead of me with Doug on the hot July afternoon. The pair of them laughed outright when I explained my spontaneous jig of victory.

It felt like a coup and an auspicious start. Lewis wanted me to know he and Landsberg had been signatories to a public letter that, prior to the 2014 provincial election, accused Ontario NDP leader Andrea Horwath of running to the right of the Liberals in an attempt to win Conservative votes and coercing supporters "to vote against their principles" (unsuccessfully, it turned out, Kathleen Wynne and the Liberals having gone on to win an unexpected majority) but also that he'd do anything the party asked.

"Holy Shit!" wrote Pratt when I told him my news. "I'd probably just give him my wallet." Get Lewis to do the fundraising ask, he importuned.

Part of me wondered how it was the party had not done the obvious and arranged for Lewis to speak at Mulcair's and the party's rallies already, but I chose instead to feel relief I had not kicked up some wasp's nest of internecine party differences. Most of all, I was elated that a man so important to the political left and such a champion of pressing international causes was speaking on behalf of a neophyte.

"F'in huge," emailed Heller. "Worth more than a 'little dance.'"

"You're entirely free to let people know I'll be speaking at the nomination," wrote Lewis. "Given the current polling data for Toronto, I genuinely feel that St. Paul's is a seat we can win."

. . .

Ten days later, I had lunch with Lewis at Mashu Mashu, a Middle Eastern restaurant in Forest Hill Village. He was brimming with determination, optimism and knowledge of campaigns to which I was not yet privy.

"What's really important is we make no assumptions about where your vote is coming from," said Lewis. "Let the Conservative do whatever she is doing and you'll take advantage of the trend. Nobody's saying a vote for the NDP is wasted anymore."

Lewis smiled. That excited him.

"The campaign manager is crucial," he said. "But so is the campaign organizer."

"I don't know how much I'll be in a position to choose," I said. "I asked the party to foot the bill and it seems they might. But if they do, it's their call, really."

"We must run the name of your campaign manager by my brother," said Lewis. "Michael ran campaigns no one thought he would win."

This was good news. Michael had worked with the NDP for twenty-four years, and with the United Steelworkers Union for another eighteen, where his job was to liaise with the party. He'd worked in riding development and on campaigns from B.C. to Nova Scotia.

The bill came, I reached, Lewis took it.

"The candidate never pays," he said. "These months will cost you enough."

Two days later I received an email from Lewis. Ever the producer, I worried he was writing to say he'd be out of the country and unable to speak at my nomination. But it said:

Dear Noah: I've spoken at length to my brother, and he's checking on people. Unfortunately, the two party types whom he would wish to consult are on vacation. He'll continue to try to reach them. In the meantime, perhaps you can suggest that you'd like to wait until you're the formal candidate before settling on a campaign manager. On the other hand, if it becomes too awkward, or difficult with constituency colleagues, then take the suggestion of the establishment, and if necessary we can try to work around it.

Truth to tell, most of the sterling campaign managers are already committed (rather like members of your own executive).

I thoroughly enjoyed our lunch. Michele and I will enthusiastically put up a sign and we'll contribute financially. But I'll be goddamned if I'll canvass. I'm too old.

I had more than a speaker: I had a patron.

. . .

In the meantime, Marno had arranged for the Election Planning Committee—several members of the riding executive and an equivalent number of friends of mine—to meet. The riding list had been taken out of my hands for others to call, and we discussed fundraising and campaign logistics. Marno presented two slim-line budgets: one for $50,000 for a five-week campaign, and another at $70,000 for ten weeks, "a Cadillac for Toronto—St. Paul's." Each took into account signs and a staff such as Heller had delineated, the difference lying principally in higher wage costs for the paid positions of campaign manager, volunteer organizer and office manager, extra campaign literature and extended rent for an office, desks, phone lines, computers and so on. Marno said photographs of me were needed if we were to meet the party deadline for discounted orders of lawn and window signs and candidate literature. I was raring to go and, though the election writ had not yet been dropped, set about the task of fundraising immediately after the meeting was dissolved. I certainly wanted to have some sort of pamphlet at hand when, if only for training, I began canvassing. We had started our preparations late, and if literature was to be ready for August then photographs would need to be taken as soon as possible. Ray offered to arrange for Ilich Mejia, a professional photographer and a soccer-playing pal of his, to shoot them over the weekend— and, even better, said Ilich would do so pro bono.

"You have to tell the official agent," said Marno.

"It was free," I said, pleased with myself.

"Everything has a value that has to be recorded, or we'll be in trouble. We can't exceed the statutory limit."

"That's unlikely," I said.

A campaign is not allowed to exceed the dollar limits stipulated, when the election begins, by Elections Canada, and gifts in kind—from chairs loaned to a campaign office, to donated room space or specialized labour—are evaluated in dollar terms and applied against the ceiling. We expected the limit to be in the region of $90,000 for a five-week campaign starting in the first week of September.

JULY 24

CPC	NDP	LPC	BQ	GRN	OTH
31.3%	31.3%	26.3%	5.0%	5.3%	0.8%

. . .

Sarah, the spouse (not the "political wife"):

I wasn't prepared in supporting Noah's run for just how sexist the political world is. One of the first things Julian Heller said to me was "It's often harder on the spouse than the candidate!" This seemed crazy to me. In the beginning I'd talked about taking a sabbatical, but Noah insisted there was no need, and I fully expected to continue to go to work and do my job while Noah was out there knocking on doors, talking to strangers and trying to engage people. Canvassing and debating other candidates in public fora seems like a kind of hell to me, but I wasn't going to be the one putting myself on the line—he was. Still, people would ask me, "How does it feel to be a political wife?" and I'd stop myself from saying, "If I defined myself in terms of what my husband did then I suppose I might feel more put upon than I actually do!" I'm married to Noah, he's my partner in life, but I certainly do not see myself in the position of being "his" anything. I resist labels, and "political wife" was never one I was going to take on. It amazed me that even people I'd known for years used it.

. . .

Friends in places right and wrong: Heller telephoned to inform me of a fundraising event that one of Toronto—St. Paul's two city councillors, the "unaligned" leftie Joe Mihevc, was hosting to aid not my cause but those of neighbouring NDP candidates Andrew Cash, the sitting MP for Davenport, and Jennifer Hollett, the opponent of Liberal Chrystia Freeland in University—Rosedale.

"Their war chests are way ahead of ours," said Heller.

"And they're doing it in our riding, the one with a whopping $350, our constituents about to be sapped for other candidates?"

"Yes."

"And Mulcair is going to be there?"

Silence.

"It's unconscionable," said Heller, "that the leader would countenance a councillor playing both sides of the fence."

"What do you mean?"

"Mihevc is supporting the NDP, but not where he lives."

"What the fuck," I said. "I'm going to call Hollett and Cash. Some party."

"Don't," said Heller. "Jennifer's organizer called. They want to cooperate."

I was livid. I couldn't imagine that residents in a riding with poor chances would give twice, and felt shackled before I'd started. Some debut.

As if sensing trouble in the ether, Marno called to talk me off the ledge.

"We're not sure Cash and Hollett had access to our members' lists," said Marno.

"Come on. If they had any decency they'd give me a third of the money that they raise."

"The event was planned before you were on board."

"But it's in our riding."

"Yes."

"Whatever."

"Listen to me," said Marno. "You're going to go. You're going to be seen. And you're going to be nice to Joe Mihevc."

Which was what Sarah, hardly enthusiastic about her first appearance as the "political wife" she was not, was also telling me to do. Come the Saturday, the pair of us drove along St. Clair West, found a parking spot by the nearby McDonald's, and walked up a pleasant residential street in a district I barely knew to the house where some young volunteers in NDP-orange T-shirts were milling in the driveway.

The party was in the backyard. Another volunteer, sitting at a desk by the garage, asked me for my name.

"Noah Richler," I said. "I'm the NDP candidate for Toronto—St. Paul's. That would be here."

Sarah gave me a stern look and telegraphed the smile I was to wear just as the woman standing next to me asked if I lived in the riding.

"No," I said.

"Where do you?" the woman asked.

"Cabbagetown."

"Don't you think that's a problem?" she said in ornery fashion.

"You know how expensive and difficult it is to move house in Toronto," I said. "But if the vote goes our way I'll be putting roots down here."

This was news to Sarah, and to me, though I was confident she would have clocked the undetailed stating of my commitment—an office would constitute "roots," no?

"Don't you think you need to be in the riding now?"

"Well," I said, gathering up the arguments I'd practised with Boutilier, "it seems to me most of the challenges Torontonians have to contend with are true across the GTA— transit, infrastructure. Of course there are some issues particular to Toronto—St. Paul's and I'll see to those, but the truth is that you've not had a serious NDP candidate in the riding for a long time and I aim to be that."

Say *we*, never *you*, I thought, as Sarah nudged me on into the garden.

"Remember not to cross your arms," said Sarah.

In the backyard, I recognized Cash. He was standing with the musician Jason Collett and Jennifer Hollett. A former MuchMusic VJ, Hollett had studied at the John F. Kennedy School of Government at Harvard University and was in her element. The political adventure that was, to me, an exercise in democratic participation I did not expect to win (at least at the outset) was, to Hollett, a vocation relentlessly pursued to which all of her social media experience needed to be applied. Jennifer had a couple of people with her, one of them her campaign manager.

"The campaign manager is the most important person on your team," said Hollett. "Make sure you get the right one."

She said to call if I needed anything and, from this first moment of our meeting, proved to be the most helpful of my fellow GTA candidates. I felt suitably chastened. Then Tom Mulcair entered the backyard with his French-born Sephardic Turkish wife, Catherine Pinhas. A burly, bearded photographer in his fifties followed, motioning for the candidates and party leader to gather for a group shot. I stepped back—despite explicit instructions from Heller to get a photograph that could be posted on social media—but, as I did so, Mulcair took my hand and said how pleased he was that I was a part of the team. "Are you going to be okay?" he joked. I introduced Sarah and, not missing a beat, Mulcair smiled broadly and said he would telephone if he needed publishing advice, what with his auto-biography *Strength of Conviction* having just been released.

The photographer, Marc de Mouy, introduced himself and told me how excited he was I was running in his riding. Mulcair was ushered past and I headed to the bottom of the garden in anticipation of his speaking. On my way, I was stopped by a middle-aged woman wearing a small blue porkpie hat and hold-ing a dog on a lead.

"Do you live in the riding?" she asked.

"No," I said.

The woman's smile spoke to a certain agitation and I braced. I was about to be put on the spot again—had better get used to it—and needed not just my wits but a generosity of spirit if this politicking gig was to work out at all.

I embarked on the same answer I had provided minutes before. Once sorted, a politician's words are quickly repeated.

"And Toronto—St. Paul's is actually extraordinarily diverse. Would you feel I had more in common with this part of the riding, that strikes me as being quite a bit like Cabbagetown, if I lived in Forest Hill?"

"*Keep it simple,*" whispered Sarah in my ear. "Remember what Atwood said. You're getting too complicated."

"Do you have a dog?" the woman asked.

"Two."

"You should bring them to the dog park. You'll meet the riding that way."

The suggestion seemed familiar and I realized that, follow-ing the publication of the *Toronto Star* piece, the woman had already tweeted her dissatisfaction that I was not living in the riding at me. It was evident that nothing I could say was going to be particularly winning—or needed to be. There would be more significant issues.

"Did that get you down?" Sarah asked.

"No," I said. "I think folk just want to have made the point. And besides, it's all they know about me so far."

Mihevc stepped up to the microphone standing on the small riser at the foot of the garden. He welcomed Cash and Hollett and then mumbled a thrown-away fundraising ask before introducing Mulcair badly. Delivering a paean to Jack Layton, with whom he'd worked when the late NDP leader was a Toronto city councillor, Mihevc mentioned none of Mulcair's own bona fides, like he wasn't even a guest at the party. But the NDP leader, polls in his favour, took to the stage with a broad smile: a new day was dawning.

"It's amazing what leading does for a person," said Sarah. "He's so confident."

This was true. Mulcair was beaming. He embraced Cash and Hollett and congratulated the Davenport MP for the work he'd done getting the Conservatives' tax on tampons lifted.

"He reminds me of an old-fashioned political statesman from the fifties," said Sarah. "I like him—and I love that he's talking about tampons."

And then Mulcair did what Mihevc had not and gave the riding's candidate a shout-out, looking for me in the small crowd and asking that I join him on stage.

"He's smart, too," said Sarah, nudging me forward.

Mulcair congratulated his team but left quickly after that, his campaign already on. I mingled and chatted with a few guests who mentioned, apologetically, they'd given money to other ridings (information not solicited by me), and with a father and son polling duo from Alberta who told me, excitedly, how they had known a good week ahead of the result that Rachel Notley would win.

"Ninety percent of the vote depends on the performance of the leader in the last three weeks of the campaign," I said. "Notley is fabulous."

On our way out of the garden, Cash's partner, Michelle Shook, stepped away from the group gathered around her husband to have a quiet word.

"Don't believe people who say you can't win the first time," she said. "Andrew did."

I appreciated Michelle's friendliness in what had otherwise been a curious debut, and appreciated that her husband had been forthcoming too. My frustration about the event, I realized, had been out of order.

But the councillor was a problem. I looked for Mihevc, to say goodbye, and found him with a couple of constituents at the foot of the garden. When finally he did break away, I suggested that we meet sometime and asked how best to be in touch; he said his office number was on his website. It was clear there was to be no support there. Safely out of earshot, I told Sarah, "I'm going to have to win this riding without him."

. . .

The nomination meeting less than a week away, I pushed on with fundraising. This was not so easy. As with any writing I do, the first matter of business was to determine what was my authority to put pen to paper in the first place. What gave me the right to ask for other people's money? What was I offering? What made my project in any way distinct? Targeting *whom* to ask for money was fairly straightforward; figuring out the *how* was another story. It took me a good few days to determine whatever were plausibly the grounds that allowed me to ask for people to spend money they would not see back. The conversation—about why I was running at all—was, in the first instance, with myself.

. . .

DRAFT OF TEXT FOR (MAJOR) FUNDRAISING ASK

Hi _____

[PERSONALIZE FIRST PARAGRAPH, GIVE DETAILS OF NOMINATION MEETING AND FOLLOW WITH]

I am, like many, profoundly disturbed at the changes in the way Canada is being governed, the divisions that have been deliberately used to divide the community and the damage that nearly ten years of "Harper Government" has done at home and to our international reputation, too.

I believe that the reliance of the "Harper government" upon enmity for political expediency's sake is hurting the country in numerous ways but I am also not satisfied with Justin Trudeau as an alternative.

I believe that Tom Mulcair and the New Democratic Party offer the best, most progressive and exciting way forward. Finally Mulcair is being recognized as the force that he is in Parliament, a man of integrity and the impassioned leader of a party replete with talented and dedicated MPs that have already proved themselves so capable in opposition, and who are eager and ready to serve. I think of Niki Ashton, who represents a riding two thirds the size of France, who speaks four languages and is studying Cree; of the so-called McGill Four, twenty-somethings that have only impressed; or of Paul Dewar, Megan Leslie, Craig Scott and a host of others. Ever since the leadership campaign of 2012, when it first occurred to me to run, the NDP has revealed itself to be a party of diversity, intelligence and vitality. I am not easy on my bosses, and I can tell you that watching Tom last Saturday at a local fundraiser, I absolutely knew that I had made the right choice.

[GET TO THE MONEY ASK, YOU'RE TAKING TOO LONG]

The truth of a political campaign is that it costs money—$70,000 to $100,000 for a good one. The situation I am facing in Toronto—St. Paul's is that both my Liberal and Conservative rivals have very substantial amounts of money, likely the maximum, and I have—well, at last count, $350. I am asking you to make a donation not just for the riding to be able to pay for the campaign of which we are worthy—one in which we can afford the printing and the signs and office quarters and staff—but to ensure, no matter your affiliation (I am making no assumptions), a contest in which the serious issues of our day are rigorously discussed. Let us, together, work towards a better, healthier debate and democracy and away from Harper's Canada, in which science and statistics and contrary opinion are reviled.

The next election is one of the most important that has ever faced Canada. The money you give will ensure not just a vigorous local campaign but combat electoral apathy. It will help get out, as I shall be working hard to do, the young and the marginalized and to ensure that whatever course the country chooses, the decision will be one in which the population at large has participated.

For these reasons, I am asking you to donate to my campaign.

[ADD DONATION INSTRUCTIONS AND FIND
PERSONAL WAY TO SIGN OFF]

. . .

Such an easy index, money is. Money is vindication, a barometer of friends' and colleagues' confidence. Already, I was
scouring my personal contacts lists with a view to identifying
who was likely to pony up. Writers, I'd warned the team from
the start, were rarely flush and prone to complaining about
not being paid for this or that even as they indulged in the
"culture of free." No great expectations there, but I knew I'd
pitch writers anyway, they were the pals I had, though I
marked them down in Category Three on the "Noah's
Contacts" Excel sheet I was preparing for my fundraising asks.
Category One stood for "wealthy and powerful and likes me,
so go for it"; Category Two was pretty well the same but for
people perhaps living out of the riding or unlikely to give for
various reasons but give it a try anyway; Category Three was
for impecunious, what the hell, but don't dwell on it; and
Category Four was for those who've already given, or who are
broke, or not well, so try last of all.

Quickly I was proved wrong. Among the very first to
donate—the draft of my fundraising ask still on my hard
drive—were a couple of novelist friends from Newfoundland,
a legal thriller writer from Nova Scotia and a radio champion
of Canadian writing living on the West Coast. In many of
these letters, sentiments were expressed that I would encounter throughout the campaign: "I am so proud of you"; "Kudos
for trying what I would like to be able to do, but cannot"; "I
believe (really) and hope that the NDP will form the next
government." This was encouraging. Whatever degradation of
parliamentary democracy I feared the Conservatives had
managed was not deep-rooted; there were still people who
believed politics could be redeemed should the right folk find

their way in. I wanted to be that person, to live up to that ideal, even if a part of me also knew I would be most free to be the person of integrity—the inspiring and decent politician promising to bring a clean slate to tawdry government—during the period of time in which lack of title meant I was no more than a pretender. Did history not teach that *office* would, by its very nature, put an end to the sincerity with which most candidates begin?

How much, I wondered, did Mulcair or Trudeau actually believe any new party could bring "change" to Ottawa? "Change," as a slogan, should have been as tired an idea as decades of television advertisements for better detergents, more lustrous hair or youthful skin. How was it that we were still fooled? A satirical political advertisement on YouTube ("This Is a Generic Presidential Campaign Ad," created by the stock footage company Dissolve) compiles, quite perfectly, all the tropes that innumerable candidates have depended upon to sell themselves as society's panacea—farmers' fields, hard-hatted workers, doctors with stethoscopes about their neck, but also soldiers, brooding skies and hooded evildoers, etc. The messages of Hope and the Change that returns the gift of it to us (Clinton's, Obama's, Trudeau's and Mulcair's pitch) or, conversely, the stoking of fear that society will not be secure, or the economy not soundly managed (Bush's, Harper's, Trump's), are so inveterate we should be embarrassed that we are not yet inured.

. . .

And maybe you imagine political allegiances are about party platforms, class or the money we think the taxman has snatched? Not so. "Political identities," says the *New Yorker* writer George

Packer "are shaped mainly by irrational factors that have nothing to do with rational deliberation: family and tribal origins, character traits, historical currents." Our political affiliations "form in early adulthood and seldom change. Few people can be reasoned into abandoning their politics."

We have a whole set of reasons for choosing the parties we do: logical ones informed by platforms and the ideologies that, long ago, spawned them, but also resolute, personal ones. People talk of being "lifelong [*fill in the blank*] voters" because, such loyalty as inviolable as one to a sports team, voting as the family has done is a reflex and makes them part of a tribe. Makes them *belong*. Or maybe we identify with a party leader because we feel a kinship derived from a sense of being hard done by—but in our personal lives, rather than our *political* circumstances. Perhaps aspiration is the driver, and so we adhere to an aura of celebrity and success that could almost be ours because we voted for it. There's always baggage—a piece of carry-on, at least.

. . .

London, England, 1996.

My shrink looks like Medusa. She has long, curly russet locks that, in the hind corner of my vision, could pass for snakes. A classicist, I find this fitting. And so I am lying on the couch, eighty pounds sterling a session. There is a Rorschach print very deliberately positioned on the wall in front of me and, today, it looks like a padlocked rib cage. I am discussing the bad play I have been working on, a rewrite of Aeschylus's *Agamemnon*, in which I have made the brash Mycenaean leader of the Greek flotilla a foreign correspondent. I have given his long-suffering wife, Clytemnestra, a child that may or not be his. In the scene I am describing to my psychoanalyst, the infant boy runs and embraces Agamemnon, returned home after ten years.

"Agamemnon is your father," Medusa says.

"Oh no," I say. "He's just an absent hero to the boy."

. . .

In the start-up that was the Toronto—St. Paul's NDP campaign, my father's friends constituted another target in the search for early investors, so to speak. Almost all of them were not simply card-carrying Liberals, but full-on Liberal Party pushers. It was a useless pursuit—for money, that is. But it proved to me that I was charting my own course, this nagging of an Oedipal itch.

. . .

"J., how are you? It's Noah."

"How come you're not on the hustings?"

"Well, I walked into a riding that's absolutely broke and there's a little prep to do first. As it was put to me by one of the team, 'my time no longer belongs to me.'"

"I wish you luck."

"Also, I'm phoning because . . . well, I sent you a letter and didn't hear from you and I thought I'd better check that—"

"I know you're running against Carolyn Bennett in a difficult ward."

"I'm thoroughly fed up with Harper—"

"So are a lot of people. I wish you luck."

. . .

From: M.

Sent: July-28-15 5:33 PM

To: Noah Richler

Subject: Re: I had to ask . . .

Dear Noah,

Thank you for a very thoughtful and intelligent letter. I agree with much of what you say.

I actually met Mr. Mulcair at CTV and chatted with him and his executive assistant about cultural issues. I was given his card and actually wrote him. The silence was deafening. I never heard back. Where does the NDP stand on cultural policy?

I am appalled by his stance on the Clarity Act and 50% plus one. I am deeply pro-French and profoundly anti-separatist. How can I interpret his remarks other than pandering to soft nationalists in Quebec?

As to tomorrow night, I would be there to support you personally but am off at the crack of dawn for lunch with Mayor Nenshi in Calgary and simply do not land until 1 am Thursday. I like Stephen Lewis very much. His dad was a great friend of my late father.

Sadly, I cannot support you financially because I committed my full legal allowance weeks before you entered the campaign to two other friends—Seamus O'Regan and Chrystia Freeland.

I am sorry not to be more helpful on the short-term practical front.

Best regards,

M.

. . .

Wednesday, July 29, came and Laura arrived early for the nomination meeting at one of the Tarragon Theatre's rehearsal halls with bus trays of soft drinks, a couple of fold-up tables and, just in case, a laptop computer and printer—all of this without planning on my part. Kari Marshall, a friend who worked at the House on Parliament, my Cabbagetown local, had set up outside with a cart of the eclectic Pop Stand popsicles she crafts and was handing out orange ones to welcome folk in. Inside, volunteers from the riding were taking down names, the first of many times I'd shake the hand of men and women coming out to work for the campaign whom I'd meet no more than once. In the upstairs rehearsal room that we'd been provided, the kernel of what would become my team had set up a small stage and lights and a PA and had blown up orange balloons. The room of sixty was filled to capacity, the overflow watching through the open doors at the back, when Stephen Lewis rose to speak.

"Let me suggest to you that the moment the election is called, we unleash the potential of Toronto—St. Paul's and you *don't wait*," said Lewis. "Come to the committee room in advance, choose a poll and go out that night and start knocking on doors—the later the better, because it attracts voter attention. It's a simple proposition: my suggestion is you go out any time between eleven and midnight, you knock on the door and, as generously and in as dignified a manner as you can convey— because people will be staggering down the hall to greet you— you say, 'Good evening sir, I represent Carolyn Bennett.' And you will find by the morning, the campaign is over!"

Lewis was in fine form. He complimented the NDP's "formidable array of talent" across the GTA—Craig Scott and Linda McQuaig in the room, and Andrew Cash, Olivia Chow, Jennifer Hollett, Peggy Nash, Mike Sullivan and Rathika

Sitsabaiesan among those outside of it. "My father David Lewis [one of the founders of the NDP, David had been leader of the federal party during the first four years of his son's time as Ontario NDP leader] always said to me, 'Son, not in my time, but perhaps in yours.' And I've always said to our own three kids, 'Not in my time, but perhaps in yours.' Well I'll be damned! It looks as if it could be in my time after all!"

Some elections, said Lewis, were vastly more auspicious than others, this one particularly so. Harper's government was the "most ignoble that Canada had ever experienced, lacking sincerity and honesty and run with reprehensible cunning." Canada was "being shredded before our eyes."

Lewis's attack was as unrelenting as it was enthralling. And it was being viewed by more than those in the room. I had assembled the beginnings of a social network team for the campaign: Carolyn McNeillie, who'd helped build my author's website, and Neil Wadhwa, another employee at the House of Anansi. In our moment of start-up, Carolyn was the invaluable lynchpin, the overseer pushing essential things forward discreetly and purposefully. It was Carolyn who, at Sarah's suggestion, had set up Slack, the campaign's intramural communications program on which I would come to depend, and now here she was attending my nomination with Neil and broadcasting the event on Periscope, a Twitter-powered live video-streaming app not yet in widespread use. Thanks to the set-up, ten times the number in the room were able to hear Lewis speak and then the Sudanese-Canadian musician Waleed Abdulhamid play, at a cost to the riding association of exactly nothing. The first congratulatory comment to come in was a tweet from Milan, irrelevant in terms of votes or donations but auguring well for the campaign's reach. I had elected not to speak immediately after Lewis (why ambush myself?) and, instead, the television writer and comic Anne Fenn stepped up to make the money ask. Craig Scott had come out and my mother, sitting next to Linda McQuaig, the NDP's Toronto Centre candidate, raised her hand pledging the maximum $1,500 to get the fundraising going—and it worked. Doug followed and then more friends gave, a number of them from outside the riding, and then constituents of all ages did. Within fifteen minutes we had raised over $16,000—already exceeding the $10,000 we'd set as a target and a good portion of the money we required for the skeleton budget that Marno had drawn up during the July 23 meeting of the EPC. We had more than enough money to order lawn and window signs and a first pamphlet.

We had a campaign.

From the wings, I stepped up to the microphone to deliver the first speech of my campaign. Looking back, I see how easy a target the Conservatives had become—and how the language of a Canada to be restored was sufficiently in the air that it spanned the parties.

The Canada I know, the Canada you and I love—the Canada in which those who can take care of themselves take care of the people who cannot; that seeks through such long overdue measures as affordable child care, not to maintain but improve the lives of working people; that treats the environment sensibly and engages with and seeks to learn from the gift of our First Nations; that sees racism and does not turn away from it; that should never have to be told "Black Lives Matter"—this Canada, the country for so long held in high esteem all over the world, the Canada that stands as an example to other countries and to ourselves— the Canada of encouragement, of peace, prosperity, good government and goodwill—this country, I tell you now, is coming back.

But a campaign is, to a very significant degree, cocooned. The focus is intensely local, and what messages do seep in from elsewhere have been pushed through the party filter. That process had already started. First order of business: knock the competition.

It is the NDP that is going to help you retrieve it—not a Liberal Party still hopelessly entitled—a Liberal Party that, in its cynical and self-serving support of the odious Bill C-51, has shown yet again that, as shamefully as the Conservatives, it regards power as its just desserts; a party that has willingly sacrificed the interests of Canadians on the altar of its slavish pursuit of power, as if we hadn't noticed their true character already. As if we hadn't watched the ridiculous imposition upon a riding that wished otherwise of the hapless Eve Adams as candidate—or, worse, of Toronto's former police chief Bill Blair, champion of carding and the man who, during the G20 Summit five years ago, turned this city into a security forces' training ground stripped of dignity and civil rights by overzealous officers. No, no, neither is this country for me.

Then sing the party's praises.

No, instead I choose you, I choose the New Democratic Party, I choose its leader, Tom Mulcair, and its plethora of bright, exciting, dedicated MPs who do not take their position for granted—assume anything is rightfully theirs—but instead work each day to convince you, to learn from you, to serve you. I choose Canada, and I choose the NDP because the NDP is Canada, the NDP is you.

And put the platform in.

I want a party that will heal, not divide—that will provide transport for cities and affordable child care for working families, that will hold in respect all constituencies, even ones that may not, this coming October, immediately see the light. I choose the party that knows its job is to make Canada the best place, the fair country, the caring country. This is my pledge.

Whatever the necessary intrusions, the voice was mine, no question about that, and the points I was making were ones I wished for the party at large. I had not yet learned these were sentences, not sound bites, nor that it was not my place to make speeches of this kind—to behave, I suppose, as a party leader would. Lewis was wonderful but ultimately misleading. I was speaking above my station, and at fault was my own romantic imagination.

. . .

But I did not know that then. The evening ended, spirits good, and an email from Pratt appeared on my iPhone.

16 grand!?!? That's amazing. Well done.
　　Also, Penny shook me down last night and we're gonna float you money for the deposit for the office.

Josh Moraes, the regional organizer responsible for several of the GTA ridings, had coached me through the early stages of the nomination process and took me into a backroom to sign a couple of mandatory forms.

"When this whole thing is over," said Moraes, "people will

ask you if you're going to run again. But you don't ask yourself that. Not for at least a month."

. . .

Larry, my bank manager, has left a message: now that I'm a candidate, I'll need an account. Sarah's driving when I return the call and am put through to his voicemail.

"Hey, Larry, Noah here. Hope all's well. Listen, I've just been through Mount Pleasant Cemetery—it's in my riding—and I've sent you the names of five dead people not on the rolls. So we're good for five twenty-grand deposits, okay? Bye!"

"*YOU CAN'T DO THAT!*" Sarah screams.

"Sorry, love."

"You're a candidate! You have people out to get you now. You don't know what happens to that tape or who is listening. No jokes. *Stop yourself!*"

. . .

Three days later, on August 2—and some five weeks ahead of the September day that was expected to be the start of the 2015 campaign—Harper announced the issuing of writs for Canada's forty-second general election. The early start put an end to expenditures that did not count towards parties', party leaders' and candidates' election limits, as it did the quasi-campaigning that had been in effect for several months. The contest, culminating on October 19, was to be 78 days long, the longest in 143 years—and, certainly within the NDP, the suspicion was that Harper's early instruction for the 338 writs to be issued was intended to put the more resourced Conservative Party of Canada at an advantage. The longer campaign meant, for instance, that the $96,756 each riding would have been allowed under Elections Canada rules to spend on a 37-day contest was increased to $203,972. This was money the Conservatives and Liberals, but not the NDP, had. And it was hoped that not just the NDP's coffers, but its human energies, would be exhausted. Within the NDP, the instruction was not to fall prey to the manoeuvre—for teams to pace themselves and not panic.

AUGUST 3

CPC	NDP	LPC	BQ	GRN	OTH
30.9%	33.2%	25.9%	4.7%	4.7%	0.7%

. . .

A few days later, Marno called to say that I had two excellent campaign manager options to choose from. I knew I needed someone with experience, but also wanted a person who would be open to new tactics and strategies. Marno had already informed me she would not be managing campaigns this time around, and Deb Parent had said the same. Marno, my good fortune, was offering one of the few proven campaign managers still not booked—somebody boasting a terrific track record but who was asking to be paid—or, in his place, a triumvirate of three respected party veterans: Phil Carter, whom she described as an excellent speechwriter; Wendy Hughes, a former principal of Clinton Street Junior Public School, in Toronto; and Janet Solberg, a former vice-president of the Ontario NDP, daughter of David Lewis, and sister to Michael and Stephen. (Wendy Hughes had been married to Michael for a time and all were close.) All had agreed to come out of retirement, and to work for free. Carter, said Marno, would likely only be on for a short time, and Hughes and Solberg would alternate from August on. I felt Stephen's hand at work, and said right away that the triumvirate was what I wanted. And it's what I got.

. . .

Janet, campaign manager:

I've worked in campaigns all of my life. And that's not hyperbole. Being a Lewis meant that all of the children started working in campaigns when we were old enough to distribute leaflets, print signs, address envelopes. Sounds so old school now! Stephen wrote me about Noah running and told me he was speaking at his nomination. He also said he didn't know who the campaign manager was. That got me thinking. I didn't know Noah but I did know I couldn't run a good campaign by myself—it's been a while—so I asked a couple of experienced friends and that formed the nucleus of the campaign management team that expanded into an energetic, hard-working and fun group.

. . .

Phil, campaign manager:

Why, after decades of refusing to ever organize another campaign, did I agree to co-manage the TSP campaign? Because Janet made me do it. The party had asked me in the spring to manage another campaign, offering "lots of money." I told them no amount of money would induce me to manage a campaign again. But then, in midsummer, it felt like history was in the making and I mentioned to Janet that I wished I could play a part by helping out with speeches, leaflets or whatever. She said there were a number of priority seats still without campaign managers and I said the only way I'd ever get involved in that again would be co-managing with her. Since she was crazy busy with the Stephen Lewis Foundation, the campaign in Toronto Danforth and the provincial party, I thought that would put an end to that. But then she called and said she'd agreed to take on the Richler campaign in Toronto—St. Paul's. Brother Stephen had spoken at the TSP nomination and was enthused about the candidate. So there we were. Janet brought in Wendy as well, and we got off to a good start.

. . .

Wendy, campaign manager:

And why did I get involved? There is something miraculous about how quickly a group with common cause comes together and gives so much effort. In a short period of time—because of long hours, every single day—you get to know your co-workers as intimately as family members. In a week you know more about their strengths and vulnerabilities than casual or regular workplace friends you might have known for years. I'm sure this is the same intensity war veterans feel about their combat relationships. You quickly figure out whom you can trust and rely on, and there are always those who surprise and delight you with their optimism, dedication, hard work and insights.

. . .

They say an alcoholic never remembers his first drink, and if
the tumult of that road is anything to go by, maybe that's why
I can't recall the first moment of meeting my campaign management team—all of whom, contrary to their wary pledges,
worked full-time from beginning to end. What I do remember
is that by the time I was back in Toronto—I'd taken a few days
to be with my family in Nova Scotia—the Bathurst Street
office was in business, Janet, Phil and Wendy hard at work
within it. I'd suggested looking for premises in the Oakwood–
Dufferin west end of the riding, an area Debbie Parent had
identified as one of NDP strength, or even setting up a mobile
office in an Airstream or Winnebago caravan, cheaper to run,
and that we could move about the district as an old-fashioned
circus troupe as indeed my late friend Terry Wall might have
done, but that didn't wash. We needed facilities for people with
disabilities, a bank of telephones and computer stations, and
fortunately, a member of the executive had found the perfect
site, Penny negotiating the lease for a highly visible former
retail space on Bathurst Street just north of St. Clair Avenue
West. The junction was almost exactly in the geographical
heart of the riding—easy to span out from—and busy with the
passing traffic of shoppers, TTC riders and commuters. Our
very first sign could not have been more strategically placed.
At a first meeting that Laura had called, arriving with two
friends and a strategist from her husband Michael's office
who thought they might be interested in working with the
campaign, the office had still been empty and without desks or
phones or furniture but for a few folding chairs we pulled
across the bare, unfinished concrete underfoot into a small
circle. One wall of the office was made entirely of mirror,

though the front was a floor-to-ceiling window that filled the place with light. The office had air conditioning, and at the back there were a couple of washrooms—one for people with disabilities—and a room that would do nicely for private meetings. A boon for volunteers canvassing and posting signs, or a candidate arriving from Cabbagetown, there was an exit to the lot behind the building, and free parking there as well as underground. Posters of Tom Mulcair were pinned to the window storefront—a banner with my name had been ordered to go above it—and several desks of different sizes, corralled from members and friends and garages, already had people working at them. Phil, who'd insisted on being "backroom," if he was to work on the campaign at all, had set himself up nicely at one of the larger desks farthest away from the front door. Wendy was seated at one of a few desks with a telephone, and if I have an abiding visual memory of the office it is of this soft-spoken and thoughtful woman with her head down, speaking into the telephone to voters in the riding as she would do from nine in the morning to seven at night and later, virtually every day of the campaign. And, too, of Janet, pacing in the front. On the wall behind Phil were sheets listing the 190 polls (there was also a mobile one) in the adjusted riding, as well as a calendar and list of tasks. A candidate's office is much like the green room of a stage play, and for the long hour of strutting and fretting that was our election run, I would learn how a campaign is an undertaking of the many and the candidate is certainly not the boss of it. I'd come to appreciate the distinct qualities of my colleagues—all those other pieces of the machine. There was Young Ethan, a political science graduate and, years back, the grade school classmate of one of Sarah's two girls. He'd anticipated working for the Liberals, but I'd leaned on our family friendship to have him work for me. A wise move it was, Young Ethan being a model of dependability and resolve. So too was Data Ethan, a member of the riding executive who'd moved over to the Bathurst Street office on Day One, busy at the computer dedicated to the entry of polling information and liaising with Populus, the federal party database. And there was Elizabeth Glor-Bell, of course, another member of the Toronto—St. Paul's executive, who, at that first meeting I'd attended back on July 8, declared she was too busy to work for us but subsequently agreed to come on as the pre-election organizer. The first of the two washrooms at the back had been appropriated for storage and was filled with candidate signs. The second had her bicycle parked in one of its two stalls. Beside it was the backroom, which would be used for telephone canvassing and confidential meetings. For eleven weeks, these premises were ground control and home.

. . .

Wendy and her common-law partner, Bob Meddings, ushered me into the backroom. Phil, who had asked me to bring in a variety of suits and ties, stood by the door.

"Don't dress for the job you have," Phil had said. "Dress for the job you want."

Bob, whom I'd become accustomed to seeing step out of a beaten-up car with a full load of signs and a mallet in hand, was the campaign's photographer for the reshoot we'd decided was necessary for less harried material for the election proper. The three urged me to smile, not very successfully, then to come forward like Snoopy wanting to shake a hand, and soon gave up—but they were good, the shots. Dress the candidate for the job you want him to have. He's all you've got.

. . .

Brochures on the go, the next task was to create a viable organizational structure (and communications to support it) with a view to seamlessly melding the working practices of the experienced NDP members of the team with the ambitions of a mostly younger bunch with new methods and ideas and an aptitude for the social networks. Barnaby Marshall, a social networking specialist, Neil and Carolyn had been with the campaign since before my nomination. The two Ethans; Krista Kais-Prial, a young lawyer whom I'd convinced through Twitter to come see us; and Becky Elming, special assistant to Andrea Horwath and helping to nurture the TSP team along, were added subsequently. Krista was handling tweets, Barnaby my NDP candidate's page and the mail that came into it, and Becky and Young Ethan the liaising with my Facebook Events page. The Slack program Carolyn set up had been working well for us, both as a security measure—worried about Conservative or Liberal infiltration, I had acted on Laura's wariness—and because, free of unsolicited messages, there was no whacking through a bush of emails to find the ones worth reading before they were lost in the undergrowth of a smartphone retaining just the last fifty communications. There were only the messages that mattered, sorted by subject, by person or by group. Slack also provided an easy monitoring of who was dipping in and completing tasks and who was just visiting. I decided that hangers-on—folk I could not rely upon, who'd not been in touch for a while or had decided, for instance, that they were above canvassing—would be dropped from the program, ergo the team, and that was that.

Our structure, replicated in the channels of the Slack program, looked like this:

CAMPAIGN MANAGEMENT TEAM
Philip Carter   Wendy Hughes   Janet Solberg

Riding Association Julian Heller	**Handler/Scheduler** Becky Fong	**Official Agent** Erinn Somerville

CANDIDATE
Noah Richler

ELECTION PLANNING COMMITTEE	OUTREACH/ VOLUNTEERS	OFFICE	STRATEGY	SOCIAL MEDIA	FINANCE
B. Ross Ashley	**Pre-Election**	**Office**	**Strategy Group**	**Web Admin**	B. Ross Ashley
Sean Caragata	**Organizer**	**Manager**	Doug Bell	Rebecca Elming	Erinn Somerville
Kristian Chartier	Liz Glor-Bell	Susan Marcus	Sean Caragata	Barnaby Marshall	
Liz Glor-Bell			Kristian Chartier	Carolyn McNeillie	**Fundraising**
Ethan Hoddes	**Volunteer**		Sarah M.		**General**
Joyce Rankin	**Contact**		Josh Scheinert	**Audio-Visual**	Catherine Drillis
Molly Reynolds	**Organizer**		Michael T.	Carolyn M.	Julian Heller
	Ethan F.		Laura Watts	Neil Wadhwa	Colleen Siles
				Ilich Mejia	
	Election Day		**Speechwriting**	Marc de Mouy	**Fundraising**
	Organizer		Philip Carter	J. Rotsztain	**Cultural Events**
	TBD		Michael T.		Sandra C.
				Video Team	Sarah M.
				???	Ray Perkins

If I bother you with this information, it is for two reasons. First, I was quite surprised, given the number of elections the NDP had contested before this one, that I was not handed a simple handbook and told, "Here's the template for building a campaign, get to it." (The "traditional knowledge" of campaign teams is, as with Inuit, oral.) My second reason may be an answer to the first. Every campaign is, as I have already said, a fresh invention, and every election demands new techniques mostly determined by advances in technology. *Shopping for Votes: How Politicians Choose Us and We Choose Them* is a useful text by the veteran Ottawa correspondent Susan Delacourt that mines the obvious parallel to be made between the pushing of political candidates and the evolution of marketing techniques. A chapter on the 2015 campaign (the first edition of the book stopped after 2011) could have been written months before the forty-second general election even started, for it was common knowledge across the country that social media—in particular, Facebook, Twitter and YouTube—would provide the means for the next landscape-altering technological advance. Phones were still important, of course (though landlines less); and knocking on doors more so, but the new technology meant cheaper outlays, less costly research, the possibility of significantly greater reach—and a dividend to be reaped on imaginative work. From the beginning, we were aware, hardly an original thought, that the last condition favoured campaigns like ours with next to no resources. A draft social media team and a stream of good audio-visual material to feed our network platforms were of the essence from the very start. To that end, one of my first recruits had been Jonathan Rotsztain, a cartoonist and graphic artist with whom I had collaborated at Luminato, and he agreed to produce cartoons and "The Candidate" graphics—dare I call it "branding" —as required. We also needed a video team. But before meeting that challenge, I had a strategy team to put to work, eager to become a candidate impeccably in command of the facts. In Toronto—St. Paul's, the fact of Liberals having represented the riding since 1993 meant we were under no illusions about whom to target, and first order of business was to create a SWOT chart listing the assets and liabilities of Carolyn Bennett's run and my own, a task undertaken by Sean Caragata and Young Ethan. Defeating Harper was of course paramount, but, at the local level, the Conservative candidate Marnie MacDougall (no relation to Barbara MacDougall, the Progressive Conservative who had occupied the seat from 1984 to 1993) did not yet come into it.

. . .

One of Laura's friends was Catherine Drillis, a communications and PR professional, and, early on in the campaign, she arrived with a PowerPoint presentation. Catherine talked about fundraising strategies and targets, and it was clear she was thinking big—much bigger than the party was used to. The NDP, version 2015, was sending out multiple e-blasts a day from proxy addresses of top party figures, each asking for five dollars at a time, most duly discarded. President Barack Obama's grassroots fundraising success was the model, but in truth the emails spoke to a party with an ingrained resistance to exactly the sort of splashy events and bigger asks both Catherine and I were envisioning. As if to illustrate, an email was circulating of a cocktail reception that Barry Sherman, a Liberal in the riding, was hosting for Justin Trudeau at which a donation of $1,500 was necessary just to get across the threshold. I wondered how much the NDP dared ask for the privilege of meeting Mulcair. What was he "worth," and what did that hypothetical figure say? As for the Conservatives, it was generally believed they were campaigning in the riding more to raise money for the party than to win the seat. But the NDP tradition of events was to hope visitors might leave a little more than the ten dollars it cost to feed them shrimp platters, sandwich quarters or dim sum. This approach was a reflection of the reality of many NDP supporters' limited means—the very reason the party exists—though also of a certain failure of ambition. So, despite my knowing we had too little time to put into place things we'd like to see happen, we discussed the merely vaguely possible: an arts gala at Casa Loma, perhaps a cocktail party during TIFF, but also schoolyard, park and community events and the series of pub nights Ray and I were keen on.

Catherine, not one to be cowed, was suggesting an outlay of $20,000 to gain $100,000, while Heller was holding his peace and not telling her—not immediately anyway—that this simply would not happen. But I really wanted her on the team and could see that she was expecting to be paid and that whatever I did agree to pay her, if indeed that authority was mine, would need to be built into the targets. Fundraising had never stopped being key, and her data analyzed the 2011 fundraising of the four parties operating in the riding and the financial resources each was on record as having to draw on. MacDougall had $200,000 in the bank; Bennett, $150,000. Catherine had put together graphs illustrating past campaigns' successes—the amount of money raised, the number of contributors, the sizes of donations. Whatever funds the NDP had raised in the riding in 2011—less, even, than the Green Party—did not register. More graphs attested to equally dispiriting data. Then Catherine flipped to a pane called "Advantages."

It said:

NO DONOR FATIGUE

. . .

Peter, a donor (and to the max):

Why did I give?
For the following reasons:

    1. I enjoy supporting insurgents over incumbents—in just
       about anything.
    2. Especially a disruptor or activist—someone who is also
       humorous (I love lightness of being, especially where
       lightness is challenged.)
    3. I believe in karma.
    4. I'm a BIG fan of the spouse.
    5. Alcohol probably had a small role.
    6. And the tax deduction helps.

. . .

Things I was planning from the start:
  Funky town halls
  Fundraisers
  A cartoon crew
  A skateboard gang
  Videos
  Meet and greets

. . .

I'd been working since before my nomination on the first of the meet and greets with Shannon Litzenberger, a dancer and advocate working with the Canadian Arts Coalition and the annual Canadian Arts Summit organized by Business for the Arts, a fundraising body pairing patrons from the corporate community with cultural causes. Shannon had put me in touch with a number of her contacts, one of them a resident of a small and very wealthy enclave in the Toronto—St. Paul's riding known as "the Republic of Rathnelly." (This part of the city was previously known, less glamorously, as South Hill, but playfully declared itself an independent republic during the country's 1967 centenary celebrations, hence the moniker.) Such is the way of things in Toronto: a part of the city that was once the *pied à terre* of journalists, professors and writers—it lies just north of the railway tracks of the Canadian Pacific Dupont Line that mark the southern edge of the riding—the Republic of Rathnelly is now home to a more moneyed set. My contact was Nichole Anderson, in her late thirties and CEO of Business for the Arts. In July, she had congratulated me for throwing my hat in the ring. "A disruptive force . . . for the good," she wrote.

The pair of us had arranged to meet for coffee before Nichole's departure to cottage country, with a view to staging a meet and greet in the riding in late August or early September.

"There are a few NDPers in Rathnelly," emailed Nichole, "and the standard Liberal voters."

I waited on a blisteringly hot Friday afternoon at Seven Grams, a coffee shop at the corner of Avenue Road and MacPherson Avenue to meet Nichole for a chat and a tour of Rathnelly. Much as I would have liked to imagine a future in Fisheries (that portfolio already pledged, apparently), common sense said that *were* I elected, *were* I offered a ministry and *were* any of the NDP MPs who had worked so hard in opposition not ahead of me in the queue, then Heritage was a role to which experience suited me, so that the tenor of our meeting made sense. Besides, it was good practice, a rehearsal on friendly territory. But when Nichole sat down at the small patio table in the shade to which I had staked a claim, it was the NDP in general that we discussed. Nichole was wary. Her husband, Alain Bergeron, a senior vice-president and portfolio manager with Mackenzie Investments, had met Mulcair when the NDP leader was the minister of the environment for the Quebec Liberals and had found him "warm and friendly," said Nichole, but rude and arrogant when, as NDP leader, he was "attacking his sector in the media."

"We need someone at the helm who is going to work with business to improve society rather than attack," said Nichole. "Most people of our generation—even those working in finance!—care deeply about the social good."

This had not been my experience of Mulcair at all, I said—noting, as I did so, the uncomfortable first of having to apologize for my party leader. What impressed me, in fact, was just how keen Mulcair was *not* to alienate, and to bring all parties to the table: he'd discussed the prospect of biannual meetings with the provinces—congresses that Harper had effectively eliminated—and was promising to take not just the premiers but also mayors, NGOs and even critics to the Paris Summit of the United Nations Climate Change Conference scheduled for October.

"What about taxes?" asked Nichole. "Is the NDP planning to raise taxes?"

"Yes," I said. "We'll be cutting stock option tax loopholes and asking corporations to pay more."

"If you do that you'll drive corporations out of town. Toronto will lose jobs. It's already so hard."

Here was the familiar coercion of big business, a constant in politics, that I'd anticipated having to combat at the door.

"What keeps corporations in place," I said, "are cities where income inequality does not create an insuperable divide, and it's incumbent upon corporations to understand it's in their own best interests that people living right next to the one percent are not wracked with envy or a bitter sense of unjust desert. For the sake of community, we need to make cities liveable—for everybody. Look, I walked the riding just south of St. Clair and west of Spadina yesterday, and was stunned to discover a full-on gated community. I couldn't believe it. I had no idea Toronto had a single one—"

"There's Wychwood."

"That's different, it's historic. This had a manned barrier checking the cars that went through. I felt like I was in a government embassy compound, or a gated community in L.A. Is that what you want?"

Nichole suggested we take a walk through Rathnelly. We crossed Avenue Road and turned left just north of the railway bridge, where she showed me the CP tracks that were a source of tremendous local concern. Residents were worried, with cause, that a train wreck could devastate the area through fire or the release of toxic chemicals, an anxiety heightened by the train derailment disaster that, two years before, had demolished the Quebec town of Lac-Mégantic and taken forty-seven lives.

"All politics is derived from principle," I said, "and the first one is that government exists to take care of those that can't take care of themselves. The second is that government is there to act as a hedge against big business—to speak for communities that may not be heard otherwise. This is not a comment *against* business but simply a recognition that when corporations overreach, ordinary people need a hand. You believe that too. It's why you're asking for help in the face of Canadian Pacific bringing all their toxic materials through."

Nichole smiled, her manner as unrevealing as it was serene, and took me along the street that was home, introducing me to a few passers-by and homeowners as we passed. You could feel the city emptying out for the weekend. Alain, home from work, joined us and spoke of an open letter sent by a league of investors' groups, controlling trillions, to the G7 ministers of finance in advance of the UN Climate Change Conference, urging support of the "ambitious agreement" to limit global temperature increase to 2°C. It was an interesting document— and the fact of its origin in the financial sector was encouraging. I'd been developing the notion of a "moral moments" pitch at the door and this demonstration of environmental concern by an accomplished investor was playing into it. This was certainly not the bullish world of uncompromising advocates of the oil patch at all costs.

We arrived at the family house. The city had erected temporary fencing to protect the tree in the front yard.

"We'll have to have our meet and greet somewhere else," said Nichole. "We're having renovations done."

I wondered if my heavy-handed defense of the NDP had prompted a change of mind.

"The fence is orange," I said. "I figure that's a good omen."

. . .

August 8, and the first of the election debates is being broadcast online. Mulcair appears a little stiff, but who, in the unnatural forum of a television debate, would not be? Elizabeth May, that's who. She is the star, tolerating none of Harper's obfuscations and appearing terrifically on top of her material.

I say to Doug, "Wouldn't it be something if right now, live before the country, Mulcair said, 'We need your intelligence, Elizabeth. I don't care what colour you wear, come on over. Be our minister of the environment.'"

"Will never happen."

"But it's a thought."

AUGUST 10

CPC	NDP	LPC	BQ	GRN	OTH
30.8%	33.0%	27.2%	4.2%	4.2%	0.6%

. . .

The national campaign is heating up and in Toronto—St. Paul's, the fledgling team is feeling buoyant. Trudeau has pledged to build the Canadian economy "from the heart" and is being ridiculed in newspapers and on social media by pundits wondering what this could possibly mean. The Liberal Party leader and his top advisor, Gerald Butts, are scrambling to explain on Twitter that by "heart," the leader meant the "middle class." There are chortles all around as B., a fashion magnate, calls. Trudeau had visited his Toronto factory earlier in the year and he wants to know what the NDP's position on marijuana is.

"Justin's gonna legalize it," says B.

"We're planning to decriminalize it. That's not quite the same thing, but a necessary first step."

"I really like his plan. But Noah, I love what you're doing, so I'm going to give you three thousand and my wife—well, she's giving two, but that's five grand all in all and should do you well, no?"

"That's amazing, B., thank you."

"We're doing it ourselves—not in the name of the company. It's got to be anonymous, okay?"

I thank him profusely, make excuses about a bad line and say I'll call back. I know B. to be easily distracted and there is not much point in talking about maximum donations, or explaining that companies aren't allowed to give and large donations are, by law, not anonymous, as he is driving. Time for that later.

"That's fantastic," I say very sincerely. "That's really great."

"I love your friends," says Janet.

. . .

The next day, a cheque arrives from Nova Scotia for $1,500—that's a $2,000 tally for the day, what with the cheque for $500 that was pushed through my door in the morning.

"I'll never vote NDP," says the donor when I call to say thanks, "but we need people like you in Parliament."

. . .

A spritely, balding fella in a red T-shirt, a successful fifty-something entrepreneur, bounds into the campaign office. He introduces himself as Tom.

He says: "I've been a lifelong Conservative. I want to write you a cheque—and I want the biggest sign you have."

Tom, hopping about with excitement, fills out a cheque for a grand and then asks if he can take an iPhone picture of me holding it up to my chest.

"Wow," he says. "This'll really piss off my Facebook friends."

DOORS OPE

Disillusioned
Working
Young People

TCHC
Old People
East

UPPER
BENNETT
COUNTRY

CPC
OLIVERLAND

ISIL–Anxious
Forest Hill Jews

ISLE OF
MACDOUGALL

Locally
Disinterested
Condo Dwellers

MID BENNETT COUNTRY/Rich Old People

Dog Walkers for Bennett

Joe Mihevc Avenue West

LOWER
BENNETT
COUNTRY

Pierre Trudeau's
Jamaica

Euro
Contractors

Cookie Roscoe
Territory

Liberals
in Big Houses
Worried About
Trains

NDP NOAHLAND

TCHC
Old People
West

Artists
for Deficits

LIBERAL
FREELAND

NDP
CASHLAND

Poor People
Worried About
Trains

CHAPTER THREE

, TORONTO

Elizabeth, volunteer organizer:

Canvassing is a strange beast. It puts a person in the unusual circumstance of approaching someone at home—where people are most comfortable but also, the encounter being so personal, they feel most vulnerable too. A politician is a bit like a door-to-door salesman, and this local aspect of an election is essential because the news cycle is dominated by the interparty air war. On the ground you have to come off as likeable, trustworthy and inspire respect. You have to show you're engaged with the community and familiar with it. A common complaint in politics is that politicians only come around when they're looking for votes; when you need them, they're nowhere to be found. So showing face after you've chosen to run is the single most important thing a candidate does. Because then you become real, you're more than just a name on paper. If you're seen, if you're known, if you're liked, you've probably gained a vote. Canvassing is important to the election process—but it's not that easy. Noah's head was in the big game—making big moves, being heard beyond our little corner of Toronto and helping the NDP's run beyond the borders of a nigh-unwinnable riding. Having the drive, ambition and

know-how to get the big projects done can make a great political
candidate. It doesn't necessarily translate into being a candidate
who wins elections.

. . .

The brochures have arrived. I like that the office phone number
is my name, 647-348-NOAH. The volunteers and staff at the
office are getting to know each other. The atmosphere is good.

"This election, there's a clear choice for change," says the first
leaflet I am to hand out. It has a photograph of smiling Tom
Mulcair at a rally on the front and my strange, doctored happy
self (not used to that) on the back. The Conservatives are "wrong
for Canada." Trudeau isn't "up to the job." Mulcair offers "experienced, principled leadership" and "our best chance for defeating Stephen Harper." A graph displays the first- and second-place
tallies of the three major parties back in 2011: 166 Conservative
MPs elected, 65 ridings where they came second; 103 and 121 for
the NDP; and 34 and 76 for the Liberals—a distant third. The
inference—one that will be relied upon heavily in the NDP's
campaign—is that in a plethora of races our party placed, not
showed, and just a little push will convert close calls into wins
and a majority.

Bennett is my target and I have no issue saying she's *past*
ready—eighteen years is too long for any MP to be in office,
surely. Sarah's worried. She thinks I'm not cut out for this. But
I'm an old radio hand and I like talking to people. I promise
myself I'll be gracious at the door—not be negative, do my best
to be charming.

. . .

AUGUST 17

CPC	NDP	LPC	BQ	GRN	OTH
29.4%	33.5%	26.7%	3.7%	5.8%	0.9%

. . .

Outing number one: Poll 143.

Elizabeth accompanies Young Ethan and me out on our first canvass. Liz, born in Calgary and raised in Ottawa, is in her late twenties, naturally ebullient and, well, pleasantly ruthless. She has been working as a personal support worker (or "PSW") since her graduation from the University of Toronto in linguistics and gender studies, and when I ask how one thing led to the other she responds in a simple, matter-of-fact way that her younger brother has Down syndrome. Vigilant as a hawk, her routine is to watch relentlessly for moments in which I may have convinced myself that a bit of reflection in a corner of the office serves us better than knocking on doors. Liz knows better and, standing in plain view, makes of herself a physical reminder impossible to ignore, that I am not doing what is expected of a candidate. And if that is not enough—if I continue to take notes or send messages or speak on the telephone—she'll take one of the 190 green folders kept in accordion boxes at her desk, one for each of the electoral district's polling stations, and thrust it at me with gleeful relish.

The folders contain a street map and corresponding lists with the names of registered voters living in each household and the party preferences they'd stated in the last election marked alongside. It is the canvasser's duty to update this data by affirming voters' intentions and discovering potentially new supporters not on the lists. The canvasser marks a 1, 2, 3 or 4, denoting whether or not the voter is (1) a certain supporter; (2) uncertain but quite likely to vote the party's way; (3) undecided; and (4) opposed or without the right to cast a ballot. If the voter is in the first category, then it is the canvasser's job to encourage the resident to take a lawn or a window sign, volunteer some hours or donate. If the person is a 2, or even a 3, some attempt is made to affirm or convert. The 4s, considered a waste of time, are left to themselves. On "E-Day"—the day of the election—the contact information of the top two categories is vital to the efforts of volunteers seeking to "get out the vote"—offering telephone reminders and rides, if need be, to those who might have forgotten about or be physically incapable of visiting the polls.

On this first outing, our primary aim is to meet the Elections Canada requirement of gathering signatures of two hundred riding residents approving of a candidate's decision to run. The signature is an indication not of approval of the party but of the democratic act, and is necessary for candidates to have their names on the ballot. The sunny day is also a training opportunity in the best of circumstances. It is August. The days are long and languorous, and people at the door are generally content to pass the time in conversation. Some were even excited to do so, the election belonging to some distant time months away and the harvest of tomato plants and vines in the garden their most pressing concern. If common wisdom held that the longer campaign favoured the Conservatives and their well-oiled machine (I had not even started before I heard of a bus carrying fifty Conservative interns, each with iPads, put up in hotels to work the cause of a neighbouring riding), it is also the case that in Toronto—St. Paul's, the extra five weeks means my team has more time to get up to speed and organized. Canadians are so unaccustomed to longer campaigns that they are also indisposed to them, and a lot of the politicians' and pundits' talk (and my early speeches at the door) touch on the waste of a Conservative measure squandering an estimated extra seventy-three million dollars on an election that might as easily have been decided in the normal thirty-seven days.

The standard canvassing method is for a pair of volunteers to work ahead of the candidate, knocking on doors of adjacent dwellings on one side of the street in leapfrogging fashion. The candidate stays back on the sidewalk, pretending at a distance to make a call on the cell or some such. When a door is opened, and intuition says there is an opportunity to engage, the candidate moves forward.

"Oh, look, here's the candidate! Would you like to speak to him now?"

. . .

The days will be unbelievably long but they are also pleasantly so. We'd started knocking on doors at three, and, four hours later, there was still plenty of light. It was balmy, the sky a fiery slap-dash of reds and oranges. Poll 143 was a working-class part of the riding above Rogers and east of Dufferin, and—exceptionally, I would learn—not yet a territory lost to the city of Toronto's rapid gentrification. Here, as the writer John Lorinc pointed out to me in an ambling walk we took in the riding west of Wychwood, houses stay with immigrant families that have worked hard just to gain a foothold, before they are passed on to children of the next generation likely sharing the home already. Contractors' materials were in the driveways of several, and come seven we'd see their owners walking home in construction site gear covered in dust and paint. The first person to engage me is an octogenarian grandmother resting in a lawn chair on her narrow concrete porch, the rest of the family not yet home. She wants the catalpa tree in her neighbour's front yard taken down—it takes away all the light, she says—and I tell her in Italian (she speaks no English) that her complaint is a city matter but I'd pass it on. Not my jurisdiction, but it feels better to say this than to enter into a complicated and unfruitful discussion about municipal, provincial and federal tiers of government—and I am enjoying the chat.

The first-time canvasser notices a couple of things right away. Many front doors have neither bells nor knockers, not ones that function anyway, because fixtures like these belong to the wealthy and the secure—to people confident that opening the front door will not lead to a confrontation with police, a utility rep or a landlord demanding overdue rent. As if to prove the point, a couple of houses have collection agency notices posted above lock boxes. At others, perhaps with bells, a curtain might be drawn for a look outside, but folk are reluctant to answer the stranger using the front door rather than the back (as relatives and friends would)—at least not until working members of the family are home. And there are the refuseniks, plenty of them, residents abstaining from signing the Elections Canada form, even when I explain that their signature is in no way a vote for the party and—a rational fear—that they'd not be receiving robocalls from the NDP or anyone else as a consequence. Against better sense (I need the signatures), I am sympathetic. I am even impressed at this exercising of the freedom not to cooperate that, furthermore, strikes me as an early indication of just how many Canadians feel powerless and marginalized in a system that, says their own long experience, is excluding them. Saying no is for a significant, alienated and relatively powerless few a last way to be heard.

And, on such days, the first-timer notices the trees: apple trees, cherry trees, fig trees, peach trees, pear trees, plum trees—others I did not recognize. Purely ornamental trees such as I'd been considering to replace the useless Manitoba maple that had fallen across the back alley of my home during a winter ice storm were just that: ornamental—and *useless*. The better sense of the mostly Italian and Portuguese families that settled this part of Toronto, decades before, speaks out in the flourishing cornucopia of their gorgeously blooming, but also bounteous, front and back yards.

"Thirty seconds a door is the idea," says Liz. "Sometimes you'll need a minute because you're new to the riding and introducing yourself."

This is not a target I am easily meeting and, taking too long, I don't have to look behind me at Liz waiting on the sidewalk to feel her admonishment burning into my back. Even I can feel the cumbersome, protracted nature of August's "elevator pitch" as I hold the candidate's card with my smiling mug up to screen doors or others held slightly ajar. But there is time, plenty of it. This is going to be fun.

. . .

Things I said at the door:

"Hi, I'm Noah Richler, your candidate for the NDP."

"Okay."

"I'm new at this—"

Laugh. Extend a hand.

"So thanks for speaking to me, I wanted to explain why it is that a guy like me, a writer until now, has taken a different tack in his fifties and is running for Parliament."

Get them on board. Make your inexperience a virtue.

"You see, I don't want a prime minister that hates people."

Point one always gets a good reaction and often a laugh.

"I believe it's time for *change*."

Get the dig in.

"But I believe we also need change *locally*. You've had the same MP for *eighteen* years and that's too long. Even the president of the United States—the most important job in the world!—is only able to hold the office for two terms."

Point two: good—

"And the president of Mexico only gets to do his job once!"

Too much, man! What are you going to do? Explain the revolution that led to the law because you read the history of Mexico last week? Remember the Atwood principle! Get back on topic.

"Change is key, and it's not the Liberals that are going to provide it. Bennett voted for Bill C-51, and—"

Flip the card to the front side with the picture of Tom—

"Is that you?"

"Yes! That's me when I had a beard."

No, jokes don't work, risky but worth the try.

"I jest, that's Tom Mulcair, the leader of the NDP."

Don't lose momentum.

"You know, I didn't meet Tom Mulcair until recently and I really like him. I respect him very much. He's a good, thoughtful man."

Get to point three, hurry up.

"He's the only leader speaking for Toronto. Tom's all about investing in cities, he says that Toronto is the most important city in Canada. And I can tell you that if as a writer I said that I'd be in *big trouble* and they wouldn't be talking to me in Vancouver or Sudbury or anywhere other than here. But when *Tom* says that I know he's speaking in shorthand."

Liz is glowering, get a move on.

"He's saying what's good for Toronto is good across the country because we're living in an urban age and we need infrastructure and parks and better schools and to make cities more liveable for everybody."

All right, motormouth, spit it out.

"But what I really like is that when Tom talks about infra-structure, really he's talking about *people*—not just about con-crete and transit, but about health care and pharmacare and care for seniors and good jobs and all the things that make lives of the community better."

You're drifting. Close.

"Is there anything on your mind I should take back to the team? No? You're sure? Well, here, you keep this card. There's my number and do use it. Call and share anything that comes to mind—enjoy the evening!"

"Not bad," says Liz, "but too long."

After six hours we have completed the poll.

"Four should have been enough," says Liz.

. . .

For all its wealth, and maybe because of it, the riding had few public venues suitable for the all-candidates debates important to any campaign. For Toronto's problem is that if you have a cottage to go to, and in the winter would rather be in New York or Florida, then you're not going to be spending a whole lot of time loving the city you don't have to be in, or finding places to get together with communities you're de facto not much interested in, and that the lax sprawl of streets does not obligate you to meet. All-candidates debates are shortcuts to being recognized by more people than you would meet at the door—a chance of press cov-erage, too—and I found myself envying the neighbouring ridings of University—Rosedale and Toronto Centre that, due to their large student populations and pockets of greater community activism, had more. The Holy Blossom Temple, a synagogue with a very powerful congregation, had arranged an all-candidates debate for September 1, the date an exciting one to look forward to because it felt key and the proper moment of our campaign's debut. But, curiously, the synagogue had initially cast the debate with politicians from outside the riding: Joe Oliver, the sitting Conservative minister of finance, who lived in the riding and was a member of the congregation but represented, just to the north, Eglinton—Lawrence; Marco Mendicino, who had bested Trudeau's pick, Eve Adams, to contest that same riding for the Liberals; and Olivia Chow, the NDP candidate for Spadina—Fort York, whose team had passed the acting chief rabbi, Michael Satz's, invitation to participate on to me. There were also several big churches in the riding—notably the First Unitarian Congregation of Toronto, at which an all-candidates panel on the environment was booked to take place, and the St. Michael and All Angels Anglican Church, where nothing was booked at all. Beyond these venues were a good dozen high schools, some of Canada's most exclusive private ones in their number, interested in acquainting their not yet eligible voters with candidates on the job. The only other forum of note was Wychwood Barns, formerly a streetcar maintenance facility and remodelled to be the site of artists' studios, a small park and, on Saturdays, a vibrant farmers' market.

The Stop Farmers' Market at Wychwood Barns (its official name) is ridiculously pleasant to canvass, and today I have a mole in my ranks. She's "American Sarah," the daughter of friends from Massachusetts, whom I think of as my very own "activist funded by foreign money," or however Harper described environmentalists some time back. American Sarah, in her twenties, quit her New York job as an executive assistant to a comfortable member of the one percent and did not need the nightmare on the horizon of Donald Trump to look to Canada for redemption. She's loving the campaign and working outdoors. At the market, I've been showing off the cornucopia of August and September, our Canadian calendar's short paradise months. Even if my entreaties fall on deaf ears, I explain to Sarah, we can shop—berries, corn, peas, greens, peaches, tomatoes—who'd turn this good work down? Despite the friendliness and the banter, coming to us easily, we're baffled that the market supervisor seems to be doing everything her position allows to impede us—no signs, don't stand here, don't stand there, you're in the way, you're blocking traffic, etc, etc. So we learn to identify her coming and to move back onto grass officially the park's and not the market's and to charm as we are able. And inevitably, since the site is pleasant not just for the NDP, I meet my political rivals there. Kevin Farmer, the spritely, affable candidate for the Green Party of Canada, tells me he is having a hard time acquiring the requisite two hundred signatures for Elections Canada, so I add mine and tell him I've been making a point of mentioning at the door that he needs them, which is true. We are collegial from the start, perhaps because we understand our shared outsiders' position. Marnie MacDougall has a broad, confident smile, but is shorter than I expected and accompanied by a rather intimidating church secretary type. She is dressed in a blue blazer and skirt ensemble that must be hot but, seven years in Panama behind her, she is able to carry it off. We chat briefly, and I tell her that, regardless of how the campaign transpires, whatever comments I end up making should be understood as expressions of party, not personal, differences. And it is at the farmers' market, too, that I first encounter my Liberal counterpart, Carolyn Bennett, appearing in a blaze of red. (I'd not yet found the orange Italian bomber jacket that became my own NDP suit of armour.) I repeat to Bennett what I had said to MacDougall and then, because I want to be able to debate her and not a Liberal candidate from another riding, at Holy Blossom Temple, I ask why Marco Mendicino is on the slate. She seems surprised, even taken aback—I know my mention will be enough for her party machine to have her replace Mendicino—and, unwisely, she accepts my challenge to a game of Rock, Paper, Scissors. One of my team promptly tweets the video record of the NDP's shocking win-draw-win upset over the eighteen-year incumbent, the harmless reaction immediate:

@AdamCF: Love the collegiality between @noahrichler and @CarolynBennett on the #StPauls campaign trail #Cdnpoli

Such small pleasures. I knew how unlikely were my chances of victory—the campaign's early observers probably did too—so figured ambushes like these were permissible. We are still in the early days; no need for the tough to get going. But what I had not counted on was just how quickly I would start to believe that victory actually *might* be possible. I was learning that the candidate must believe: how else to ask a team, in good faith, to join the cause? Believing the outrageous makes it all so much easier.

. . .

It wasn't only larger community forums that Toronto—St. Paul's lacked. The smaller, intimate venues practical for the pub nights that we were planning were also few in number and clustered mainly along St. Clair Avenue, west of our office and north towards Eglinton. Catherine had figured out, by now, that we would not have the money to pay her—not for the grand fund-raising schemes anyway—but had been keen on the idea of pub nights from the start and, a good sport, was aware that time to plan them was short and running out. She hustled me into her car to look for venues where they might happen: maybe one on LGBTQ issues with the *Now* magazine writer Susan Cole, an able interlocutor and activist in the riding. Maybe an evening *bilingue,* or one with "Our Canada" for a theme. We visited a couple of the bars along St. Clair Avenue West, where we thought an evening about immigration or Bill C-51 would work, and then on to the district of high-rises around Yonge Street and Mt. Pleasant Road, where aspiring young professionals and Bay Street workers not yet with families or houses of their own tend to congregate in loud bars with overhead televisions and the notion of a sports-themed evening seemed apt.

I liked that Catherine's solution was to step up and make shit happen, and now here she was driving me up around the northwest end of the riding in which the party traditionally fared better: lower income, immigrants, working class. This was the part of the district that I knew the least but that interested me the most. There were manifold bars, church halls, restaurants and family-owned businesses—germane, as we had a small business policy in the platform and many were struggling to get by. Behind the busier thoroughfares of Dufferin, Eglinton, Oakwood and Vaughan were residential streets where houses had beguiling displays of ceramic statuary in their front yards—of the Virgin, of course, but also animals, buildings, ships and a soccer-playing boy in an Argentine uniform. At Five Points, a street junction with— well, the name makes it clear—was a tavern with its front windows open to the sidewalk. It had the air of a "local" in which a pub night with a "Black Lives Matter" or police injustice theme seemed appropriate, and among the contacts Raymond was pushing was a local reggae band—Mike Garrick and the Posse—that I thought might go down well. The place was empty but for a few regulars at the long bar and, I'd noticed too late, a makeshift altar on a table by the opposite wall. On it were cards and vases of flowers set beneath the photograph of a woman I recognized from a story that had run in the *Toronto Star* the week before. She'd been killed in a drive-by shooting near the grounds of the

Canadian National Exhibition, the fair on Lakeshore Boulevard, after a taxi had refused to pick her up. The young African-Canadian woman, it was clear, had been a server here.

"Talk to the owner," said Catherine, motioning me with a nod of her head towards the woman behind the bar. "Tell her who you are. She'll want to know."

I did so, but awkwardly, my politician's instincts not yet honed. I introduced myself, expressed commiserations, settled the bill and left. I'd been a lousy journalist on many occasions—unable to ask the big question or prompt the tears, not wanting to be a nuisance. Leaving a person to grieve privately seemed the better, more proper way to behave. But then I learned that a lot of the time people *want* to speak, want to be asked, want to share their grief; I'd make a better candidate in time.

. . .

Creedance, volunteer:

My first time canvassing for Noah was my first time canvassing for anything. I was nervous, as I wasn't sure what to expect. I walked up and down seventeen floors of an apartment building on Vaughan Road with my mom. I'd start at one end of the hall and my mom Janet at the other end and by around the tenth floor we had a rhythm going. Even the barking dogs and screaming kids didn't break our focus and it seemed like we'd get out of the building in another thirty minutes unscathed—until, that is, around the thirteenth floor. I heard a half laugh or half scream, I wasn't sure, from mom's end of the hall and walked over to see what startled her. I was greeted by a man standing in his doorway with no teeth and stark-naked except for the pool shoes. I can't say we were excited to see a toothless man's scrotum before dinner, but he was more than ecstatic to see us holding our clipboard and pamphlets at the door. He was a huge Richler fan, he said.

. . .

Outing number two: Poll 214.

The smells, I'll not forget: the stuffiness of flights of stairs in three-storey apartment buildings that, with their windows facing up to the sun but apartment doors locked, act like greenhouses, the fecund heat cooking overly worn shoes and the assorted detritus of family living left on mats. The thick air of corridors in the taller apartment blocks carries the odours of musty cabbage on the top floors, bleach in the basements. Occasionally, stairwells, unheated, offer the respite of cleaner, circulating breezes.

And when the door opens, for a caregiver usually, a wall of dead, used air comes at you in all its fetid, de-oxygenated saturation, telling you that the door is hardly ever opened at all—that the windows are locked shut, and that the air conditioning, if it ever existed, stopped working long ago or isn't turned on because it costs too much. You can tell by the hoarding that's going on the degree to which tenants have given up on the world outside—and the better part of the world on them. Oh, the odd havens apartments become.

The Persian man with the walker and a mattress stripped bare—no need for sheets in the overheated studio—but cages for twenty birds, the room cacophonous with chirping and smelling of their excrement.

The Portuguese grandfather with the white hair of his chest sprouting over the top of his black apron, it'll do for a shirt, and who, with thick Coke-bottle glasses on, appears oddly like a welder taking a break from the job. Really, he's making lunch and complaining vociferously about the rent.

The Caribbean-Canadian woman in a wheelchair, she's in her seventies and ailing, and she's a data miner's algorithmic dead end because, in all probability, there will be no one to tell I came by.

These apartments' smells are of loneliness, but their residents open their front doors and treat us with grace.

AUGUST 24

CPC	NDP	LPC	BQ	GRN	OTH
28.1%	37.4%	25.9%	3.7%	3.8%	1.0%

. . .

Mulcair has said he won't participate in a debate on women's issues without his target, Stephen Harper, there. The Up for Debate women's group spokesperson, Jackie Hansen, is disappointed, but Mulcair has proposed a "Plan B" series of one-on-one conversations instead. It's uncomfortable, the news. At the office, I pull out the "Issues" memoranda Wendy and the crew have left in the envelope pinned to the wall with my name affixed—comments and queries from voters I am to phone back and address.

Joyce is "VERY CONCERNED ABOUT INCREASED POWER AND CONTROL IN THE PRIME MINISTER'S OFFICE, THE REDUCED ROLE OF THE CABINET AND THE ELECTED MEMBERS OF PARLIAMENT, TOO MUCH SECRECY, OMNIBUS BILLS I WOULD VERY MUCH LIKE TO KNOW THE POSITION OF THE NDP ON THIS MATTER AS IT WILL CERTAINLY INFLUENCE MY VOTE."

Hayley says, "What a mess this election is! Having considered the options carefully, I am voting NDP—Noah Richler, you have my vote!"

Erin writes, "I'm disappointed and upset to hear that Tom Mulcair declined to participate in an extremely important public debate on women's issues. Although I understand he doesn't want to attend debates Harper won't be at, a national conversation about women's issues is sorely needed and Mulcair's silence at this time is seriously concerning. Please, the NDP should reconsider."

Subir is "worried about Mulcair's position on Israel," but Wendy already told him that the leader's position is balanced and "he took a large sign."

Edouardos is "concerned about politicians who forget working people between elections and wants to talk to Noah to help him decide."

Wilhelm writes, "WE THE AVERAGE WORKING-CLASS PEOPLE HAVE TO WAKE UP AND RECOGNIZE THE ONLY TRUE ALTERNATIVE FOR A BETTER TRUE DEMOCRATIC AND PEOPLE-FRIENDLY ADMINI-STRATION. REPLACING TWEEDLE-DUM WITH TWEEDLE-DEE WILL NOT IMPROVE THE ECO-NOMIC AND SOCIAL CONDITIONS FOR SOCIETY.

"TWEEDLE-DUM OR TWEEDLE-DEE?

"OUR CHOICE MUST BE THE NDP!"

Anna writes, "*We represent a wide range of voters who are interested in detailed coverage of parties and their candidates. Our communities include Russians, Ukrainians, Jewish [sic], Belorussians, Moldavians, Azerbaijans, Georgians, Armenians, Uzbeks, Kazakhs, Tajiks, Kirghiz, Turkmens, Lithuanians, Latvians, Estonians, and also Abkhaz, Adyghes, Bashkirs, Bulgarians, Buryats, Chechens, Chinese, Chuvash, Cossacks, Evenks, Kalmyks, Lezgins, Ossetians, Roma, Tatars, Udmurts and Yakuts. Please let us know when you are available for the meeting, we look forward to hearing from you soon.*"

. . .

Outing number three: Poll 078.

The streets of Toronto have about them the dreamy pace of late summer relaxing into fall. There is the sense of an impending transition, a blooming of the light that cannot keep, but the election is still far away and the canvassing still has the air of a rehearsal rather than discussions seriously considered. A couple in a souped-up Toyota pulls into the driveway of the house where I am knocking, and the pair proceeds to neck within it. Hanging about for them to finish, to linger and see who's who—if they're on the list and which way they intend to vote—feels, well, inappropriate. A few houses down and a couple of income strata up, there's a party going on. Three gay couples are drinking away the afternoon and seriously pissed. A stack of plasterboard sheets for their *Designer Guys* refit occupies the front room and the door is wide open to the summer air and to me. They invite me to choose from the array of bottles of wine and beer sitting on the kitchen island counter, and one fella makes a half-hearted attempt to debate doctor-assisted dying but it's too much of an effort and I leave the waning day to the partying bunch.

A senior Italian couple is sunning on their concrete front porch. They have kind faces and are wearing matching scarlet pullovers. "*Siamo canadesi,*" the husband says. "*Siamo arrivati cinquantasette anni fa. Essendo canadesi possiamo votare—e lo facciamo. In quanto cittadini canadesi è nostra responsabilità.*" I congratulate them, ask after their children and the part of Italy they left behind. The woman goes into the house and returns with a letter from Toronto Hydro advising her she is eligible for a rebate and how to collect it, but the letter is in English and she doesn't understand it. I call the number and mediate and it feels like one of the better things I have done all day.

(At my nomination, an Italian-Canadian friend had explained this part of the riding to me. "If someone accuses you of being a champagne socialist," he said, "tell him, *No—Prosecco!*")

The sun is setting gloriously, slowly—as if the day itself might fall asleep and forget to finish the job. I meet the barista of a downtown coffee shop where I am a regular, who laughs and welcomes me to the riding; at another house, a former work colleague, a kind and affecting woman who tells me she's working for a Christian NGO distributing aid in Africa, no surprise, says she wept when she learned I was running. Along a short cul-de-sac, two small Filipino children play. One of them has his forearm in a cast and leads me up the drive and around the back of a small bungalow where, under the shade of a vinyl awning, two women are rocking on a swinging bench as one of their husbands grills chicken, pork and small steaks on a charcoal barbecue. They insist that I join them, and the other man fetches a soft drink from a cooler inside the back door. "No election," the woman says, "*not Canadian.*" But I accept the invitation to eat anyway. It's too perfect a close of day and, soliciting as I may be for votes, I'm also doing this to meet Canada, the country I love. These small encounters—these views from the street—leave occasionally joyous imprints of singular experiences. I ask for seconds. Sarah is with me today and she is shaking her head—she knows this is not the job—but I am oblivious and mulling over how many Filipinos engage in "precarious" work and, unrepresented, are the party's natural franchise. I am eating more because I want them to know I care—and, besides, I'm enjoying the food. I shake the family's hands, sign the kid's cast and move on.

. . .

Dale and Laura-Lee, volunteers:

Canvassing gave us a sense of pride as we walked house to house with a purpose, decked out in NDP memorabilia. One home- owner even offered my partner and me some tea and cupcakes, though I also learned that politics has its own versions of your typical comic book nerds. I learned quite a bit about each party and everything they strived to accomplish in the election before now and the one before that. But there was one moment that I will never forget. We entered an area heavily populated with the Conservatives, blue signs, some lawns even had four signs on each corner of the lawn, so I turned to my partner and said "Bike faster, our orange is starting to stand out and I don't want to get shot today." You see, I'm Aboriginal, my partner is Aboriginal- Jamaican. Haha! A couple like us has to think about these things. But our exuberant display of colour was also providing us cover. It was rush hour, and we received a cacophony of honks of approval and a few celebratory thumbs up. It was a ton of fun painting the town orange. I'd do it again.

. . .

Night comes on and I petition a young black woman at her open window and, looking up, feel oddly as if I am serenading her. I like these streets, like the people—have fantasies about attaching speakers to a car or small truck and blasting my politico's mes- sage in Portuguese or Italian, not English, evoking politics as they were done in the Caribbean or the Old Country and win- ning me votes, surely. But, for the time being, more conventional canvassing will have to do. I knock on the door of one house with baskets of geraniums hanging from the brown-painted metal railings of its verandah, and a woman steps out and calls to her neighbour because I'll want to talk to Luca. A stocky man in his sixties whom I can only see vaguely in the half-light strides straight at me and, as he stands a step below with one hand on the railing, it occurs to me in the fast seconds that no one has tried to hit me yet. But, instead, Luca launches into a tirade about winter trucks that clear the snow off the streets of rich people's houses but not his. I commiserate and talk about the NDP's plans for infrastructure and the state of cities and he tells me that he knows politicians, I'll only come around once every four years, and I reply in Italian I'll be back sooner than that for us to drink wine *insieme* and eat the *pomodori* I know he is cultivating in his back garden. He laughs heartily and we're pals. He slaps me on the shoulder and then embarks, in Italian and English, on a screed about new immigrants to Canada freeloading and refusing to do the work his family did to build the country. When he starts to refer more specifically to blacks and Jews I give a discreet nod to my canvassing aide, a bright young LGBTQ student, indicating that, amused and unintimidated as she may be, it is time for us to extricate ourselves. The street slopes southward and, at the corner of the block, a couple of young men are standing inside their small garden's fence and holding glasses in their hands, one of them leaning at an improbable angle born of several stiff drinks. I introduce myself, and the fella with the beard tells me his name is Yossef and that he will be a citizen four days before the election.

"Congratulations, Yusuf," I say.

"*Yusuf?*" he repeats, making a play of stroking his beard with his free hand. "*Yusuf?* You think I am a terrorist? It's *Yossef*."

I make a joke of it, he seems game, and ask what has brought him from Israel to Canada. We talk about the impossibility of the situation in the Middle East for a while, and when he asks about the NDP's position I speak (sadly, again) of the two-state solution we'd encourage and he tells me I should put up a sign. Corner lots are choice in the signs war and this pleases me, but I feel obliged to be candid.

"A lot of Jews in the riding will be upset with you."

Yossef laughs.

"Why?" he asks. And then, making quotation marks in the air with his fingers, "because Harper's my 'best friend'?"

. . .

We feel better off inside, though the trials of community housing are testing. There is wailing in the corridor and suspicion behind doors of apartments we have seen people enter but that are silent when we knock. At one, the door does open and a squat Trinidadian man with a thick neck and stumpy legs is standing in shorts beside his Chinese-Canadian wife who covers her mouth and lets out a muffled laugh as I ask her name because her false teeth are not in. She apologizes and goes off to insert them. We talk at the threshold—he's a TTC engineer and a sympathetic man—and he invites me in. I was told never to do so, and typically I would not have done, but he is imploring me to see his paraplegic son. The father points to the scuffed walls of the neatly kept but tiny apartment and explains the son has severe muscular dystrophy and uses a wheelchair. The wife comes back with her teeth in and I say yes, I'll come in, what else was I going to do, and she ushers me in to the bedroom where a small television sits on the dresser and the son's wheelchair is wedged between the door and the side of the bed—the only place it fits. The father tells me he works nights in order to be with his boy during the day because his wife has shifts cleaning. His son is twenty-two, wasn't expected to live past fourteen, and for years the family has been on a list for a larger apartment that would allow him to navigate corridors without bumping the walls, but still they are waiting. They've been told they might have a bigger apartment in two years if they're lucky. The wife swivels the chair around and pushes the boy's head back up each time it falls to the weaker side of his atrophied neck. She is telling him to say hello, and I am struck by how brusque her handling of the son's head appears, but also that I am in no position to judge and not for a moment do I assume the action is not loving. The man asks me nothing, just tells me his story.

As we leave, I tell myself it's not true, John Donne. Some of us *are* islands. I am sick with pathos but also filled with bafflement and wonder at the love that is possible in such straits.

. . .

Mansions, townhouses, apartments, rooms; SUVs, beaten cars, buses, bicycles, scooters, canes. Beautiful and wealthy people; the lumping lumpenproletariat. As a writer, I am already aware of the fallacy of representation. All it takes is a flight from Toronto to Halifax to Vancouver to Regina, the plane descending over scattered farms and then sprawling suburbs and dense downtowns, to feel humbled at the best of times but mostly defeated. What makes me think I know anyone? What right do I have to put forward some abstraction, political or literary, on behalf of other people? Whom do I speak for but myself? And now here I was imagining that I might do so as a politician? Let it be a conceptual worry for another day: all we can do is speak what we believe to be right and hope our message rises above the cacophony of the rest at the foot of the Tower of Babel.

No, like a writer, the candidate does not overestimate whatever influence may be had at the door—though perhaps behaving as if the influence *is* already yours is what makes the winner. *Be bold.*

. . .

Things I said at the doors of tonier places:

"If Harper was my investment manager, I'd sack him. He's put all our resources in one stock and it's tanked. Think of the invisible taxes we're paying! Think of the opportunity costs of Harper's intransigence! If ten years ago Harper had said, 'Look, the oil sands are a problematic resource, but they're also a window of opportunity for us to be able to move towards cleaner, greener technologies and pay for them, so side with us, because we're going to do our best to exploit them responsibly for the benefit of all Canadians and our children,' rather than demonizing anybody who was the slightest bit environmentally concerned, then the oil sands wouldn't be the most reviled energy project in the world—and we'd not be in the trouble with pipelines that we find ourselves in now."

Or, "The politics of division are getting us nowhere—Harper not shaking Putin's hand, or looking menacingly through binoculars on the prow of a ship in the Baltic at Soviet forces he can do nothing about—that's not a foreign policy. And, again, think about the opportunities such politics have cost us. Canada has been Cuba's best friend for over fifty years, but it took Obama, of all people, to bully Harper into working with Cuba at the recent Summit of the Americas. The net result of Conservative intransigence is that the economic benefits of our long relationship with Cuba will go to the United States, not us."

Or, "Look, here's the truth about the Iran deal: we're talking about it as if we have a say, but we don't. Nothing Israel or Canada says matters anymore. The rest of the world is fed up with no progress and has put us on the sidelines of a game where once we were players. Harper has made 'soft power' and 'honest brokering' dirty words, but that's where our strengths lie. We're not big enough to make a military difference, but we used to be respected for working for peace and can be still. What the NDP knows is we're here to build bridges, not walls."

. . .

And, yes, the *moral moments*:

"History is a sequence of moral moments. Let me explain— markets may not be 'moral,' but the decisions we make in them are. In England in 1847, the Shaftesbury Act was passed, forbid- ding underage children and pregnant girls and women to be employed in the mines. The owners of capital complained, they always do, that the changes would wreck their businesses, but the law didn't—and, besides, we knew the law to be right. Then, a hundred and fifty years ago, they went to war in America over the decision that it was wrong not to pay people, let alone own them, because their skin was black, and again the owners of capital—the slaveholding plantation owners—threatened that their businesses would be wrecked. That was a second moral moment! And in Canada, when the NDP's Tommy Douglas helped introduce free health care, businesses and many doctors complained, but again we did it because we believed it was right. It was a moral moment, and, today, we have another. Tom is asking corporations to pay a bit more tax to bring in more revenue, yes, and to get what Mark Carney, the former governor of the Bank of Canada, called 'dead money'—more than six billion dollars of it!—moving again, because the environment and our need for green infrastructure is presenting us with another moral moment. Corporations will tell you they can't afford it, but they can—and don't they always tell you that?"

. . .

Things I said at the door that I did not altogether believe:

That we were in a recession.

That we should categorically pull out of the fight against ISIL.

That we needed to fully restore postal service.

That we did not need to cancel the existing child benefit.

. . .

"Okay, Janet, I have a problem with Mulcair saying we'll hire 2,500 more RCMP. There are way too many police already. Three on bicycles come down my street together just to hand out parking tickets."

"You say that hiring new officers is the quickest way to address the RCMP's gender and First Nations imbalance."

"Okay. That works."

"Oh, and say *Justin*, not Trudeau. When you say 'Trudeau' you're helping the brand."

Right. *The brand*: Justin, young and "not ready"; Mulcair, the statesman. The politician *with experience*.

"Who do you want to see standing beside Angela Merkel?" I'd say at the door. "Justin or Tom?"

. . .

Other newspapers have taken the *Toronto Star*'s cue and are paying Toronto—St. Paul's a bit of attention: the *Jewish Forward*, the *National Post* and the *Town Crier*. Gary Clement, the brilliant *National Post* cartoonist, has agreed to join me for a day of canvassing with a view to a full-page op-ed spread and Jonathan Kay, editor-in-chief of *The Walrus*, is booking time, too. In the *Post City* chain of Toronto neighbourhood newspapers, the former Liberal spin doctor Warren Kinsella, a perpetual blogger, is having his say:

POST CITY TORONTO
Federal Election 2015: A look at five bellwether races that could decide the next prime minister

Toronto—St. Paul's
What does Warren think?

Writers seldom make a happy transition to political life (e.g., Messrs. Dion, Ignatieff), but Richler carries a famous surname. Carolyn Bennett may not be well-loved, but she has name recognition to spare. That, plus a lot of on-the-ground experience, will make this a big challenge for Richler. My prediction: He'll say something controversial. Controversy is great for writers but not so much for aspiring politicians.

Eric Emin Wood, the reporter from the *Town Crier*, also calls, as arranged, saying he has just a few lines so to keep it short. But I still haven't learned how to and, besides, I am speaking as much for Phil, the seasoned speechwriter in our campaign management trio, politely doing his best to appear not to be listening. I want Phil to know that someone capable is in the candidate's seat—the one with the tiniest desk in the office, the size of a bedside table, wedged in between a pillar and the wall—and that I know how to talk to media. I am running, I tell Wood, because the Canada I have grown up in is seriously under threat. I explain that politics are derived from principles, etc., etc.

"What do you think of Justin Trudeau?" Wood asks. *Well, he's no Boris Johnson,* I want to say, but that reference, well out of the riding, would likely be held against me. *Imagine the story you'd like to see.*

So, instead:

"Canadian democracy is in a sorry state if, in a country of thirty-five million, we turn for a leader to the same family twice. And saying they did so in the States with the Bush family doesn't excuse it."

We talk for a good half hour and then finally the reporter cuts off my verbal diarrhea, saying he already has more than enough.

"Keep your answers short," says Phil in a low voice, listening after all.

"And be careful about what you're saying," says Janet. "What about Michael Layton, who succeeded his father, Jack, on the Toronto City Council?" She is too modest, or perhaps tactical, to say, "So what about me, my father David, my brothers Michael and Stephen, my nephew Avi?"

. . .

"Ready for Change," the first of the Toronto rallies, takes place at the 99 Gallery on Sudbury Street in Parkdale, where longtime NDP fixture Peggy Nash is the incumbent serving the second of two terms interrupted by her electoral loss in 2008 and a stint, until 2011, as president of the party. Mulcair's campaign bus is parked outside, Andrew Cash arrives on his bicycle and Charlie Angus, a musician, author and MP for Timmins—James Bay since 2004, scrutinizes me in not altogether welcoming fashion at the door. Inside, the atmosphere is excited and busy and Angus's well-received book of Aboriginal residential school experience, *Children of the Broken Treaty*, is arranged on a bookseller's table in the entryway beside piles of Mulcair's *Strength of Conviction*.

All is new to me: the chairs on risers on four sides of the small stage where Mulcair will speak; the wall of photographers; the supporters in NDP-orange T-shirts with signs and placards with the name of the candidate and riding each is there to represent. I find a place in the couple of rows by the stage reserved for candidates, and then Cash and Nash stride up to the stage to excite the crowd. The teleprompter begins to roll and cues them to ask, "*Are you ready, Toronto?*" Tonight Mulcair is preceded by Stephen Lewis, they cottoned on, and he delivers a barnburner of a speech—"the best of the election so far," TVO's Steve Paikin will write.

"There surely has never been a time in Canadian political history when a prime minister has brought his office into such disrepute," bellows Lewis. "Stephen Harper has played the hand of fear. It isn't that it's just unworthy of a prime minister—it's actually, when you think of it, *shocking, mortifying*, that a prime minister of Canada would descend to such political depths in the lust to retain power." Harper, says Lewis, has left "a divided and intolerant inheritance for our country." He has "trained his political guns on his own citizens." But now, Lewis repeats his mantra, he who had thought "not in my lifetime!"—who'd told his children "not in theirs"—was suddenly hopeful.

And then it is the turn of "*Tom Mulcair, Canada's* NEXT PRIME MINISTER!" The Montreal musician Sam Roberts's hit "We're All in This Together" blares from the speakers and a phalanx of party operatives and security and cameramen enters the quadrant of supporters standing and applauding, me among them. For a moment, only the top of Mulcair's head is visible, his wife Catherine by his side, until the leader appears out of the throng to smile and turn and shake each of the candidates' hands, mine included. "*Are you having fun?*" he says—he is—before he takes the stage and holds the microphone to his chest like it was a birthday gift, absorbing the love before he finally waves at the crowd to sit down. Mulcair addresses the room, but nervously. He has mounted the stage without the tactical interlude of an

Anne Fenn to make the transition to his lesser oratory easier, and he's underperforming for a moment, but we ignore it. He smiles again, the teleprompter is rolling and I learn to clap on command. Learn to clap till my hands are sore. Learn to stand up. Learn to sit down. Learn to stand up and clap again. We're at a church of the faithful with a rousing minister and a congregation ready for the miracle of an NDP government to bring *change to Ottawa!* Stand up! Clap again! You think your hands are sore? *Clap some more.*

And then my first rally is over. An aide motions me to follow and join the train of candidates heading behind a couple of screens at the foot of the emptying hall to a room where I learn—quickly, good lad—to be a mannequin, arranged in a tight row behind the federal party leader fielding questions from Canada's francophone and anglophone media. Then, my initiation not yet complete, the aide gestures to me to follow again, this time for a photo of the Toronto—St. Paul's candidate standing alone with Mulcair, *just in case*, you never know, I might win, or maybe for the files. I ask for another to be taken of us with Pinhas. I've seen what being the artist's partner is like; know that in the shadows, there is a price to be paid.

. . .

Jonathan Kay has been booked in to accompany me on a canvass of one of the riding's NDP-friendliest polls.

"He's a journalist," I say. "He's not stupid. He'll figure it out. You can't just send me into areas of support. We need to show him the gamut."

. . .

The debate at the Holy Blossom Temple is approaching and animating the team because we are still at the stage where ideas—intellect—are primary and have not ceded the ground to the "calculated algebra of poll-by-poll analyses" and the interparty acrimony that will follow. But in truth, I have no experience to alert me to the inevitability of this. There are seventeen-year-olds working on my campaign with a greater understanding than I of the "pugilism" the team will inevitably face. In this blissful, exciting moment—the closest the campaign will come to the panels to which broadcasting and the literary life have made me accustomed—it is entirely possible to believe candidates have their own thoughtful contributions to make, beyond being simple party pushers at the door. There is ferment, there is discussion, and the full import of the thirty-odd "backgrounders" distributed in piles by topic the breadth of my dining room table has not struck home. They are intermingled with academic papers on "Canadian values" and "the common good" and even more dialectic material suggesting a degree of knowledge that will, of course, never be necessary for the parroting the party would prefer. I have not learned this yet, and Janet, the campaign manager charged with preparing me, is so keen and intelligent, so honed by her family's generations of dedication to fundamentally altering ideas about social democracy at home and abroad, that my cocoon is for the time being a comfortable one. I am in my element.

With less than a week to go before the debate, Janet has arranged for me to meet with a thought gang of her own making, composed of herself, Doug, Sean, Alberto Quiroz (a Mexican-Canadian member of the congregation and the party) and Josh Scheinert, a young investment and human rights lawyer and foreign policy buff whom Craig Scott had taught at Osgoode Hall and for whom he is trying to find an NDP team. We assemble in the small, windowless backroom, where Josh is seated at the table already. A smart, good-looking Jewish twenty-something, he has an excellent c.v. and Janet's favour, I can tell. He's confident, even precocious, though maybe I am feeling my years.

"I was a lawyer for the Bilcon appeal," says Josh.

"And we lost," I say, thinking back to what Elizabeth May told me. "That's a drag."

"No. I was on the *Bilcon* team. I wanted to tell you because I know how much the story concerned you."

In any other instance, this would be a major case of Josh and me getting off on the wrong foot, but we have no time to deal with anything but the matter at hand. I'm nervous about the Holy Blossom event, remembering the sorts of responses I'd occasionally get from Canadian Jews to mistakes I might have made in columns written for the *National Post* on subjects close to the Diaspora's heart—like, say, when I misdated Jerusalem's Second Temple: YOU ARE NOT YOUR FATHER. SHUT UP AND WRITE SOMETHING ELSE.

Such charm—and what I thought we might encounter at the synagogue. We discuss ISIL and, of course, Palestine. Alberto talks of the synagogue's Tikkun Olam ("repair the world") program and the other community work it does that speaks to the congregation's actually quite progressive nature. He cites Deuteronomy, "Justice, justice shall you pursue," and I feel marvellously affected by the simple fact of Jewish scholarship. We rehearse the party's two-state solution line, and Sean reminds me of the fact of Mulcair's wife, Catherine, being the daughter of Holocaust survivors. We talk about the temple's educational programs for the community, and then the Gaza conflict. I say that I cannot brook conversation about Israel and Palestine that does not acknowledge that Gaza is, at times, a concentration camp. Josh refers to a past teacher of his who argued that the positive side to the fact of a wall dividing the West Bank from Israelis is that defining a limit in this way at least implicitly acknowledges that the territory on the other side does not belong to them.

"Give or take a few hundred yards."

"But it's a start."

Josh is anticipating that talk of the "Iran Deal"—the agreement for containment of the United States's and Israel's historic adversary's nuclear program—will come up and urges that I "reinforce Obama's point that Iran is currently a nuclear threshold state and let that fact set the frame for the necessity of pushing forward with a plan that aims to walk that ability backwards." The audience, he stresses, will want to hear first and foremost about Israel, more than "walls." He points out that the deal is supported by "many past heads of Israeli security services, including the former Israel Defense Forces Military Intelligence Director Amos Yadlin, former Mossad directors Meir Dagan and Efraim Halevy, and former Shin Bet director Ami Ayalon."

The meeting ends, and Josh tells me the NDP's green policies are what drew him to the party. My sense is that not much I've said has impressed him. It's interesting to be on the other side of this generational wall, and it occurs to me that, more than my discomfort with his work for Bilcon, I may be envious of someone on my team and the admiration Janet seems to hold the fella in. I make small talk, do my best to be nice and confide my insecurities to Doug.

"He's a Liberal looking for a job," says Doug dismissively.

. . .

It is September 1, still the summer side of Labour Day, and half a dozen members of my team, my mother too, are hanging with me in the empty parking lot of the Holy Blossom Temple. Kevin Farmer and his campaign manager, Adam Deutsch, arrive; then the Conservatives, looking wary even though this is (I assume) their natural camp; afterwards, a couple of young Liberals in red shirts. I recognize Bennett's husband Peter O'Brian, the producer of the classic Canadian film *The Grey Fox*. Bennett arrives in a loose red coat, the lapels of which are decorated in a black First Nations motif.

"It's so much easier for women to dress the part," says Sarah.

Bennett's juniors lead the Liberal MP and her husband in and I am left standing with a late-middle-aged man from her coterie. He is holding a copy of my father Mordecai's "requiem for a divided country," *Oh Canada! Oh Quebec!*

"I'm interested in what your father would have thought about the Sherbrooke Declaration," he says with an obnoxious, self-satisfied smile, the suggestion being that I am a traitor not just to Canada but to my family.

"It's a debate, not a séance," I say. "We'd have had it out."

Inside, only a modest crowd is gathered, these still the holidays and interest in the election still only lukewarm. A bald, surly thirty-something man in a double-breasted suit is sitting on the centre aisle, a PMO operative surely, or at least looking the part. He is emanating an unpleasantness effectively prohibiting any but the brave from sitting near him. My bunch is mostly at the back, waiting for the first question to come to me—about the economy, as arranged—and I handle it nervously, cramming too much in. Then Bennett, two seats to my right, starts. She leans forward and with a chortle says, "I love that every four years I have to reapply for my job!" I cannot believe what I am hearing—*your job?*—but am too slow to act, no one has interrupted anyone yet, and listen dumbfounded.

"It's what I call the 'St. Paul's model,'" says Bennett, going on about meeting constituents between elections and a proper democracy as if she—not Westminster—invented it.

I regret that I let the moment pass, though from then on, the debate goes swimmingly. Ed Greenspon, formerly editor-in-chief of *The Globe and Mail*, is the moderator. Bennett seems startled there is much of a debate on at all, and periodically throws harassed glances across the front of the stage. In between Bennett and me is Farmer, the loquacious Green Party candidate and, to my left, MacDougall.

Child care comes up and I compare Bennett's Liberal pamphlet to that of a mortgage broker selling bucket rates—this much of a rebate from the Conservatives, this much from the Liberals. Has politics been reduced to no more than such banal comparison shopping? I ask. The NDP's child care policy, I say, is not about stuffing money through the door for parents to use as they see fit, as the Liberals and Conservatives are doing, but about the children—about ensuring places as a right, and saying the just society should expect no less. The NDP will fight for children's rights in the same way that—with a higher percentile of women candidates than any other party—it is doing for women, continuing to lead the fight for gender parity and equal rights.

"*What?*" says Bennett, glaring this time in shock. She has pushed for more Liberal women candidates in her role on the party's Election Readiness Committee, famously fought for Toronto's Women's College Hospital to stay open, and I'd been bluffing somewhat. It wasn't territory I knew rigorously, and I'd made the argument to please my campaign management team, as much as anything else, and to steamroll on. It is a political technique that I'm not altogether comfortable having mastered—the lesson that the *appearance* of rectitude is often a substitute for the real thing. This I regret a little, though not at all my highlighting of the Liberal sense of entitlement that, I argue, is not a trivial matter of social comportment but a phenomenon with serious political and legislative consequences. To illustrate, I talk about the arrogance of Trudeau trying to impose Eve Adams on the Eglinton—Lawrence riding, close to where we are; of the cynicism of the appointment of the former Toronto police chief Bill Blair as a Scarborough candidate; and then of Bill C-51:

"It's not enough to say, 'Not to worry, we voted for Bill C-51 so that Harper was unable to make hay of it, we'll fix it in office.' What if you *don't* win office? What happens then?"

Bennett looks sideways with another frown, invoking the October attack on Parliament and arguing the bill's importance, alleging the police had evidence leading them to believe an incident was imminent but were unable to act. The Liberal MP Wayne Easter, formerly solicitor general, says Bennett, assured the Liberal caucus that many of the elements of the bill were necessary. I am astonished Bennett has argued outright *for* the bill and make a note of her having done so for later parries: the laws of an ousted government, no matter the rhetoric, can be awfully convenient to the next.

Greenspon asks about the Middle East and MacDougall opens her binder to a page that says IF ISRAEL COMES UP, then starts to read from the statements prescribed beneath it. I think of asking, out loud, if she needs help reading her instructions but, because she is a woman, I am worried I'll come off as patronizing rather than funny, so I don't. It has been an aim for the evening for me to be the gentleman and stay true to the pledge I made to MacDougall, in particular, at the Wychwood market. But when the subject of missing and murdered Aboriginal women arises and MacDougall starts to read from her binder again with no acknowledgment of the shame of the tragedy and the Conservatives' willed indifference towards it, instead embarking on the barely tenable sequitur of a security presence in small communities, I decide it is appropriate to intervene and do. I tell her that the Conservatives relinquished the moral right to speak of the horror of the missing and murdered when they refused to hold an inquiry and Harper described the phenomenon as not "a sociological problem." MacDougall reacts badly, says she is being interrupted and, though I have no regrets about having been rude for a moment, I feel discomfort in the congregation. There is a yearning, not just in the room, for politicians to be civil and, come the end of the evening, a young rabbi speaks for the congregation insisting on the same. But it feels like a victory.

"The best thing MacDougall can do for you is to canvass," says Doug.

We have done well—we've won, is the consensus, our triumph made all the more evident by the Conservatives' hasty exit, though Bennett and O'Brian are polite and chat a bit. Josh has attended to provide a post-mortem, and does so rigorously. "Bennett gave the impression that law enforcement is helpless in the face of terrorism," he writes. "But that's bullshit and needs to be called out as such. The Criminal Code provides law enforcement with wide powers to arrest, including preventative arrests, and Bennett should know that—many of the changes were written in by Liberals post-9/11. So is Bennett saying the Liberals did a bad job writing laws to keep us safe? The evidence suggests otherwise. Just look at the Toronto Eighteen, a plot broken up in advance by the police and resulting in charges, convictions and long prison sentences."

My own immediate reward is that the battery in our car has died. Like a scene out of Armando Iannucci's *The Thick of It*, the BBC's satirical television series on the tawdriness of political life (and a candidate's handy primer), Sarah and I spend till well past midnight in the parking lot, having sent everyone else home before we'd realized we were stuck. We contemplate ordering a pizza. We are in good spirits.

. . .

Polls, Various.

A young woman answers the door. She has a bright, happy smile and eyes that are filled with excitement, but also trust. From Nova Scotia, she is a pianist studying at the University of Toronto. The piano occupies most of the small apartment's living room. She's so excited about the election, she says, but not sure in which riding she votes.

A forty-something man tells me of the sexual abuse he suffered as a child. We discuss his subsequent addiction and rehab, and the difficulty of his finding work. He asks me, of all things, about Harper's "muzzling of scientists"—an issue that, to my surprise, is repeatedly raised in the initial weeks of the campaign. The catchy phrase, I am learning, has become the accommodating vessel of a plethora of people's discontents.

A Quebecker, a photographer, insists I step in. He lectures me about the NDP failing its radical roots—specifically vis-à-vis the environment, the biggest challenge facing the world. *No pipelines.* Vote Green, I say, I'm fine with that, but make sure you vote. And, by the way, there's a panel about environmental issues scheduled for late September. Do come.

A woman is watching the baseball game from her three-wheel scooter parked in front of a wide-screen television. The apartment is well appointed, if a bit pleathery. "Fuck the NDP," she says. "Fuck politicians. I'm from Thunder Bay and I watched that asshole I went to school with get into council and give millions to the fucking Natives. *What about me?*"

A former lawyer, seething, presents me with hundreds of sheets of his one-sided correspondence with the city, Queen's Park and Ottawa. He's been unjustly disbarred by the criminal Michael Bryant, he says, that *murderer* who got off scot-free. Here, take these and if Mulcair answers me, I'll vote for him.

On the lawn of a well-to-do home in the affluent northeast

DOORS OPEN, TORONTO

part of the riding, the southern end of Leaside, a man with
Down syndrome insists we "put a big sign right here," pointing
to the spot where he wants it. We talk for a while and I learn his
parents live a couple of streets north, get the address and make a
note to call before doing anything about the sign. But I wonder
about the ethics of this. Am I being patronizing? Is it not his
choice? If it makes him happy, why should I not?

A Russian-Canadian immigrant who has taught herself English
and also Portuguese, the language of commerce and the tavern she
owns on Dufferin Street, implores me to come by with someone
who speaks the language. *You must*, she says. But I am in luck. I
have Daniyal Ulysses Amed with me. The henna-haired Daniyal
is ruminative, exceedingly bright and a tad peculiar. He was born
in Lahore, Pakistan, raised there and in Italy, now Canada, and
bullied in a few countries, he tells me. Daniyal speaks English,
Italian, French, Spanish, Urdu, Hindi, Punjabi, some German—
and Portuguese. She is practically weeping when they speak.

A beautiful young Ethiopian mother is making coffee as she
used to in Addis Ababa: beans, home-roasted, the tool to crush
them and a brass pot and cups laid out on a mat in her tiny
apartment. Her aged mother smiles but is too shy to come out
from the kitchen. The children, perhaps seven and eight, aren't
shy at all—precocious, even. One wants to be a doctor, the other
a politician. The happiness is infectious.

A woman in her early thirties with large doe eyes has dark
hair pulled back into a thick ponytail. She's Jewish and her great
grandfather, she says, was a Toronto city councillor. She shows
me a faded newspaper clipping with his picture. I suggest she
might want to volunteer, and she does.

A woman with thick make-up and a minuscule red and black
lace bra and matching panties opens the door a few inches: she's
a working woman, it's pretty clear.

"Hi," I say. "My name's Noah Richler. I'm your NDP candidate."

"Not a good time," the woman says, gently smiling as she pushes the hair back from her face.

"Oh, sorry."

Before closing the door, she pulls one of the candidate's cards I'm holding out of my hand.

"But I'll take one of those," she says.

November 4, Ottawa.

Cabinet's been settled for the morning's Rideau Hall reveal and I'm waiting in the lobby of the CBC on Sparks Street for a quick chat with Rosie when my CTV contact calls.

> *"Noah, you know all that stuff that keeps most people from running?"*
> *"Money?"*
> *"Don't kid around. Now it's your turn."*

But he was on the company cell, so he wouldn't say more.

I look up and Heller is standing outside and gives me a high five and points to his watch and I wonder what misstep has caught up with me. Heller mouths "Rideau Hall!" and looks up to the sky like he can't believe it. Then he points to his illegally parked car, hazard lights flashing, and motions at me to get a move on. Who'd I insulted? Who'd I slept with who suddenly decided it was news? Quickly I reviewed the shitty things I'd done maybe coming back to haunt me on this, the NDP's day of victory. I'd come down hard on Jian Ghomeshi, that was true, but I did so early on and I doubted that I'd ever ranked so high on the radar of the rehabilitated sex advice columnist for me to be the one he'd come after. As for Evan Solomon, the ex-CBC host cum art pusher, I'd been careful not to pass judgment—not publicly at any rate—already worrying about bad karma and thinking that if I kept quiet for long enough maybe I'd have access to a discounted catalogue. (Note to self: have Ethan see if he'll have me on his Sirius show.) And yes, I'd knocked loudly on the door of the only bathroom of the last Porter flight I was on before a young woman several months pregnant stepped out guiding her infant daughter ahead of her and into the aisle. That was a boo-boo, me not looking back because I didn't need to, I could hear the bros who'd been drinking in the row behind me muttering loudly about what an asshole I was. But I doubted they'd have recognized me now, they didn't seem the Liberal or even the voting type and my candidacy had not yet been announced. So maybe the cashier at Sobeys in Saint John had come forward, the one I'd been rude to when a power cut meant she couldn't cash me out and I'd asked if they still teach math in New Brunswick schools or did they do so only in French. Or what about the server at the fancy restaurant to whom I'd sent an anonymous card—just a nice gesture, that was all—maybe she'd figured out the postmark or my handwriting and fed it to His Nastiness at Canadaland: "NDP CANDIDATE TOLD ME I'D HAVE CHANGED HIS LIFE IF HE'D BEEN TWENTY YEARS YOUNGER—MORE LIKE THIRTY, THE PERV."

I have no idea what is coming at me, no time to call Kinsella—he'd know—but am at least braced for something when, ushered into the studio of Power & Politics, Rosemary Barton, the dragon slayer, asks about an affair that I'd forgotten even as she assures me they're not yet taping and we're off the record—like that's ever true!

"Never happened," I say, as images come to mind of a wimpy Jimmy Carter professing adulterous thoughts and Bill Clinton so easily getting away with more. "But hell, it's only 2015, there's still time."

No jokes! I can see Sarah telling me now. I look over Barton's shoulder into the control booth and Levy is covering her face with her hands. Heller is rolling his eyes. Solberg points to the red light overhead and mouths the words, "We're live."

Okay, okay, so that didn't happen either—but this did:

"Noah," said Pratt. "We need you to stay home."

"What do you mean?" I said.

"You're not to take calls from anyone."

"You know, if I'd offered the *Star* editors a piece about celebrity culture sucking up attention on the social networks at the expense of people dying in Africa, they'd have sucked it up and been thrilled by the hits."

"Noah," said Pratt, "you don't get it. *You're on the wrong side of revenge porn.*"

THE CANDIDATE IS IMPOSED IN LIBERAL
PARTY AD WITH TRUDEAU GETTING
NOWHERE ON ESCALATOR.

THE CANDIDATE PASSES TRUDEAU AND
LOOKS BACK OVER HIS SHOULDER,
PUZZLED THAT JT IS STATIONARY.

"THIS IS WHAT'S
HAPPENING TO
MILLIONS OF
CANADIANS IN 10
YEARS UNDER
STEPHEN HARPER"

THE CANDIDATE TURNS TO WATCH JT
BEHIND HIM AND REACHES FOR THE
EMERGENCY BUTTON.

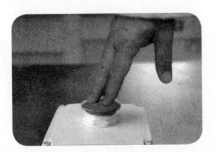

THE CANDIDATE HITS BUTTON,
ESCALATOR STOPS.

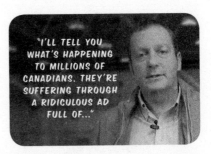

THE CANDIDATE SPEAKS TO THE CAMERA.

HOLDING LIBERAL PAMPHLETS.

THROWS PAMPHLETS OVER SHOULDER.

AS LIBERAL PAMPHLETS LAND
ON TRUDEAU'S FACE.

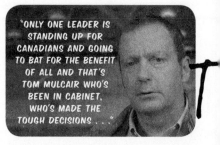

THE CANDIDATE DELIVERS POLITICAL
MESSAGE AND CONCLUDES,

"I'M NOAH RICHLER, THE NDP'S CANDIDATE
IN TORONTO-ST.PAUL'S. THERE'S ONLY ONE
PARTY TO GET THE COUNTRY MOVING
AGAIN, AND THAT'S OURS."

THE CANDIDATE LOOKS OVER SHOULDER
AT TRUDEAU.

THE CANDIDATE AGAIN HITS BUTTON,
TRUDEAU SENT BACK DOWN STAIRS,
SPEAKING ACCELERATED REVERSE
JIBBERISH.

CHAPTER FOUR

E CANDIDATE
ADE A VIDEO.

You won't believe what happened next.

In my thirties, not a bad-looking fella and living in England at the time, I bought a motorcycle—an exquisite, canary yellow 1973 Norton 750cc Commando Combat. I'd wanted to ride a bike for years, imagining that, on days when maybe I felt a little blue, I'd put on my leathers and helmet and take to the country, leaning into the curves of the road: just me and the elements, fields and hedgerows passing at the level of my eyes as I leaned forward, left and right, alert and looking for the conditions that might undo me. I liked that sometimes the journey took longer than planned because I was not travelling in the shell of a car where you don't even see the sky, or that I'd have to pull in at a roadside pub for a pint and a bed for the night because the weather had turned. I liked that the route of a journey, not the time it would take, was all I could reliably calculate. I liked that I was in the world—and lesser.

And the thing I liked most of all was that when I did buy the bike, everything—but everything—was as I'd imagined it: on days when maybe I felt a little blue, I'd put on my leathers and helmet and take to the country, leaning into the curves of the road: just me and the elements, fields and hedgerows passing at the level of my eyes as I leaned forward, left and right, alert and looking for the conditions that might undo me. Sometimes the journey took longer than planned because I was not travelling in the shell of a car where you don't even see the sky, and I'd have to pull in at a roadside pub for a pint and a bed for the night because the weather had turned. The route of a journey, not the time it would take, was all I could calculate. I was in the world—and lesser.

And I liked cleaning my bike. I liked that the engine of my kick-started Norton, all pretty chrome, was a mechanical sequence easy to follow, and to pinpoint the dysfunction of, when something was not quite right.

Politics—politics was not like that.

SEPTEMBER 1

CPC	NDP	LPC	BQ	GRN	OTH
29.4%	31.2%	27.7%	4.0%	6.1%	1.7%

. . .

Through July and most of August, Trudeau was saying his party could make no budget predictions until it was clear just what "mess" the next government would inherit from the Conservatives. Then, on August 25, Mulcair told media that, were it elected, the NDP's "first budget will be a balanced budget."

"Maybe we're not completely fucked," said Phil.

Deficits were a sore point for Phil but he was feeling optimistic. He'd been a speechwriter for Ed Broadbent in 1983, when as leader he was arguing it was time for the Liberals—Pierre Elliott Trudeau, at the time, ready to campaign for a fifth term—to reduce the deficit, and that an NDP government would do so. The economy was in recession and, advising Broadbent, Phil had argued (as the Nobel Prize–winning MIT professor of economics Paul A. Samuelson was also doing) that what the economy actually needed was stimulus, not restraint. The austerity program had been an about-turn not cleared by the party's federal council, nor with the major union bodies. Phil had said the reduce-the-deficit stance was "bad policy and worse politics" without effect and had given his notice.

"Ironically, on the day I left the Hill, Ed was forced to reverse himself—nothing to do with me and everything to do with the party and labour movement going ballistic," said Phil. "But at least Ed didn't have his deficit brain cramp in the middle of the highest-stakes election campaign the federal party ever had."

But Phil was giving Mulcair a pass because the numbers were holding. In fact, the numbers were very good.

Then, two days later, Trudeau declared his party's intentions to run deficits to the tune of $10 billion per annum for three years as part of a $125 billion spend on infrastructure, vaguely defined. The announcement was made in front of the requisite assembly of workers in hard hats, though the party's broad definition of infrastructure included green energy, clean tech and social services.

"Our economy needs investment in order to create growth," said Trudeau. "Our plan features three years of historic investment in the Canadian economy. That growth will eliminate the Harper deficit and we will balance the budget in 2019."

Phil was at his desk. Behind him, the accumulating strokes and numbers and colours of the grids showed our canvassing progress, though also the vast number of polls we had yet to visit. The numbers were starting to slide and he had the Liberal news up on his screen.

"Ah," said Phil. "We're fucked."

Later, Trudeau would describe going home after the announcement and saying to his wife, Sophie Grégoire-Trudeau, "I'm pretty sure we just won the election." But we define all our adventures in retrospect, it's too easy for the loosely remembered story to ascend to the mythic, and the truth is that about the issue of deficits there was only moderate fanfare at first. At the all-candidates debate at Holy Blossom Temple, no one had addressed the subject of deficits much. The opening statement about the economy had been mine, and I'd talked about the difference between a resource economy and a resource mentality and not treating the land as a bank vault to be pillaged without making any effort towards the creative industries.

"Look," I said, resorting to what I figured was one of my catchier lines, "if Stephen Harper and Joe Oliver were my stock-brokers, I'd sack them. They've put all our money in one stock and it's tanked. High-risk portfolios are for cowboys; what a steadily growing economy needs is *variety* in its portfolio—diversity, proven resources in manufacturing, and the small and medium-sized businesses that provide eighty percent of the jobs in this country, with openings to future earners in the form of tax breaks for innovation. Harper can blame the global economy as much as he wishes, but to do so is missing the point. We'd endure the lows and ride the highs infinitely better if we'd laid the way for a diverse economy rather than relying disproportionately on resources."

MacDougall had threatened, as was her party's habit, dire consequences were the economy in anything but Conservative hands, and Bennett had praised Trudeau for being a leader, not a boss, and surrounding himself with good people, an attitude that I wished had been the NDP's. I was ready to say, "There is no need to resort to accumulating deficits because the cash exists already— Canadians have already handed over some $600 billion of 'dead money' to corporations hoarding it, so it would be criminal to exhort them to have to pay to kick-start the economy a second time," but the Greens' Kevin Farmer beat me to it, good man. Hundreds of billions in non-working capital is a "disease of hyper-right-wing thinking," said the notes Michael Tamblyn and my team had prepared for me. "There's no need to resort to accumulating deficits because the cash exists already. We'll not be having government do what the private sector can but nudging the corporate sector into doing its bit and spending. That's how you get an economy going—through the velocity of money that's stagnant right now. Trudeau was a champion of balanced budgets until July, and now he's telling you he'll run deficits and that's dandy because it relieves him of the need to tell you whether or not his plans are affordable, even as he plans to lump great big debts on our children—as if they don't have enough they'll be paying for. Trudeau can promise you the moon, anything, but you'd be daft to believe it'll come without a crippling cost.

"We're confident we can institute our plans and balance the budget," was the party message.

That worked for a while, encounters at the door not yet shining a light on the altering political landscape. Deficit spending was not yet Trudeau's winning card, and balancing the books not yet the NDP's Battle of the Somme. During the better part of the month of August, the predominant question had been "How will the NDP do in a coalition?"

"Tom's a collaborator by nature," I'd say. "He's always said he's prepared to work with the Liberals—but Trudeau! Trudeau has said that he won't! Of course, he has to say that, doesn't he?

Don't worry [*deliver, sotto voce, a knowing chuckle*], he'll change his mind closer to the day."

But faces at the door were evolving away from August's happy-go-lucky to something more ... well, *concerned*. Voters were listening more intently to the case being made, it was September and the contest was now serious. There was less time to waste and "E-Day"—October 19—was no longer a date in dreamtime. Auguring as much, on Wednesday, September 2, the day after the Holy Blossom debate, the Syrian infant Alan Kurdi was washed up on the Turkish beach of Bodrum, dead. The image that was the encapsulation of the dreadful news quickly undermined whatever may have been the political advantage enjoyed by the Conservative Chris Alexander, the MP for Ajax—Pickering and minister of immigration, refugees and citizenship. His hostile performance on CBC News Network's flagship political program *Power & Politics* was the norm for him but, on this day, it was another Conservative tactic suddenly inadequate to the task. Alexander's shaky demonstration—his talking about refugees from Iraq, not Syria, and the complete implosion of his numbers—was deftly handled by Rosemary Barton, the program's host, and seized upon by his opponents as obfuscating and inhumane. Quickly, the Ajax—Pickering MP was dispatched to Ottawa, ostensibly to deal with the Kurdi family case but surely to be put through a direly needed crash course in voter-sensitivity training. It was a watershed moment. Alexander, previously a UN diplomat, had become one of the CPC's nastiest spokespeople, unpleasant, short-tempered and accusing—and, pretty well for these reasons, was acclaimed by party loyalists and a lazy press as one of its rising stars. But the *Power & Politics* undoing was one of a series of events showing just how deeply the rot of insensitivity had infiltrated the Conservatives and was a symptom of the party's peculiar malaise. Even Harper, a man increasingly perceived as a leader without friends, was beginning to seem curiously un-anchored and adrift of the task. Out of reach, no life-buoy thrown to him, the minister of immigration, refugees and citizenship was floundering in the water.

Alexander was on air at 5 p.m. I'd not seen the Bodrum photograph yet, but was following the fracas, as I was able to, on Twitter. An hour later, I was welcomed at a private home in Rathnelly for the meet and greet that Nichole Anderson had put into play, the first of my campaign. The Rathnelly guests, well-to-do and eager, numbered about twenty-five. My hosts—one a celebrated painter whose work I'd bought long before we'd met, and the other a former colleague from the writing world—were welcoming and convivial and had laid on a good spread; I could not have made my debut in more optimal surroundings, but botched it. The point of a meet and greet is for a candidate to engage constituents and to deliver a message, but also to raise money. It doesn't have to be much, but not to do so is an opportunity missed. I'd arrived without pledge forms, though, and without an assistant able to work the room. But these turned out to be just a couple of the ways in which I discovered myself—*pace* the PMO—"not ready." I'd come prepared to address residents' worries about volatile bitumen being transported along the Dupont Line and spoke well, but failed to fathom the full significance of one woman's question about refugees. I was distracted. The stage manager in me was worrying about keeping the campaign's photographer busy and getting him shots that might be useful to the campaign, more for his satisfaction than mine, and I suggested, fairly disastrously, a group picture on the back garden steps. Immediately, I realized how untoward had been my assumption that the group, many of them strangers to each other, would be cajoled into de facto support of a candidate they'd come simply to hear out.

Within hours, photographs of the drowned three-year-old Syrian went authentically viral, the BBC and other media reporting that the Conservative government had stalled the Kurdi family's application to immigrate, news that Harper and the PMO vehemently denied. The drowned boy's aunt lived in Vancouver. The Kurdi story had a tragic, domestic face.

The next day, the prime minister held a press conference and said he and his wife, Laureen, had seen the picture of Alan Kurdi on the Internet. "The first thing that crossed our minds was remembering our own son Ben at that age," said Harper. "That brings tears to your eye. That is the reaction of every parent, anyone who's ever had a two-year-old, or been near a two-year-old, been a parent in Canada or anywhere around the world."

I did not doubt Harper, but marvelled at his unfortunate capacity to appear dispassionate when a display of feeling was so pressingly called for. The prime minister was unconvincing because the only thing he knew how to state with any urgency was the not unreasonable position that came next: "Refugee policy alone is not remotely a solution to this problem, it is of a scale far, far beyond that," said Harper.

"We are also doing what we have to do to try and fight the root cause of this problem. That is the violent campaign being led against millions of people by ISIS. That is why we are part of the international military coalition." In the "interparty air war" of an election in which images—hands on hearts, tears—would matter more than they ever had, Harper's words were neither sufficient nor appealing. And this was true despite significant concessions in the prime minister's rhetoric that went unnoticed: his reference to a "root cause" would have been anathema to the Conservatives during all the years of the conflict in Afghanistan, and his description of Canada "as one of the largest donors of humanitarian aid relative to our size in this part of the world" stood in stark contrast to his characterization of such work, only three weeks before, as "dropping aid on dead people." These small alterations had no bearing. The steady resolve, the placing of the incident within the greater context of the war with ISIL, did not satisfy the burgeoning need of Canadians to be able to respond as unequivocally and immediately as the country (including the prime minister) had done after the Haitian earthquake five years before.

In Montreal, Trudeau was repeating his open-ended pledge to bring in twenty-five thousand government-sponsored refugees by the end of the year and saying, of the Conservatives, that "you don't get to discover compassion in the middle of a campaign, you either have it or you don't." And at the Café Diplomatico, a popular College Street spot in Toronto's Little Italy neighbourhood to which the NDP's loose-knit coterie of downtown MPs and candidates had been summoned, Mulcair was prefacing the series of platform announcements concerning seniors he was due to make with a necessary acknowledgment of the Kurdi photographs and what they said about the refugee crisis. "As a dad and a grandfather," said Mulcair, "it's unbearable that we're doing nothing." Mulcair, visibly moved, compared the photograph of the dead Syrian infant to the equally iconic one of "the Girl in the Picture"—the pre-teen, naked Kim Phúc fleeing an American napalm attack during the Vietnam War. Mulcair warned against using the situation for political advantage, though not without a discreet swipe at the minister in the news. "Canada has a responsibility to act," said Mulcair, "and it would be too easy to start assigning blame. Chris Alexander has a lot to answer for, but that's not where we are right now." It was the sort of deftly delivered remark that had contributed to the leader of the Official Opposition's august reputation in the House, but it did not work so well in the larger public forum in which Canadians were needing to have emotions, not rational arguments, vindicated.

. . .

The early call at the Café Diplomatico had been easy enough: an espresso, a sunny morning and none of us in the Aegean. Count your blessings. What with Hollett reading the tele-prompter introduction of the party leader for the cameras, there was a fair sense of where the party figured its meaningful fight was going to be. Toronto—Danforth and Davenport were in the can, University—Rosedale was for the taking; Toronto—St. Paul's—well, there were NDP candidates in the Don Valley, in Markham and in all the ridings of Scarborough, too. Mulcair announced his plans to roll back the retirement age from sixty-seven to sixty-five, to protect public and private pensions, and to create affordable housing and "a larger federal role in areas like long-term care, palliative care and dementia" in ways that did not saddle future generations with massive social and economic debts. Then, at Bathurst Street, word came from Davenport of a demonstration that Lifeline Syria was planning for outside the Government of Canada Citizenship and Immigration offices on St. Clair Avenue East that afternoon, where Andrew Cash was going to speak.

"Jesus," I said to Janet. "What's with this party? Nobody knows how to play as a team? This is my riding! Tell them *I* have to speak."

Janet decided not to point out that Cash was the party's critic for immigration.

"Ethan," I called out. "Get me the name and the date of that ship of Hindus that Canada turned away. The *Moramagatu*, I think it was. And the MS *St. Louis*—was it 1939?"

My adjutant was sitting at the front of the room with his laptop perched upon his knees, and I went to the tiny desk by the pillar that I'd appropriated as my own to prepare a pithy address that I'd be delivering, I was sure, to hundreds if not *thousands* of distressed Canadians gathered at whatever was the park by the citizenship offices.

Except that when I arrived at the rally, there was no park and the hundreds if not thousands I was imagining had not assembled (I really should have known my riding better). There were perhaps a dozen protestors along the sidewalk, three or four of them holding up a banner. CP24, CBC and Global television crews had SUVs parked on the other side of St. Clair, where one of the teams was filming an intro with St. Clair's traffic and the small demonstration as a backdrop. I knew the drill—they were biding their time, making the most of their own labour as they waited for a bigger crowd and public figures. Cash had not yet arrived. The two other cameramen-reporter pairs were mulling about, idle.

"I'm the local NDP candidate," I said to the CP24 duo. I recognized the cameraman from literary events at which I'd provided pieces to camera on occasion, but this was a new context and his expression was disconcertingly blank.

"Sorry," he said, pointing to the reporter beside him. "She makes the call."

She looked up at the interloper, then down again.

I approached the cameraman from the CBC.

"I'm the local NDP candidate," I said. "I do a fair amount of work for the CBC."

Another deadpan expression. He looked past me to where the CBC reporter with him was gesturing that they should collect some vox pops, the demonstrators' number having increased to about thirty. The woman holding up a placard that read MY DOOR IS OPEN TO REFUGEES said she recognized me, good news.

"Are you working for us?" I asked, ready to thank her, learn her name (and not forget it).

No, she said, she was working in Cash's Davenport office because she thought the NDP had no chance in Toronto—

St. Paul's. I was figuring out how to take my leave without sounding sour and told her, "You're volunteering for the NDP in Toronto, that's what matters"—which, of course, was true, but it hurt. Then Cash arrived with an assistant to manage the media and the cameras turned towards him. This was not the scene I'd been banking on for my Canada-rallying rhetorical turn before an impassioned crowd. The reality was that I was unlikely to manage a word for the cameras, but Cash took my arm and pulled me to his side. He spoke fervently about the necessity for action and introduced me as the local candidate. That was good of him; maybe the GTA NDP was a team after all. I knew I had only a few seconds and that it was likely no one in from the networks would review the footage (digital stuff that didn't even need to be physically dumped), but spoke anyway. I said Canada had turned away the *Komagata Maru* back in 1914 and then, in 1939, the MS *St. Louis* and its boatload of 907 Jews, some of whom would later die in concentration camps. I spoke of Mackenzie King's declaration that the refugee crisis of the day was "not a Canadian problem" and cited the infamous words of one of the immigration agents of that era, saying of the fear-inducing immigrants of the day, "none is too many," all in twenty, maybe thirty seconds, before rushing to add the more recent example of the MV *Sun Sea*. In 2010, the rickety boat had arrived on B.C.'s shores with a cargo of some four hundred Tamils promptly described as "terrorists" and "migrants jumping the queue" by Harper, Vic Toews and Jason Kenney reflexively—no, vindictively—using the moment to increase Canadians' fears and boost their own anxious cause. Now, I said, was the time of the Syrian people's need and for Canada to behave differently—now was the time to reclaim "Canadian values" and the humanitarian traditions Harper had described as *dropping aid on dead people*. This, I said, was the moral moment!

I knew this stuff, I'd written about it, and the crowd of maybe fifty now was not really a crowd, but I was in my element and able to speak, able to do the politician's thing—the first speech since my nomination—and perorating beautifully as . . . as the cameraman packed up and joined the reporter who'd put away her microphone and the pair waited for an interval in the traffic to cross the busy street to where their van was parked.

. . .

Monday, September 7, the holiday morning of the Labour Day weekend, was gorgeous and sunny and blue. This was, in Alistair MacLeod's marvellous phrase (that was the Cape Breton writer's title for perhaps the best Canadian story ever to be written about work), "The Closing Down of Summer." I cycled down University Avenue to join the Labour Day parade, where, in bright orange T-shirts, an NDP cohort of volunteers from across the GTA was gathering at the head of an assembling crowd (and this time, it was actually a crowd). There were placards for Andrew Cash, Laura Casselman, Olivia Chow, Jennifer Hollett, Peggy Nash, Rathika Sitsabaiesan—and even a few for me. The cameras would be at the front, the candidates and NDP incumbents leading the phalanx. Liz tapped me on the shoulder—she had been dispatched by Sarah, aware I was unsure of what to do—and took me up to the top of the line, where I joined candidates holding the NDP banner the breadth of Queen Street like a skirt to their waists. Hollett was my neighbour as we moved forward and we talked for a while about the campaign and our prospects, and after several blocks Mulcair appeared out of the crowd taking hold of the banner and marching next to me. *Click-click. Click-click. Click-click.* I'd barely said hello before a check from behind shoved me to the left and Peggy Nash appeared between us. Mulcair fell out like a paratrooper to a waiting black SUV.

"Don't worry," said Sarah, who had been walking backwards in front of me. "I got the shot."

. . .

I'd taken advantage of the moment to talk to Nash about the urgency, in Toronto, of a position vis-à-vis the arts, and the former NDP president told me that she and Cash were concerned the party had no credible position on Toronto beyond the promises about infrastructure being made. A few hours of walking later, I found myself standing next to several NDP candidates on risers arranged along the west side of Dufferin Street, there for us to wave our solidarity to the mile-long parade of workers and floats filing into Centennial Park. The district associations of assorted unions strode by and a CUPE bigwig I'd seen making nice to Bennett at Wychwood Barns shook the candidates' hands and was introduced to me as "someone important to know." It was around about the time when the IAMAW Local 2323—or was it Local 128 of the International Brotherhood of Boilermakers, or maybe the United Steelworkers, or was it the Workers United of Brockville or Belleville or Oshawa or Orangeville?—marched past in duck-hunting camouflage shirts, that some part of me wondered what was the 1950s drama of which the NDP imagined it was the star. What bygone world was the NDP living in, that it thought people voted in blocs and organized labour was its bed-rock? Why was it assuming the allegiance of groups of highly paid carpenters, nurses and teachers, et cetera, who, their revenue guar-anteed, were surely as likely as anyone to choose the party that taxed them the least (their union management among the provin-cial Liberal Party's biggest donors); or of workers from small towns as wary as Westerners of the party's please-all-comers vacillations on gun control, and fine with all that environment stuff as long as it did not lead to carbon taxes and hikes on the price of gasoline? *Dis*organized labour—part-time and "precarious" workers—I could see. But this long line of workers in closed shops with eighty-inch TVs and home cinemas and gas-guzzling trucks, these teachers with pensions—would they be voting our way?

. . .

The NDP's five core franchises were, I figured: labour; so-called soft Québécois nationalists wanting a better deal within Confederation than the moribund Bloc Québécois could offer; First Nations; new Canadians; and youth. The last three groups, maybe I could reach. I'd had some fairly detailed ideas about video advertisements of a satirical nature that I'd wanted to be a part of our campaign from the start, but had only a layman's idea of cheap ways to produce them. My plans of last and maybe even first resort were to shoot a series of videos with handheld iPhones, but I knew that even the appearance of amateur must be designed and planned. To that end I'd been communicating for a while with a documentary filmmaker I knew—someone on the fringes of the Toronto arts circuit to which I was privy. His posts on social media were often as virulent about the Conservatives as mine, but he'd messaged to say that "even though my political leanings are pretty evident I think it will threaten my own livelihood to actually do work for a campaign," which was a drag. In lieu, he'd put me in touch with a couple of other directors, and it was clear from initial communications that started,

Hi Noah

We have some ideas. But before we develop anything further, we need an idea of what the budget is. What are you thinking?

D___

to which I'd replied,

Hi D.,

Well, let's see. I'm the guy that walked into a riding with $350 in the bank for a $97,000, now $200,000 campaign. But I also have quite specific ideas about the two sets of vids, each taking half a day I'd say. So I figure if you're open, then a talk about what items we're costing and how to cost them is in order before we put a price on things, no? Because right now it's not even fair to ask what your own minimum would be.

Best, and hoping to chat,
Noah

that no charitable or even discounted work would be forthcoming and our conversation quickly petered out. Without scripts, props, cameras, crew or money, even iPhone plans seemed unrealizable.

Then, on September 8, the day after the Labour Day parade, chance came into play.

SEPTEMBER 8

CPC	NDP	LPC	BQ	GRN	OTH
27.0%	32.3%	31.3%	3.5%	5.1%	0.8%

. . .

I was taking a break for tea at one of the streetside tables in front of the Starbucks outlet at the corner of Bathurst and St. Clair, drafting an email to Pratt and Levy about lessons I was learning from down below. Not my place, I knew, but, what the hell, I hit "Send":

From: Noah Richler

Date: Tuesday, September 8, 2015 at 9:32 AM

Subject: A note from the floor

Hi Greta, James

I know we are holding well in the polls, but I would like to bring to your attention the feeling that we are being outpaced by Trudeau's rabbit-out-of-a-hat PR strategies that appear to be working for him. As people are repulsed with Harper and Alexander et al., folk are forgetting about C-51 and looking to his boyishness and feeling relief. Even intelligent folk I know are game for his deficit talk. And he is getting out ahead on humanitarian issues too, and even on stuff where Tom has come out first—like the Syrian question being non-partisan and not about apportioning blame, or restoring funding to the CBC. So now we see Monday's *Star* with not one, but two huge adoring pics of Trudeau, and none of anybody else, and (I defer to you if it is your strategy), the leader of the opposition coming third in the sequence of Mansbridge debates.

Should we not be giving the newspapers a bit of hell? The sum of it is that we appear to be the trailers in arguments that we have initiated, and it would be nice if we could get out ahead of other issues too.

I have sent, through my campaign management team, a team-oriented suggestion for getting ahead at least about arts talk. In this realm (and sports) we are perceived at the moment as having no position. The word I had recently, from a prominent member of the Arts Coalition, was that Trudeau was going to make his arts announcement on the Monday but then the Syrian photos hit.

I'm reattaching it.

Of course it pales in importance next to the refugee plight but at the appropriate point (and TIFF is happening now) we need to come out ahead. I have offered plans for your excellent Toronto cohort, and these arts ones would naturally be an announcement for my riding, what with its bevy of filmmakers, etc. It would be nice to see a little explicit attention from the centre.

Liz, I knew, would be waiting for me at the office with a clipboard in hand and I was procrastinating, reasoning that it was important to take what chances I had for a little air and composure. St. Clair and Bathurst is an ugly junction, busy with traffic in all directions and the proto–*Blade Runner* growth of high condominium towers sprouting without sense erratically in the landscape. The far towers east along St. Clair Avenue were daunting—gleaming white and new and, from this distance, utterly without charm. Their apartments with selling views would soon be blocked by other high-rises, and they were home to thousands upon thousands of residents who'd vote for a party leader and not a local candidate because their residence in the riding was fleeting and they weren't going to live here long enough to care about railway tracks or better local home care delivery. Don't bother canvassing the condos, I'd been told; their residents have conversations with televisions and not their neighbours. Their allegiances would be in the abstract. They'd vote for a colour or a leader, having been here for just a fraction of the eighteen years that Bennett had been incumbent. They were a precursor, really, of the dysfunction in which the parliamentary system already found itself. Canada, a country overwhelmed by the influences of its neighbour to the south, was voting and behaving presidentially—but without any of that system's institutions or controls. The towers spoke to the riding's anomie and the pit stops these apartments were to professionals briefly halting on the way from starter homes to more permanent digs; to pensioners in the last comfortable shelters they would own before moving on to assisted living, slow oblivion and death. There's a fifty percent turnover in the riding between elections, said Bennett to me in one of our Christmas Truce moments, and it's largely because of the condos. We didn't have plans to breach the lobbies of half of them—better the community housing and co-ops and seniors' residences.

I'd been starting to enumerate the pros and cons of this strategy when a young, lanky, but solid-looking fella sat down at my table.

"Are you Noah Richler?" he asked.

"Yes," I said.

"I'm glad you're running," he said, introducing himself only as Nick. He was blond, slouched in the other chair and likely in his mid- to late twenties. He had the naturally fit build of a guy who played pickup hockey effortlessly. He wore glasses and a plaid shirt, his arms crossed and legs stretched out before him like he was waiting for nothing in particular.

"What do you do?" I asked.

"I'm a film editor," he said.

"Oh?" I answered. And then, without a great deal of conviction, "Maybe you could help us out. I'm looking to make a few videos and could use someone who knows the software."

Which was all I was expecting: another piece of the puzzle on the cheap. But he was affable and a constituent, and I was relaxed, and so I explained the ideas we had for a spoof remake of the Conservatives' attack ad "The Interview," in which a boardroom table of dour accountant types is considering the Liberal Party leader's job application and decides "Justin's not ready" but he has "nice hair, though." We'd imagined a rewrite using much of the same script and a lot of the footage but, rather than Trudeau's, having Harper's application repeatedly come up for a variety of positions—as CFO (cueing "Are you nuts? He ordered a thir-teen-week election for one that should have taken six. All he does is waste money"), as VP of human resources ("Are you crazy? All he does is make enemies. He'll treat every Muslim in the building like a threat"). With each, the prime minister's headshot thrown down and added to the pile of discarded Trudeau applications already on the table in each version. We'd thought of adding celebrities to the table and having the original video's agitated South Asian, instead of complimenting Justin Trudeau's hair, ask a question about legalized marijuana. And, I said, we'd been contemplating a second set of "substantive" Charlie Rose–style interview segments in which I'd pronounce on platform issues against a black background as if edited from a conversation with the PBS broadcaster, the point of these to act in counterpoint to the satirical ad and to show that our campaign had substance.

"Sure, I could do that," said Nick. He said he did a little animation and had his own studio. "If we need somewhere bigger," he said, "I have a friend's we can use."

Nick was as appealing as he was understated, though I did not yet know just how much this was the case. We exchanged numbers and he scrawled down his full name—Nick DenBoer—and, hard to forget, the URL of his website: www.smearballs.com.

. . .

Back at the office I checked my envelope of telephone calls to return, and on my desk was Sean and Young Ethan's SWOT analysis that I'd commissioned more than a month before but none of us had followed up on. It had been an exercise in delegation as much as anything and the single page of hyperlinks to which finally I was casting an eye did not appear to amount to much. Their research confirmed that Bennett had voted against Bill C-51, and contained other rudimentary information about my Liberal and Conservative opponents that was also common knowledge. At the foot of it, Ethan and Ethan had cut-and-pasted a few of my Facebook posts:

February 27, 2015
So Chelsea football fans have natural partners, n'est-ce pas?
May they meet in the Paris Metro and push each other onto
the tracks. (What is it about blue and white livery that gets
racists going?)

February 6, 2015
[a video of Montreal snowplows efficiently at work]
How I miss this. In Toronto the overpaid incompetents just
push the stuff around.

January 27, 2015
I blame Stephen Harper PERSONALLY for this. He is a
pathological psychopath who I believe wants an attack on
Canadian soil to vindicate his paranoiac view of the world
and his idiotic policies. We as Canadians are to blame. He
brings out the worst in us, has made a travesty of our reputa-
tion abroad, but we swallow his bullshit rhetoric and his
reward is that we are about to re-elect him. No language is
too strong. If this man was leading South Africa during
apartheid he would have been unrestrained and history
would have vilified his hateful policies and their result. But
he leads Canada, we have certain vague traditions he has not
yet undone and there he is, still. A vile miscreant who
announces foreign policy at high schools rather than
Parliament and who pretends to be a champion of free speech
even as he ruins it and uses all the thuggish means of govern-
ment to shut people up. When a bomb blows up here, I put the
blame squarely on his shoulders. I have been a champion of
Canada all my life. But I wonder if that Canada even exists.
Please, please, show me it does.

Sarah, I recalled, had complained about a couple of these as I was writing them—this the usual scene:

INT. KITCHEN—MORNING

The WRITER is in his pyjamas, chuckling to himself and ignoring his wife as he types on his iPhone. SARAH, who has a steady and important job, is smartly dressed.

SARAH: What are you doing?

NOAH: Nothing.

SARAH: What are you doing?

NOAH: Nothing.

SARAH: You're lying. I can tell.

NOAH: It's going to be sunny in Nova Scotia.

SARAH: You're posting. *Don't.*

SARAH gets up from the table, clearly exasperated.

SARAH: I'm going to take that machine away from you. The social networks are no place to be funny. Nobody thinks it's funny except you. How many times do I have to tell you to stay away off the networks? Facebook is for family, Twitter is for cats. Delete what you're writing, *now.*

NOAH: Sure. Okay.

SARAH leaves. NOAH keeps tapping.

But I'd altered the settings of my Facebook page from "Public" to "Friends" in early summer and presumably "Fred Checkers" had vetted the posts before I'd been cleared. Not an issue, surely my "Friends" were my friends—and, besides, taking posts down implied a cover-up, the sort of action that had always struck me as more censurable than whatever may have been the original offence.

I tossed the paper in the bin and checked my email.

. . .

On September 8, 2015, at 5.36 p.m., Nick DenBoer wrote:

Hi Noah,

If you want to shoot some interview style Charlie Rose stuff it's totally doable here. I also have the compositing and animation skills to augment Harper's attack ads where we could alter or replace the actors to present a new narrative and maybe even sprinkle in some comedy for viral effect.

A proper skewering of the cringe-worthy messaging the CPC has been putting out this election is sure to resonate with any Canadian with half a brain in their skull.

Let me know if you want to come by.

Cheers

Nick

. . .

Nick showed Doug and me the coach house in a back alley that he'd converted into a modest shooting studio for "green screen" work—in which, as happens with weather broadcasts, an actor is filmed against a green backdrop that, using techniques of "Chroma keying," allows one background to be substituted for another. Downstairs, where the Corvette parked outside would ordinarily have been stored, was a small studio space with lighting rigs, a couple of single lens reflex cameras on stands, microphones at the ready and green and black backdrops. Upstairs were Nick's editing suites and a music and audio production setup. Beyond this were his kitchen and living quarters and a pile of laundry he explained a local Portuguese woman came by regularly to pick up, launder and press for a bargain price, "so I don't need to put in a washing machine or a dryer. Cool, eh?"

Doug and I were hard put to contain our excitement. We figured out a schedule and left.

. . .

At the Rally for Change that evening, it was the usual jockeying for seats behind the stage and in the cameras' view, this time at the Harbourfront Westin, and the turn of Quebec MP Ruth Ellen Brosseau and B.C.'s Mira Oreck, the candidate for Vancouver—Granville, to rouse the faithful and welcome "*Canada's next prime minister!!*"

Murray Brewster, a Canadian Press correspondent who'd been good to me when Afghanistan was his beat, was on the platform of reporters and cameramen. So was the CBC's James Cudmore—a friend and, years before, the intern I'd hired at the *National Post* and nicknamed "Sergeant" because the former cadet's voice boomed so. I'd always liked James a lot, enough so that I'd given him the BBC Radio travelling box that had been with me in Haiti, Rwanda and who knows how many troubled places, as if it were a talisman. Now here he was in the zone and it was my turn to be the intern.

"What's going on here?" I asked. "It looks to me to be the same folk every time."

"It's a big game," said James. "It's a show organized for the television networks. It's not made for voters. It's not even made for newspapers, because the parties have learned that the days when newspapers could afford to cover the rallies are done. Only the networks can. The buildup, the music—the signs people carry—it's all for television and the hope that the big guy will make the news."

"Does the conversation change?"

"Not really," said James. "It's the same conversation, the same people, the same potted protest. Sometimes what we write, maybe what we say to a leader or his aides privately, might change what a party does, but not often."

. . .

The next day, Anthony Green and Emma Knight came out to canvass Vaughan Road, where large signs for the campaign were multiplying at pleasingly short intervals. Anthony and Emma, now adults, were children of friends and had become friends in their own right. Handily, both were very interested in film and for a while they'd been working on a screenplay together. Anthony had directed several short films and documentaries, including one about the Rolling Stones' "Bigger Bang" world tour (*Salt of the Earth*, with Jacob Cohl), and Emma had worked at the *International New York Times* in Paris for a time. Together, they were co-founders of a cold-pressed juice retail startup and were still finding time to volunteer. They were young and industrious and had organized minds, so I'd asked them if they'd help me out on the video team.

Emma said, "You know I was delivered by—"

"—Carolyn Bennett. Yes, yes, of course you were. Who wasn't?"

"Do you think that's an issue?" she said teasingly.

Anthony asked if I had checked out Nick's show reel yet. He said, "It's amazing, what he does. We're in a whole other stratosphere with this guy."

It was true. Nick's show reel was out of this world and the stuff of a very plastic one—a hilarious and bizarre collection of comic sketches. Footage from late-night interviews and the like was manipulated by savagely distorting the features of celebrities (Hillary Clinton's eyes, Miley Cyrus's tongue) or by inserting loosely similar lips of an actor to deliver whatever lines Nick had scripted so that his subjects—Bill Cosby, Brad Pitt, Alex Trebek, Donald Trump—would speak the ridiculous and absurd.

. . .

Nick said his short film *The Chickening*, already booked in several other festivals, was opening the wildly popular Midnight Madness series of the Toronto International Film Festival, and it was probably not a good idea for him to schedule anything for the weekend. No scripts had been written, so there was no time to do anything on the video front but move forward as if the team had been up and running for weeks. I told Nick we'd be ready to shoot five videos on the Wednesday—three days before his premiere and less than a week off. Now we had an editor and a studio, and the boon we did possess was production experience. Anthony and Emma were keen and on board, Doug had worked on *The Newsroom* with Ken Finkleman and co-written (with Patrick Graham) *Afghan Luke*, an underrated dark comedy about a maverick Canadian reporter in Afghanistan, and I'd produced and written radio features and documentaries for years.

And we had a plan. We'd already settled on Bill C-51, the environment, the plight of seniors, the muzzling of scientists and the general degradation of Canadian parliamentary democracy as subjects for the substantive videos, but we'd taken too long to spoof "The Interview," the Conservatives' attack ad, and the parodying of it was already hackneyed. The Liberals themselves had turned the slogan "Justin's not ready" to their advantage in the first advertisement of their campaign ("I'm not ready to stand by as our economy slides into recession; not ready to watch hard-working Canadians lose jobs. . . . I *am* ready to do what my opponents won't") and, in the week preceding our planned shoot, NDP headquarters had put out its own limp spoof of the CPC video, neither effective nor amusing, but convincing us to look elsewhere for material. So, instead, we decided to use the interview Peter Mansbridge conducted with Stephen Harper for the CBC's *The National*, that had been broadcast two weeks before as the basis of something. But if the central NDP apparatchiks were convinced the Conservatives were the target, a conviction that would eventually undermine the NDP campaign, in Toronto—St. Paul's there was no question the Liberals were. Thus, we studied the various videos Bennett's and Trudeau's teams had produced, Nick uploading ones for us to select, transcribe and revise. We'd found, on YouTube, a badly shot video of Carolyn Bennett inviting the residents of Toronto—St. Paul's to the Liberal Party Canada Day celebration a few years before, which suited our purposes because she was facing the camera from a fixed position and the movement of her mouth would be relatively easy to rework. We knew Anne Fenn, the comedy writer who'd done the fundraising ask at my nomination, to be a terrific performer, and she had a mouth that could substitute for Bennett's. Quickly I rescripted Bennett's lines for us to have the eighteen-year incumbent say change was necessary and urge her supporters to vote for the only candidate that offered it—i.e., me. Then we looked for a suitable video with Trudeau in our sights, deciding on the Liberal "Escalator" advertisement that was by far the most successful of the election so far, the Liberal Party leader using his stationary position walking up the down escalator as the metaphor of a stalled economy and a country in crisis.

"So," I asked Nick, Doug and I paying a second visit, "if, say, we took a part of Peter Mansbridge's interview with Harper for CBC's *The National*, could you put me in that?"

"Sure," said Nick.

"And could you have me pass Trudeau on the escalator?"

"Absolutely."

Doug went off to produce a first draft, deadline yesterday.

"I can also animate Trudeau falling down the escalator by using the first wide shot of him from afar," wrote Nick after we'd left. "It could be a funny kicker at the end. Looking forward to it!"

. . .

Nick said he'd put a shot list together once we had finished scripts. Doug and I had a first go at them, and then we met with Anthony and Emma for a couple of hours over two afternoons to compress the back-and-forth of drafts within the minuscule time frame the campaign was allowing us. "The Escalator Works" would show me passing the Liberal Party leader treading on the spot, throwing a puzzled look back at him, before arriving at the top of the escalator, halting it and launching into a tirade about the danger of the Liberal Party plans for deficit spending. Then I'd toss some of Carolyn Bennett's campaign flyers over my shoulder, these landing on Trudeau, and start the escalator up again with Trudeau tumbling to the bottom of it. In the Harper spoof, "That's My Seat!," a figure not immediately identifiable as me would approach

Harper and Mansbridge in unctuous conversation, remove the Canadian flag pin from the prime minister's lapel and give the prime minister's chair an almighty kick to send him flying up and out of the picture and onto the ground. Then the figure, revealed to be me, would take the prime minister's seat and explain to Mansbridge why the Conservatives' and Liberals' talk of change, Bennett's too, was meaningless and the NDP the only genuine opportunity for the same, the prostrate Harper concurring from his position on the ground. Jonathan Rotsztain's "The Candidate" livery—the same we were employing for all the cartoons, graphics and photographs we'd been posting on Facebook and Twitter— would conclude the video and an orange wave (a visual reference to the 2011 Quebec phenomenon) would wash over the CBC logo at the top of the video so there was no confusing our product with a genuine broadcast. That was the plan. We knew it would evolve— we were doing everything in a considered way but on the fly—and to that end it was crucial to have Laura Watts and others in the room to offer instantaneous views—and censorship. What was important to me, above all, was that all players felt they had a stake, for we needed everyone to come through with their contributions, no matter how small. No PR or advertising agencies were being employed (though plenty would call to ask who made the videos afterwards), nor focus groups, and neither was there money to draw on: a campaign depends upon a lot of people doing a little for nothing and reliably so. You only get to make a first movie once.

. . .

September in Toronto is a heady time: the light gentle, the days hot but not sweaty, the leaves turning and the city's canopy of trees at its most beautiful—and the social season picking up. The ten-day Toronto International Film Festival had started and the

Blue Jays were playing so well that they would win the American League East division and go on to their first League Championship Series in twenty-two years. The city was in an excited frenzy, Sarah was looking for her 1993 vintage Jack Morris pitcher's jersey, and I was wondering just how much interest there would be in the federal election—"getting out the vote" always any party's abiding concern. Baseball was an opportunity not for riff-raff like me but for party leaders, though the Blue Jays were losing games that leaders were attending, so the politicians made an informal pact and stopped showboating at the Rogers Centre. But TIFF meant parties and the chance to mingle and show an interested NDP presence. At one such party in the riding a very successful retail fashion mogul was hosting, Gerald Schwartz, the usually reserved CEO of the private equity firm ONEX Corp., was surprisingly effusive about Mulcair. He said he'd met Tom and been very impressed, and encouraged Heather Reisman, the CEO of the Indigo bookstore chain and his wife, to do an interview. "I think Tom's very sensible," said Schwartz.

"Wow," said Sarah. "That's something. But you might want to be careful whom you tell. I don't know how much his thumbs-up will please the party radicals."

The Schwartz endorsement was intriguing for a couple of reasons—because of Schwartz's financial wizardry, of course, but also because he and Reisman acutely monitored the parties' positions on Israel and the Middle East. The Jewish residents of Forest Hill (Reisman and Schwartz lived out of riding) were almost categorically hostile to the NDP's fiscal capabilities, and wary of extremists they perceived as having a historical home within the party—particularly of ideologues supporting the Boycott, Divestment and Sanctions (BDS) movement, regarded by its detractors as not just anti-Israel, but anti-Semitic. It was always going to be a tough, if not impossible, battle for the Jewish vote in

Toronto—St. Paul's, despite Mulcair's measures to address the old prejudices. The party had booted out candidates prone to careless or ignorant statements about Israel and Palestine, while letting it be known that Catherine was Jewish and the daughter of Holocaust survivors. I did not find the party's position of a two-state solution with Canada as an enabler (though not the definer) of negotiations at all hard to argue—it was also my own—and despite or even because of the skepticism and hostility, I actually relished such conversations at the door or in the Forest Hill Village boutiques and salons I would make a point of popping into.

. . .

B., our host, came over.

"Hey, Noah," said B., "let's go see my sign."

B. motioned for me to follow him past the celebrity crowd in the lobby and out the front doors to where car valets were meeting guests pulling up in front of the magnificent corner lot. On the floodlit lawn, planted in the bank sloping towards the street, was a bright orange "NDP Noah Richler" campaign sign installed that morning for all the evening's music, sports and screen stars—k-os, Kardinal Offishall, Director X—as well as Toronto film folk and guests from the riding, to see.

B. looked at it. Smiled.

"Does it come in any other colours?" he asked.

SEPTEMBER 15

CPC	NDP	LPC	BQ	GRN	OTH
29.3%	31.5%	30.0%	3.2%	4.9%	1.0%

. . .

Rosh Hashanah, "Days of Awe."

Over morning coffee with Doug and Sarah—"Don't be seen doing too much" was Janet's instruction—I opened up *The Globe and Mail* to see that leading NDP lights had taken up the Jewish New Year's traditional instruction to "raise a noise":

"LEAP MANIFESTO" BACKED BY PROMINENT NDPERS, ACTORS, ACTIVISTS CALLS FOR UPENDING OF CAPITALIST SYSTEM

BY MICHAEL CHEN, THE GLOBE AND MAIL

Author Naomi Klein on Tuesday released a political agenda that urges the next federal government to wean Canada off fossil fuels in as little as 35 years and, in the process, upend the capitalist system on which the economy is based.

More than 100 actors, musicians, labour union leaders, aboriginal leaders, environmentalists and other activists have signed the document, called the "leap manifesto."

Environmentalist David Suzuki, former Ontario NDP leader Stephen Lewis, Mrs. Universe Ashley Callingbull, Canadian Union of Public Employees president Paul Moist and Greenpeace campaigner Melina Laboucan-Massimo were among 15 speakers who read the manifesto aloud at a news conference in Toronto on Tuesday.

"We cannot have a political class in this country floundering around for another four or five years," she said. "We just don't have the time."

Other manifesto signatories include actors Ellen Page, Rachel McAdams, Sarah Polley, Pamela Anderson and Donald Sutherland, singers Bruce Cockburn, Neil Young, Gord Downie, Sarah Harmer and Leonard Cohen, novelists Michael Ondaatje and Joseph Boyden, anti-free trade activist Maude Barlow, artist Robert Bateman and film director Patricia Rozema.

"Send that to Schwartz," said Doug.

. . .

The next day, Wednesday, September 16, was a biggie. First order of business was a 7 a.m. canvass of a TTC station in the riding (I dreaded working transit stops, but mercifully the Heath Street entrance of the St. Clair West station was at the top of the Cedarvale Ravine, and there was at least a small chance that commuters' early morning miseries would be abated by a touch of green); then our day of video shooting; afterwards a bit of door-to-door work; and a meet and greet scheduled for the evening.

Before heading out, I sent a quick note on Slack to the office confirming my unavailability for the better part of the day—I knew my absences were beginning to grate—and another to the team assembling at the studio.

> With profound apologies for the prep I know that especially Anne and Nick will have done, I am killing the Bennett video. I am doing this because our campaign is going well and I don't want to jeopardize that or to be seen as picking on a woman who is generally liked. Its tenor and focus is different from the two others and could (and may well be) an exercise in bad taste. And so I think that we should not do it.
>
> Once again, sorry to have put you through unnecessary paces but, on the other hand, merely imagining it and pursuing the idea was a good exercise. Best not to censor yourself in the creative moment but to pull in the reins afterwards. That is what we did.

Nick was waiting with Davy Foss, his sound man for the day. Davy (who goes by the working name of Davy Force) was, said Nick, a "skilled video maniac from Los Angeles." He was in Toronto because he'd been the co-creator of *The Chickening* and was "intrigued and happy to help out." The pair had set up the green screen and cameras and laid on a light breakfast spread, and put in an order for pizza come lunchtime—unreceipted campaign bounty that might land me in deep water with Elections Canada after my victory over Bennett but, hell, I'd deal with that afterwards. Laura brought make-up and our single prop—the red button she'd picked up at Staples to resemble the emergency stop on an escalator—and, a lawyer by trade, offered usefully cautious comment. Anthony assistant-directed, Emma and Doug did some on-site editing and then reformatted the scripts in 48-point font on a laptop positioned behind the camera for me to read, scrolling through by hand in place of a teleprompter for the benefit of a candidate who'd never done TV. We shot my parts in the Trudeau and Harper videos and, in the scant time that remained, recorded the texts of seven substantive videos, if only to have these in the can as audio for community radio (a tip provided me at Gerry's Fast Food, an excellent local jerk eatery and frequent canvassing stop).

It had been one of the best days of the campaign, despite everything we were unable to manage. I departed Nick's studio impressed and enlivened, but above all moved by what had been achieved by several people working to very specific ends on a campaign that, soon enough, would have a distinctive stamp. But I had no intention of our being a maverick element of the greater enterprise that was the party's national campaign, and was not about to proceed without the NDP HQ's approval; winning the support of my own management team would be the first step. Janet, Phil and Wendy had deliberately not been asking after a video project I'd not kept secret, leaving me to my own devices, and I wanted them to know their laissez-faire attitude was not misguided. Besides which, it would be Janet and Phil liaising with party brass.

. . .

I'd barely left Nick's studio when the NDP revealed its budget, long awaited by candidates shilling for an un-costed party platform. ("We're putting out a detailed plan soon! All will be explained!") The face of the NDP's fiscal document belonged to Andrew Thomson, the former Saskatchewan NDP minister of finance landed by the party with all the hoopla it could muster, what with his proven financial bona fides. Reminding the public (and particularly the Conservative public) that a couple of the party's top players had previously been ministers—Mulcair having tended the environment portfolio in Quebec, and Thomson finance in Saskatchewan—was the implicit tactic the NDP leader was using to thwart Trudeau, teacher and back-bencher. And so, a few weeks prior, the leader had attended the opening of the party's campaign office in Eglinton—Lawrence, where Thomson was up against Joe Oliver and Marco Mendicino. I might have been annoyed at Mulcair's popping into neighbouring ridings and not mine, my original entreaties ignored, but I was also aware that outlying areas of the GTA—Scarborough especially (where there had been a single rally in July but none during the campaign proper)—were being similarly neglected. The strategy of the NDP leader in Toronto, to the extent that any existed, was constantly baffling: incumbents Dan Harris and Rathika Sitsabaiesan had tough battles on their hands in Scarborough, where new Canadians constituted a natural constituency and a vital swing vote, but, to all intents and purposes, it was solely downtown Toronto that was practically in the party's sights. And yet, but for statements about infrastructure and Mulcair's slightly awkward declarations that Toronto was the "most important" city in Canada (the latter statement problematic), the country's media capital was being used for announcements about national policies rather than ones honed to it. Really, I did not envy Thomson—a bright, proven and appealing man—one bit. His Eglinton—Lawrence parachuting seemed, even in the best of circumstances, destined for defeat, his prospects there making even mine look fabulously rosy.

On the day, Thomson spoke of the NDP's "prudent and responsible approach to balancing the budget." Not only would the "progressive" plan balance the books, but an NDP government would run surpluses. The NDP budget would not, as Harper was doing, hit the "snooze button on the economy"; it would not, as the Liberals were doing, "hit the panic button."

"Man," said Phil, "we are really fucked. And we've done this to ourselves."

. . .

The bells, the bells!

Am buzzed into the meet and greet, on Farnham Avenue where some twenty people have gathered on the rooftop of a handsome 1930s apartment building at the corner of Avenue Road. I am addressing a group I know is inherently skeptical of the NDP's ability to manage finances, about the affability of the party leader, his responsible fiscal policy, the experience Mulcair has as a minister and his plans for infrastructure and investment in Toronto. Instead, the topic of the refugees arises, expressed with more alarm and precision than had been the case at Rathnelly. I speak of Canada's humanitarian traditions, again invoking the

Komagata Maru, the MS *St. Louis* and the MV *Sun Sea*. I deride Public Safety Minister Vic Toews's characterization of Tamils as "criminals," "terrorists" and migrants "jumping the queue"; reiterate Harper's condescending view of the country's humanitarian tradition; and condemn Defence Minister Jason Kenney's having described the refugee crisis as "a challenge for European and African countries" with Canada having no obligation to help.

The phrases roll easily off my tongue, but it is not the high and the abstract that my listeners want to hear. They want *numbers*. Trudeau has been saying that Canada should take 50,000 by the end of 2016 and 25,000 immediately. Mulcair has proposed that Canada should accept 10,000 government-sponsored refugees before the year is out and another 9,000 per annum through 2019, for a total of 46,000 over four years.

"Why not more?" I was asked.

I talk about logistics—about speedy process and officers in Syria on site—explaining the NDP's number is in concordance with the UN's request. I share my vision of Canada, saying that with its gift of space, of course the country can absorb massive numbers of people in distress—this is the story of the very foundation of the country, from the United Empire Loyalists (refugees of the American War of Independence) forward. A few questions about the effect of a large intake of refugees upon national security do come up, but the atmosphere is generally one of skepticism—either the NDP's views are too lax (ISIL is a problem), or conversely they are not open enough. My answers are not convincing, and neither is the going on too long that is typically my response, in difficult straits, helping. Becky Fong, previously the producer of political and cultural commentator Allan Gregg's program at TVO, had come on as the campaign's scheduler and candidate handler after the Rathnelly and Lifeline Syria demonstration disappointments, and I can see her in the distance giving me a caring, rather than wholeheartedly approving, glance: not good. On the campaign trail, the challenge of the refugee crisis and how Canada should act to alleviate it is another early harbinger of the NDP's electoral destiny. Beyond the straightforward foreign policy imperative, the issue is allowing politicians of all parties—though, more to the point, ordinary Canadians—to articulate their vision of home in the most emotive and rousing of terms. The refugee crisis is letting Canadians remember themselves, and in the circus's high striker of feeling that was the party leaders' contest, Trudeau's 50,000 scored better than Mulcair's 46,000 and the first hit of the bell was the winner. Even I could hear "50,000" ring out. It was the better number: it divided well, it doubled well, it remembered well. The NDP's "46,000" was not a number at all. It said, "Why not 45 or 42 or 39 or, indeed, 50?" It spoke to the details of government and not to the art of the possible; it spoke to the technocrat and not the impassioned man.

. . .

The campaign is gathering momentum. Video production is in high gear and the "funky town hall" pub nights are turning out to be more than plans on paper. At Dave's on St. Clair, Juno Award–winning Mexican musician Quique Escamilla, a Toronto resident and a friend, is our featured artist. Young Ethan, a bright and witty theatrical arts student of Cree descent named Dale, and Diedra, an enabler of up-and-coming Canadian musicians at the independent music label Arts & Crafts, are minding the door. Inside, Quique, with whom I'd worked at Luminato Festival, is being, as ever, delightful. The Conservatives' Bill C-24, the law facilitating the stripping of Canadian citizenship from dual passport holders, had been the spur for having fun. During Luminato, I'd asked Quique if and when he was planning to take out Canadian citizenship. "Why would I do that?" he answered. "It costs a lot of money and the government can just take it away." It had not occurred to me until then how greatly the value of Canadian citizenship had been reduced in the eyes of potential future citizens able to contribute much. Quique could contemplate living in the United States, United Kingdom, France, Germany or his native Mexico, and in the supermarket of citizenship that is the new world, Bill C-24 had made of the Canadian passport a diminished product. Quique plays, and in the interval between sets, local author Nazneen Sheikh reads a pertinent election scene from a novel of hers set in Pakistan, and then Quique and I discuss Bill C-24 and the concert he is planning for Leamington, Ontario, for Temporary Foreign Workers (TFWs) in the agricultural sector paid, with the consent of the law, a lesser wage than Canadian citizens would be for equivalent work. A good crowd has turned out, but we've guaranteed Liz Guerrier, the owner of the popular bar, a one-thousand-dollar food and beverages till for reserving the premises. I watch anxiously as NDP activists nurse single beers or glasses of water, just a few sticking around after ten. Kindly, Liz forgoes the $350 we might have owed, and we clear more than a thousand dollars in donations and at the door. But the pub nights are intended to spread word of our campaign as much as to fundraise, and if they are to do so effectively, then we need to reach out into the riding for people not already party members. We decide that the Wychwood Pub should be the venue for the next pub night, and to have another somewhere in Little Jamaica. Still, we feel like winners. I mean, what do the polls really say?—they're still using landlines, don't you know! Who bothers with those anymore? Not the young, certainly!

SEPTEMBER 21

CPC	NDP	LPC	BQ	GRN	OTH
30.3%	29.7%	30.5%	3.8%	4.8%	0.9%

. . .

At Bathurst Street, the team is saying (as loudly as silence permits) nothing at all about the videos, the contents of which I have been asking them to take on faith. But the chill in the air is palpable, so I decide it is time to assemble the crew and give a pep talk. I explain that the reach of the videos will be greater than anything I am able to deliver canvassing, and while I'd needed to absent myself for the small amount of time the videos were taking to produce, the requisite hours did not mean I was avoiding knocking on doors or taking that primary component of the campaign any less seriously. To my mind, I say, the NDP's social networking tactics are a failure. What political parties generally do, I explain, is choose party-friendly stories reinforcing party-friendly messages and push these at party-friendly people so their incremental reach is practically nil. At best, the statements, articles and videos posted to social media reinforce the convictions of the existing base and, at worst, they alienate it—as I believe the central NDP's constant barrage of five-dollar solicitations is doing. Of all the parties' web strategies, I go on, the NDP's most unfortunately illustrated the patterns of cognitive dissonance and consonance that are endemic features of Internet exchanges. Users display, in their choices, an innate disposition not to engage with "dissonant" stories challenging previously held points of view, and instead open and pass on ones "consonant" with their beliefs, the new information neither threatening nor effective because it buttresses these directly or takes down opponents and their contrary arguments. So the NDP picks up party-friendly stories and passes these on in groups that intersect neither with Liberal nor Conservative circles, fooled by numbers of likes and shares that reflect only these messages' circularity into believing they are having effect. By contrast, the videos we are making are designed to vault over the barrier of dissonance by using humour—the property I'd always believed to be a barometer of the confident. The jokes of the Trudeau and Harper videos will, if they are successful, allow content to penetrate the minds of voters that ordinarily we would not reach and find the undecided among them. We were also, I add, making substantive videos that do not share the humorous ones' viral possibility, their more pedestrian purpose to remind whomever we reached that we could not be dismissed as simple jesters.

I'd been keeping the campaign managers in the know all along, and I'd asked Phil to come round to the studio on the following Wednesday, September 23, to view rough cuts. I did so knowing, even at the time, that, had my team been working for another party, we almost certainly would not have had the relative freedom we were enjoying to invent as we saw fit. A more organized electoral machine would surely have been more dictatorial; would probably not have let me use Jonathan's designs, our slogans— "Spread the Word," "Your Vote Matters"—or my moniker, "The Candidate." Even I was aware the label—the *brand!*—might be thought of as maverick or lacking humility or conflicting with the *national* one. For the time being, our heads were beneath the parapet, but we needed the office to be on our side of it, with us.

Phil watched, taciturn—but I knew, by then, this was his *happy* taciturn face. He liked the Trudeau and Harper videos a lot, but, while not disturbed by the essential action in the latter of kicking the prime minister out of his interviewee's seat, he did worry that the frame of him lying prostrate on the ground as I took up the conversation with Mansbridge made Harper's still body look like a corpse. Nick fixed the frame, at least in the interim, by having Harper, lying on the lawn a distance behind Mansbridge and me, nodding his head in approval at what I was saying. Phil also worried that my face looked tired and haggard—as indeed it did, after intense hours of shooting and rewriting. Make-up had achieved little and my eyes were darting about visibly as I read lines off our ersatz teleprompter. But Nick found a software program that was his genius editor's equivalent of blush and wrote to say he'd applied it to the tired candidate in the videos "with great results, it'll send you back in time a good decade." That was enough to allow us to use the short appearances we'd left of me, as we'd decided to use topic-related footage to illustrate the substantive videos, effectively reducing my to-camera contributions to short introductions at the start of each (with a map of the electoral riding behind me) and a reappearance at the end before Jonathan's "The Candidate" graphics concluded them. The videos for which we had not found images, we kept in reserve.

. . .

Later, I asked Nick if, during our Starbucks encounter, he'd expected to say, "Sure, I can help."

"No," said Nick, "it wasn't on my mind until you expressed interest."

"Do you ever worry about crossing the line?"

"Well," he laughed, "I've probably crossed the line a few times, but it wasn't my line. I've made a lot of videos that have been shelved by clients out of fear of fucking with reality a bit too much."

"But what are your own signals for—umm, maybe not?"

"I guess my messing with reality always has an obvious comedic fakeness to it," said Nick. "But I'm not really pulling the wool over most *intelligent* people's eyes, so I don't feel like as much of a trickster as the people who cherry pick sound bites to push whatever is their agenda. My motive is comedy. Ethics would come into it more if deception was my motivation. That said, I've been asked to make a video where I replace a politician's mouth with a puckering asshole, so who am I to talk?"

. . .

We'd decided on Friday, September 25, as the launch date of "The Escalator Works." In Montreal, the night before, the debate organized by the province's consortium of French-language broadcasters had taken place, with reports beginning to filter through of the trouble that Mulcair had landed himself in on a couple of counts. He'd sparred with Harper and Gilles Duceppe, the Bloc Québécois leader, over Zunera Ishaq's right to wear the niqab at her Canadian citizenship ceremony, and with Trudeau over the Sherbrooke Declaration. We were paying attention—I was proud of the stance Mulcair had taken vis-à-vis the niqab—but preoccupied with developing an appropriate strategy for our video launch. We knew that simply dropping a video into the ether and hoping for the best risked oblivion, so we'd compiled a list of about thirty web "gate-keepers." The list included journalists working in mainstream media; bloggers of digital and literary as well as political events; and habitual tweeters with substantial numbers of followers. Crucially, pundits disinclined towards the NDP's messaging were in all of these groups. The sequence of the videos' rollout was also critical, and so we planned to follow the launch of "The Escalator Works" with several of the substantive videos—the Bill C-51 attack ("*We cannot afford that #LPC architects and supporters of C-51 and the G-20 fiasco fade from view: @justintrudeau @carolyn_bennett @bill-blair #cdnpoli #NDP2015*"); another supporting the party's policies towards the environment; and then a *cri de coeur* on behalf of the freedom of scientists; before pushing out "That's My Seat!" as a finale. Whatever videos were left we'd use ad hoc or as a coda.

Wendy—by nature the most reserved of the campaign management team and, what with her hours' work every day on the telephones, the campaign manager on the front lines—was ambivalent about the Harper kick. But the consensus had been to move forward, and Doug and Ethan and I were deciding which to prioritize when Janet asked to speak to me in the backroom. She and the NDP's director of media, George Soule, had been discussing the videos we'd sent along.

"The good news is they loved the Trudeau one," said Janet. "They won't give us official permission one way or the other, but they said do it. They had a little discussion about the pamphlets landing on Trudeau's head, but George and I agreed it's not funny otherwise, or funny in a different way, so that one you can use as is. As for the environment video, he'd prefer you to take the photo of the tar sands out of it and put something else in there. He said it evokes too much controversy at the moment."

"They're nixing the Harper vid?"

"Right, they're nixing the Harper for a whole bunch of reasons," said Janet.

Soule, said Janet, was afraid the Harper video would become a news story and that Mulcair would be asked about it.

"So they should tell Tom to say, 'It's funny, go ask the candidate.'"

Janet appeared sombre. At this point, she was only reporting.

"George says, the questions won't be 'What do you think about this obviously funny and yet very insightful video?' but 'What do you think about your candidate kicking the prime minister?' or 'Did it go too far?' The networks won't show you creatively discussing our positions, they'll clip the kick and show the PM on the ground."

"I want to speak to Soule."

"Okay," said Janet.

. . .

What are we worried about here, I wondered—being nice to one of the most punishing politicians in Canadian memory?

. . .

"George Soule here."

"Hi George, it's Janet—with Noah. Do you have time— well, no, let's just make time for this conversation, okay?"

"Okay."

"So you don't want to run the Harper video," I said. "Can you tell me why?"

"It's not something that we can put out there. I think it crosses too many lines."

"I just want to understand what the lines are. Seventy-five percent of the country wants to boot him out of office anyway—"

(Well, 68 percent actually, if truth be told—but, along with the maybe 7 percent siding with the ridiculous *Globe and Mail* endorsement of the "Conservatives without Harper," that would be 75.)

"I'm sorry," said Soule, "but it's unanimous here."

"I need to understand why—"

"We'll be sued. It will derail the campaign for days."

. . .

"So what did you say?" asked Doug.

"Nothing. I didn't want to be told not to bother adjusting it. But we're putting out Trudeau—and we're doing it today, before anyone changes their mind."

. . .

At four o'clock on the Friday, Doug and Ethan started the launch of "The Escalator Works." Using my Facebook page as well as YouTube to embed the videos, and my NDP Twitter address as the initial source, we tweeted,

> Couldn't resist: had to take on @justintrudeau and his budget fantasies http://bit.ly/1OXfVJA Elections are no excuse for fictions.#TM4PM

And then we waited.

We'd had a notional sense of what it meant for a video to "go viral." Ten-thousand views was a target that can only be described as notional. And then our smartphones started pinging. Lots.

> David Akin @davidakin
> Gotta watch NDP candidate Noah Richler spoof justinpjtrudeau escalator ad

> Paul Wells @InklessPW
> Why, Noah. You scamp.

> Andrew Coyne @acoyne
> Heh

The video garnered 1,000 Facebook views within an hour, 50,000 in eight and 100,000 in twenty-four before its rate of acceleration diminished and, after thirty-six days, it settled at 117,000 Facebook views and another 15,000 on YouTube. By E-Day, it would garner 175,000 Facebook views and a further 25,000 on YouTube. Before the weekend was out, the video had been liked more than 600 times, with over 1,700 shares. Trudeau's initial "Real Change" ad had been launched August 30 and achieved only 43,000 Facebook views, with 1,954 likes and 788 shares, though the reach of the Trudeau ad that "The Escalator Works" parodied did, of course, far exceed ours: in the month since its launch, it had accumulated 157,000 views on Facebook, with 5,200 likes and 1,961 shares, but also a whopping 1.7 million YouTube views, attributable to Trudeau's national profile and the television and radio broadcasts we were never in a position to afford. Our own party had issued seven videos, none of which had cracked 100,000 views on Facebook (though "Performance Review," released two weeks prior, reached 95,000 Facebook views and accumulated a further 361,000 views on YouTube).

I was being recognized on the street, a boon to a campaign unable to pay for lawn and window signs with the candidate's headshot. The video was also providing other benefits: it was putting the Toronto—St. Paul's campaign on the map of the party brass, and it was doing its own small part to lift a national campaign caught in drudgery. The video had vaulted over the traditional boundaries of the Internet's political echo chambers and was being enjoyed by gatekeepers forgetting their own allegiances for a while. David Frum and Ezra Levant were other pundits that had pushed it, and CTV's Don Martin showed a part of it on the network's television program of political review, *Power Play*, and tweeted, "This hilarious Richler ad is wasted on just one candidate. Why Mulcair didn't seize it for himself is odd."

By comparison, Carolyn Bennett's "Toronto—St. Paul's Model" video—a treatment of the nonsensical contention that an MP's consulting of constituents between elections was a matter of her invention—had accumulated fewer than fifty Facebook views, and less than half that number on YouTube. Here was something to gloat about, though the pleasure was not universal.

Our Twitter feeds were offering early signals that we were getting under the Liberals' skin, even as we were enjoying that from coast to coast, in English and French, media were reporting on it.

NOAH RICHLER'S PARODY OF TRUDEAU ESCALATOR AD INJECTS SOME HUMOUR INTO THE CAMPAIGN
—*The Huffington Post*

NDP CANDIDATE MONKEYS WITH JUSTIN TRUDEAU ESCALATOR AD
—*The Straight*

UN CANDIDAT DU NPD PARODIE LES PUBS DE JUSTIN TRUDEAU
—*Journal de Montréal*

Hell, even one of my CBC television contacts called:

"Loved your video!" said the producer. "Why didn't you give me the heads-up? I do a roundup on my show."

"Didn't think of it," I said—but, sensing an opportunity, "we made another with Stephen Harper for a target. What about using that?"

"Sorry, Noah, no. I can't have it on the show."

"Why not?"

"We know each other."

"But you just said—"

"Breach of ethics."

"Right."

"But, really, it was great!"

. . .

If I'd wondered on occasion about the NDP's failure to act in concert, then I did not need to wait longer than September 27 for more obvious and damning evidence of the party centre's disinclination to get behind local campaigns working the trenches. On the Sunday, the NDP held a town hall on the subject of the environment at the Daniels Spectrum in Regent Park. This was the downtown riding of Toronto Centre, historically Liberal, in which Linda McQuaig, the former *Toronto Star* columnist and best-selling author of *It's the Crude, Dude: War, Big Oil and the Fight for the Planet* and *The Trouble with Billionaires*, was putting herself forward federally a second time. She'd lost against Chrystia Freeland in the November 2013 Toronto Centre by-election and now here she was running in a constituency of slightly adjusted boundaries against the Bay Street alumnus Bill Morneau, another well-resourced, well-accredited political newcomer, this one tagged to minister of finance in the event of a Liberal win.

A hand from the leader showing off his team's pedigree was in order. Back in early August, McQuaig had been challenged on CBC News Network's *Power & Politics* by the Conservative Michelle Rempel concerning an article she'd written years earlier about the cost to the environment of oil sands development and the need for some sort of carbon pricing. McQuaig, to her credit—presumably these views were part of the reason she'd been selected as a candidate—did not rescind her position. "A lot of the oil sands oil may have to stay in the ground," responded McQuaig. When pressed, she'd said just how much was to stay below ground would be known "once we properly put in place a climate change accountability system of some kind."

The Conservatives and their allies in the media jumped on McQuaig's statement with alacrity. What the Toronto Centre candidate said was proof, said Harper, that the NDP would "wreck our economy." The Alberta Business and Taxpayers

Coalition declared that it would travel to the riding to campaign against McQuaig (no cowboys or roughnecks were spotted outside the Daniels Spectrum on the day) and, predictably, there was fury on the social networks. And yet there'd been nothing particularly controversial about what McQuaig had said, and, in the weeks following, even some to the right of centre would support her point of view—as a senior BP oil executive also would.

Oftentimes, the furor and venting of pundits and Internet denizens are simply to be waited out. Truth is the tortoise to the hare of sensation, and it catches up eventually. But at this NDP town hall, the tortoise was locked out—or at least kept safely to the side of the stage and the action. I'd arrived early and was enjoying pats on the back from party members and others in the audience who'd seen "The Escalator Works," and that was pleasing. I'd also cornered George Smith, one of Mulcair's handlers, before the town hall started, to plead with him for a moment with Mulcair. It seemed to me a blatant omission for the NDP to have nothing at all to say about sports—or, more naturally my field, the arts. These were two realms mattering greatly to the people of Toronto and beyond, but about which the NDP was markedly silent. Trudeau, delayed for a time by the headline news that was the Syrian refugee crisis (as I'd been warned), had since made a big announcement about arts funding and the NDP could not afford to be mute, I told Smith—did the party leader have a moment?

On the stage were two high stools waiting for Mulcair and his interlocutor. As my colleagues arrived and the public were let in, I watched for the usual bagging of premium front-row seats in plain view of the cameras' lenses. Surprisingly, McQuaig took one of these.

"Aren't we talking about the environment?" I asked.

McQuaig nodded.

"It's not you up there?"

"No."

McQuaig was not so familiar to me that I was reliably able to gauge her mood, but I sensed a measure of despondency and I was certainly unsettled. The Spectrum filled, we waited, we clapped, we stood, we sat, we stood, we clapped some more, well rehearsed by now in the routine of an ecstatic rock-star entry for "Canada's next prime minister!" "We're All in This Together" blasted through the speakers again, Mulcair and Pinhas made their entry again, the NDP leader took the stage again and the teleprompter started to roll again. Then Mulcair was joined by Jennifer Hollett for a brief chat about the NDP's environmental policy. Apparently more utility was to be found in Hollett's VJ experience than McQuaig's credentials, the local candidate shunted just as my environment video's image of the oil sands had been. Certainly we were not seeing a leader extolling the talents and virtues of one of his 338 in situ. Mulcair took a few planted questions from the audience, a "town hall" is anything but, before telling supporters there was certain to be a place in his cabinet for Hollett.

Mulcair was performing well—the best I'd yet seen him—but what kind of support was this, I worried, that a leader should distance himself from a candidate arguing exactly what the party and a majority of Canadians believed? I was appalled, and not even on my own behalf. Welcome to politics.

. . .

On my way out, the NDP leader's chief of staff, Alain Gaul, took me aside to tell me that Mulcair would telephone from the car. I was almost home when he did.

"Hi Noah," said Mulcair. "You're keeping out of trouble?"

"Trying."

Mulcair laughed, I told him he'd performed well, and made the case for some kind of event about the arts:

"Trudeau pledged to double Canada Council funding and restore CBC money that the Tories cut—"

"We did that in January."

"Sure, but no one remembers and we should get out in front," I said—and then, putting a word in for my team's cause, "you could come to Toronto—St. Paul's. The riding is filled with very powerful arts players and the arts community is a very vocal one. Or go to Davenport, but do something."

"My people are telling me nobody cares. That the media won't pay attention."

"They're wrong," I said. "And look, a lot of people say one of the reasons Olivia Chow lost the mayoral race is because she had nothing to say about the arts."

"Thank you," said Mulcair. "I'm up here looking at the country from thirty thousand feet. It's great to hear from our people on the ground."

. . .

That evening I called George Soule, hoping the success of "The Escalator Works" would bolster the case for a release of a revised version of "That's My Seat!" I'd already emailed a list of proposed revisions with excerpts from columns by author Michael Geist, a digital media expert, on the subject of the Copyright Act. The first video release had been a success and I could sense in the decidedly more agreeable tone of Soule's voice, acknowledging as much, that ground had been won. I started by addressing the party's anxieties about the use of the image of an oil sands project in the environment video and, my loss leader, offered to replace it.

"If we could find a way," said Soule, "to make this video stay only in your riding, in Toronto—or frankly, only in Ontario, I'd say it's all good. My concern is that, with the image in, it goes from being an excellent video to, 'Oh, another Toronto candidate talking about the oil sands.' I agree with you—if we were a rational people, a reasonable people, it would be fine. But this is politics and reasonable people go out the window."

"So, if I have, say, stuff spilling into rivers, is that okay with you?"

"If it's not oil, that's fine."

Then I offered to coordinate the other substantive videos with whatever was the central party's agenda, suggesting that the Bill C-51 short come next. I alerted Soule that I'd described Bennett as a "vocal supporter of Bill C-51 even now" and let him know this was not rumour but substantiated by what the Liberal candidate had said at the Holy Blossom Temple debate, witnessed by many, and therefore defensible.

"I have no concern," said Soule.

Then we talked about the Harper video.

"If Tom is asked, 'Hey, do you know your candidate is making very funny videos?'" said Soule, "he can say, 'Yes, I do, it's funny, you have to laugh!' But the thing we want to avoid is that the question becomes—regardless of whether the video is legally actionable—'Do you think that ad went too far?' Then that's the question you have to answer and it becomes a story for a day or two and you're off message."

"Of course, I don't want to do that. Tom's the reason I'm here," I said. "A part of me does think if someone asked him about the videos and he just said, 'They're pretty funny, go ask him,' that would defuse it. But I can tone down the kick and then I think we'd be all right."

"Look," said Soule, laughing, "if we were watching this on YouTube or on a late-night talk show, we'd think it hilarious."

I felt an opening. We discussed a few other amendments, and Soule said, "That sounds better."

The opportunity for "That's My Seat!" to go out was still on.

SEPTEMBER 28

CPC	NDP	LPC	BQ	GRN	OTH
31.8%	27.7%	30.8%	4.2%	4.7%	0.9%

. . .

The next morning, Sarah and I cycled over to Soho House to meet Sandra Cunningham, part of my events team, a relentless canvasser with her husband, Rens, and the president of Union Pictures in her working life. Sandra had set up for an 8 a.m. breakfast with several prominent players in the Toronto film world: Hussain Amarshi, the CEO of Mongrel Media, Canada's premier distributor of independent and foreign films; Martin Katz, the founder and president of Prospero Pictures and a frequent collaborator with David Cronenberg (who lived in the riding); and Helga Stephenson, then still the CEO of the Academy of Canadian Cinema and Television.

I liked this bunch and appreciated the opportunity that Sandra had created, but doubt had started to creep in and I wondered whether I was guilty of hubris—or, as I preferred to see it, was doing something for a party in need of a hand. It was stunning to me that in a country in which, no matter one's position, the importance of arts and culture was the fulcrum of manifold arguments, the NDP was demonstrating no noticeable interest towards the sector in Toronto. In 2008, Harper's Conservatives were, in all likelihood, kept to a minority by Québécois rage against the CPC's cuts to the arts and the prime minister's view of its practitioners as "a bunch of people at a rich gala all subsidized by taxpayers claiming their subsidies aren't high enough." A given of the current election—and of the preceding decade—was the cost to the Conservatives of their antipathy towards the CBC (a repository of "progressive," if not NDP, votes), so that the NDP's seemed such a silly and easily remedied omission, all the more remarkable from a party leader who'd been a minister in Quebec. Of all the provinces, Quebeckers have understood the Gramsci-esque messaging potential of both sports and the arts the most. But whereas Trudeau knew how to play it, the NDP was only indifferently courting the sector. To my mind, the oversight spoke not only to a failure of vision but to a certain Calvinist streak in a party that seemed to uphold a very old-fashioned idea of work as its covenant. Even in the autumn of 2015, the ethos of the party was rooted in (Ontario) factories and (Western) fields and (Quebec's supply-side) farms; in closed-shop unions and assembly plants rather than the modern-day fact of a world in which technology and disintermediation have promoted very different kinds of labour—problems, certainly, but also founts of ingenuity and a new lexicon of terms. Making a very personal appeal to historic ideas of labour was routine for Mulcair. Saying that he was the second of ten children (then rapidly naming his brothers and sisters according to age), remembering how his father had been laid off, or how, before becoming a lawyer, he'd worked in construction to get by, were all staples of Mulcair's stump speeches, when perhaps a reference to Amazon warehouse workers unable to afford the goods they stock might have had more clout and a ring of the present. The party's insistence on balancing the books was designed to appeal to wavering Conservative voters and others anxious about the financial mess attributed to Bob Rae when he was NDP premier of Ontario. But the policy was also rooted in the NDP's long history of not having had any money to spend in the first place, and believing that debt and interest payments borne of deficits are a direct threat to ongoing funding for health, education and social programs. So if there were any interest in the arts, it was only expressed through ties with unions and notions of stagehands and carpenters that the party's socialization made familiar. (A powerful Toronto film mogul, not at our breakfast, had written Sandra to say, "Noah is running an election campaign and should not waste time on a hopeless case like me—but everyone else on my set is probably voting NDP.") The party balked at anything beyond that; the gambles and risky outlays of directors and producers who are by nature big spenders borrowing big sums with a view to repaying investors and, ultimately, earning fat fees—this sort of ethos lay outside the borders of the party's imagination. Concomitantly, the arenas of sport were perceived solely as ones of chauvinist national-ism and individual accomplishment—both phenomena with which the old-fashioned Dipper is ideologically uncomfortable—rather than extraordinary theatres in which, in Canada, the fron-tiers of inclusivity, equality and human rights are constantly and thrillingly being pushed out on behalf of women, people with disabilities and the ethnically and religiously diverse. Not one but two of the political circuit's greatest avenues to popular appeal were no-go areas, their social resonance only dimly understood. (I've never forgotten being sent to pick up Sarah's younger daugh-ter at primary school and watching her beat the boys she was playing with at basketball well aware that, when I was a kid, the response of boys would have been to take the ball away from her. These ones were just casually losing: the symptom of a social bar-rier broken down. How exciting—and how *important*.)

And so, for a morning, I played a game of pretend—I was the minister of heritage designate, why not. Amarshi was distressed by the dominance, in the world of film distribution, of just a few inordinately powerful international corporations—Amazon, Apple and Netflix—and the effect this was having on domestic production. Helga Stephenson's preoccupation, a topic not mentioned by any of the party leaders, was with the preservation of film—and, more broadly, the National Archive that Conservatives held in disregard (unless the subject was military). Martin Katz was restless; he'd likely calculated the odds and was less interested in playing the game.

"Marty is mad at the NDP for vote splitting but he thinks you are a good candidate," Sandra had warned. "Baby steps."

. . .

Evening came and my iPhone rang as I'd finally made it through the crowds and into the Roy Thomson Hall lobby for the Munk Debate. It was a 613 area code: Ottawa, James Pratt.

"Noah, I have some bad news."

"You do?"

"We just got the heads-up. *La Presse* has been through your Facebook and there's going to be an article tomorrow."

"I'm going to lose reception. I'll call you later."

. . .

At the Munk Debate on Foreign Policy—the fourth of the 2015 election's televised debates and the third in English—Mulcair walked into the forum, a gladiator with the wrong armour. Outside Roy Thomson Hall, a great pressing throng of social activists was taunting ticketed patrons in their finery, and for once it was the sartorially splendid kept in line by police manning barricades and waving leaders' campaign cortèges through. I tweeted how encouraging it was to see politics and not just Toronto International Film Festival events get a crowd at the Hall, the 2010 G20 Summit the memory, and thought little more of it. But, once inside, Sarah and

I sat in gobsmacked silence. In the stands were Liberal and Conservative barons baying in league like bloodthirsty Romans for the end of the Orange Pretender. "Change" was what the day's patricians knew was coming—they could sense its inevitability in the angry faces of the plebs outside—so "change" would happen, but not so much change that they'd be out of pocket, or the order that had served them be threatened. If there needed to be a change of costume, then its finery would be red, not orange.

Never, during the campaign, did I feel in the presence of so much hate as on this day; never so much relish at the gall of one man's trying. Blue ties, red ties; the silver-haired incumbent or the younger pretender, it didn't matter. What was so ugly and obvious in Roy Thomson Hall that night was that there would be no new order, the one of convenience would persist. Mulcair and his team had arranged for their own defeat, snookered by players better at the game and only let in to the club so that established members could watch the arrivistes' humiliation. Earlier in the campaign, Trudeau had threatened to pull out from the Munk Debate because it was not going to be bilingual and tickets were too expensive, said his team. The first issue had been resolved, host Rudyard Griffiths putting a few questions to the leaders in French, but the ticketing issue was forgotten about. The latter objection had been fought out in the media rather than directly with the organizers of the debate, a decoy of a point surely raised for political advantage. For, as the Liberal and Conservative war rooms surely knew would be the case, the tony crowd served the NDP's interests least of all. That evening, Trudeau strode on to the stage, arms open, with a confident, welcoming, come-to-me gait. Harper, still in the running, stood tall in the centre. But Mulcair looked uncomfortable from the start: stiff, dowdy, looking no one in the eye. It was as if the NDP leader knew the party had no friends in the room, and was unsure what to say or how to speak to anyone outside of it. As

Harper and then Trudeau won rounds of applause for their points, and Mulcair, sneers and approbation, he looked a beaten man, shrank into himself, and made even Harper seem trim. The hostility was unsettling. Mulcair spoke less and less. Bill C-51 came up and Mulcair sensed an opening and declared the NDP had been "the only party to stand up in 1970 when Pierre Trudeau put hundreds of Canadians in jail without trial, without even any accusations." But the remark backfired. It allowed Justin Trudeau to invoke his love of his father on a day that was, fortuitously, the fifteenth anniversary of Pierre Elliott Trudeau's death, and to lay personal claim to the Canadian Charter of Rights and Freedoms, multiculturalism and even state bilingualism ("which, as my father understood it, Mr. Mulcair, means saying the same thing in French as you say in English"). Mulcair had made himself appear petty and patronizing; he'd been calling the Liberal Party leader "Justin"— and allowed him to perorate. The audience loved it.

Sarah and I sat quietly, mildly uncomfortable and astonished. Cheers for Trudeau, cheers for Harper. Jeers for Mulcair.

"If power stays in these people's hands," said Sarah, "I don't think a revolution is impossible."

Sarah is not given to such remarks, but that's what it felt like: an establishment unfazed and not minding that eager Liberal operatives in slim-fitting suits and bowties were in their midst, congratulating each other on how well their leader had done. So what if it was the Liberals' turn now? Votes were a meaningless veneer for this plum lot. Enjoy the fresh new faces at the table. There really wasn't a whole lot of difference between the parties, certainly not at the Bay Street end of the map. They'd manage, they'd make the adjustments. They'd hold on to power whichever way the vote went.

. . .

My iPhone at zero bars in Roy Thomson Hall, I was unaware during the debate of the machinating going on behind the scenes at NDP Central but Pratt's email subject line made the prospect of impending trouble clear enough: "Fw: Red Flag need your input ASAP."

The *La Presse* reporter Pierre-André Normandin was asking about a tweet and two Facebook posts he was intending to publish. The tweet dated to February 2014, sent out by me from the floor of a Canada Council Literary Forum being held in Montreal, at which the francophone delegates had, in summation, put forward a fairly staggering list of twenty-nine "priorities," significantly more than half the number the entire national congress had tabled. "Have to admit," I wrote, "no Canadian is better than the Quebecker at demanding things."

The tweet was neither shocking nor an original thought. Any student of this country's provincial–federal politics understands completely the part that negotiating relations with Quebec's francophone (not sovereigntist) community has played in the country's political evolution. And since even before the establishment of the nation-state called "Canada," territorial and then provincial and municipal governments of *la belle province* have been particularly adept at playing their hands. Ironically, I was also making the point in admiration— highlighting the example of Quebec's *fierté*, instrumental, as I have already pointed out, in obstructing a Conservative majority in the 2008 federal election.

My second offence—a Facebook post dated to April 2014— was a share of a Jon Kay column for the *National Post* published in the week preceding the last Quebec provincial election. Its headline was "Pauline Marois an enabler for society's worst, most phobic, most parochial sentiments" and Kay's lines were, underneath, "People say weird and batty things all the time. But only in Marois' Quebec does the most powerful politician in the province provide encouragement." I wrote:

> To Jonathan Kay's credit, this is gently put. I also believe that a lot of Quebeckers understand that the rest of Canada (a good place) is fed up in a different way than it has been historically, and that it can imagine life without Quebec on present terms, and without upset. Monday's election can't come soon enough.

The idea that, in the nearly forty years of argument since the first Parti Québécois government (in 1976, under René Lévesque), a lot of Canadians were able to imagine a Canada living with Quebec on altered terms—i.e., not *without* that vital territory, but imagining what that altered arrangment might look like—is hardly the stuff of scandal either. Canada (all of it) is the country that, foremost of any democracy in the world, is persistently and expertly negotiating the constitutional terms of its very existence with itself. It is amusing to me even now that the province regarded not just by *souverainistes* as a "distinct society" should take umbrage at the shocking suggestion that the rest of Canada might be engaging with it in an evolving manner.

The Facebook post of February 27, 2015, however, was a more delicate matter—and, *mea culpa*, I recognized the text of it from the SWOT page Young Ethan and Sean had left on my desk and that it had taken me nearly a month to consider—and discard. This second Facebook post shared an article ("20% de Québécois se dissent racists") in which, at the height of discussion of the PQ's "Chartre des Valeurs"—an election platform document demanding, among other measures, the barring of any religious ornament or headgear on anyone employed by that province's government (save Christian crucifixes, or the great big one affixed to the wall of the Quebec legislature)—a full fifth of

Quebeckers polled willingly described themselves as racist. The report appeared on the same day that, in Paris, a bunch of Chelsea soccer fan hooligans pushed a black man onto the Paris Métro railway tracks, chanting, "We are racist, we are racist, and that's the way we like it!" Which was when I wrote:

> So Chelsea football fans have natural partners, n'est çe pas? May they meet each other in the Paris Métro and push each other onto the tracks. (What is it about the blue and white livery that gets racists going?)

I was not suggesting that either all Chelsea football fans or all Quebeckers adoring the province's blue-and-white flag are racist, but that the racists *within* each following represented by blue and white have a happy get-together. But the wording was definitely sloppy and I was not about to win an Internet debate on a question of logic. ("If NDP supporters wear orange, do all who wear orange support the NDP?")

Normandin falsely claimed the Twitter and two Facebook posts had "rapidly disappeared." They had not. In July, when the team had established my candidate's event page, I had altered my Facebook settings to make my posts available only to "Friends" rather than to "Public" viewing. So they must have been fed to Normandin—who is not, even in the lexicon of Facebook, a "Friend" of mine—and the posts in question were not fully removed by me until October 1, two days after the *La Presse* reporter's article appeared. Normandin did not respond to the request I made to discuss his article. Had he done so, I would have asked if the discovery was his own—and why, as a more conscientious (or, perhaps, simply less busy) reporter would have done, he did not note the tweet I put out after Pauline Marois and the PQ lost the April 7, 2014, election, which said:

Can't recall the last time an election left me so happy: voters doing the smart thing. Hell, Rob Ford can have Toronto, Quebec's back!

Or the Instagram photograph I'd shared of thousands of Quebeckers at a Montreal demonstration against funding cuts, waving pro-Radio-Canada banners, with the caption:

#SaveTheCBC #WakeUpEnglishCanada Quebec leading the way in this country when it comes to anything.

The idea that the February 2014 tweet and the April 2014 Facebook post proved me to be anti-Québécois was preposterous and insulting, but this is the sort of routine and lazy muckraking that passes for journalism in the present age.

"The whole team is on it," said Pratt. The moment I made my exit from the Munk Debate at 8:17 p.m., the flurry of emails concerning (the French text of) an apology began.

On September 28, 2015, at 8.17 p.m., James Pratt wrote:

Hey Noah,

I've cc'd Valerie Dufour here. She's trying to contain this from our Montreal office.

The statement is as follows:

I would like to offer my sincerest apologies to all Quebeckers offended by comments I have posted in the past to Facebook. My comments were injurious and inappropriate and do not reflect my views of Quebec and the Québécois. My comments were written during the last Quebec provincial election, during which Madame Pauline Marois' PQ was proposing a "charter of values" with which I was in profound disagreement. I make no secret of the fact that issues of identity are impassioned ones for me. This is not an excuse for my remarks, but places them in context. I have a visceral reaction to the politics of exclusion that is stronger than I am. In the same way, I find it reprehensible that Conservatives are trying to apply the same recipe of fear and division to the current election.

At 9.53 p.m., Noah Richler wrote:

Hi James, Valerie
Thank you for this. I will tell you straight up that I am not comfortable with the apology as written and in fact wholly understand why I wrote the posts in the first place.

The tone of the apology is also distinctly not mine and that matters. This political life has been easy for me so far because I wholly believe in the NDP platform and the cause which is why I am able to argue it passionately.

The Kay post deserves no apology. I am making a positive political point. The Canada Council tweet is funny and ironically admiring of Quebeckers' mastery of the see-saw of provincial-federal negotiation. Only the "Blue and White" post is dubious, though I can defend that easily too.

Also, I have formed a relationship with the Quebec press that is by and large good and it explicitly was not formed by walking away with my tail between my legs. I believe that confidence of the sort that Tom displayed vis-a-vis the recent niqab imbroglio in Quebec is more winning.

At 10.01 p.m., Valerie Dufour wrote:

Duceppe will hit Tom and the NDP hard. I see the nuance in what you are saying but I am afraid our opponents will not and will not want to. BQ partisans have already hinted at something on Twitter. My job is to protect the brand and the leader and I feel that apology is needed. Quebec media will make us pay and we don't need it right now.

At 10.03 p.m., Noah Richler wrote:

Hi James, Valerie,
I feel strongly about this. If you make me feel like a hypocrite, everything changes, and there is nothing in any of these posts that I cannot (and even entertainingly, eloquently) defend. The idea that Duceppe will gain advantage is absurd. And I am also not stupid. Direct your complainants to me and no-one is embarrassed. Speak to Greta. Speak to my campaign managers. Speak to the 150 witnesses who saw me beat Carolyn Bennett in my debate with her soundly.

There is no need to run scared. And in fact, in what has not been a great week for us, I'd say we would be better off if we stood our ground confidently instead of worrying at every corner. You have your apology, but I will not be false or craven without necessity.

A contracted apology is attached. No changes without me seeing them. You might want to check the grammar.

At 10.08 p.m., James Pratt wrote:

Is the apology strong enough? My experience with these is less is more. The media and our opponents will give us one line. Is the line they're gonna take in this "I'm sorry"?

At 10.54 p.m., Noah Richler wrote:

Hi Valerie
I acknowledge your expertise, and James's. I have cut the line about my visceral reaction to the politics of exclusion being "stronger than I am" which is not true.

I would like to offer my sincerest apologies to all Quebeckers offended by comments I have posted in the past to Facebook. My comments were injurious and inappropriate and do not reflect my views of Quebec and the Québécois. My comments were written during the last Quebec provincial election, during which Madame Pauline Marois's PQ was proposing a "charter of values" with which I was in profound disagreement. I make no secret of the fact that issues of identity are impassioned ones for me, my professional life having been dedicated to the study and celebration of the ties that unite us across this marvellous country. This is not an excuse for my remarks, but places them in context. I have a visceral reaction to the politics of exclusion and, in the same way, I find it reprehensible that Stephen Harper is also playing Marois's game of fear and division. I adore Quebec. I adore Canada.

At 11.05 p.m., James Pratt wrote:

I think we're good here Noah. I'll give you a shout in the a.m.

. . .

Politics is everybody else believing they know than better you. And, as with just about any job, rise too high in the profession and inevitably it comes back down to human resources and controlling uncontrollable staff. The Conservative candidate, who, previously a service technician, is caught on camera pissing in a client's mug during a house call, unwittingly provides the election its greatest moment of—well, call it bad taste. An NDP candidate is, bizarrely, reminded of a phallus by the uprights of Auschwitz concentration camp's electrified fence; another makes a slack comparison between the boorish elements of crowds following politics and sport.

"It'll blow over," said Pratt, "but we have to protect the leader."

The last candidate was in the kitchen when, the following morning, Normandin's column appeared and the NDP leader telephoned one of his 338 from 2,342 kilometres away.

. . .

Tom, the leader:

"Eh, misère!"

Chief of Staff Alain Gaul's exclamation from across the aisle on the campaign plane left no doubt: we had a problem.

"Qu'est-ce qui se passe?"

One of our Toronto candidates had made it into La Presse, *but for all the wrong reasons. Old tweets and Facebook posts had taken on a new life.*

I'd recruited Richler, enthusiastically, and realized there's something about writers—they like to write!

But every thought shared now floats in the miasma, waiting for its moment to be reanimated unannounced. As if a colleague, with perfect recall, suddenly takes issue with a phrase used in a conversation with a friend three years prior.

The new normal of election campaigns.

The niqab issue had been dogging us for weeks, but instead of changing channels with a trip to the Arctic, in Iqaluit we'd be forced to talk identity politics again.

I volunteered to make the call.

Lucid about the implications, Noah's reaction to the situation was the embodiment of the old political maxim, "when you're 'splainin, you're losin'."

And his French, it turned out, was very good. He'd attended one of Montreal's best French schools and had a deep first hand understanding of what made Québécois tick, so he got it.

We agreed that he'd apologize because 'splainin' would only put a circle around the stain.

So we turned the page successfully . . . on that one.

. . .

Mulcair had asked about my Quebec bona fides and, apologizing profusely for the trouble I'd caused, I'd supplied them. But nothing came of it in Iqaluit and, to be fair to Normandin, the column that appeared the next day reported rather than it opined, and concentrated on the apology that had been the night's work. Pratt had been supportive and stressed that the team was behind me. It looked as if we were out of the bush and into the clearing.

. . .

But I was not.

Joanna Smith, the Ottawa correspondent for the *Toronto Star*, had emailed to ask about a Facebook post from the fall of 2014, in which I'd written:

I'm not sharing the *Vanity Fair* Jennifer Lawrence story because I don't give a toss beyond finding it more than a wee bit ironic that a woman whose image has been so blatantly manipulated by the magazine for their mutual financial advantage protests of her leaked nude photos that "it's my body, and it should be my choice." Yawn.

No matter that the six-page *Vanity Fair* story about Jennifer Lawrence, whose cellphone had been hacked, was causing an explosion of reaction on the Internet at the expense of attention paid to victims of the Ebola virus, then at its apogee. The Internet does not accommodate rebuttals, and now it would be back to the apology board, unless I elected to get ahead of the story.

. . .

From: Noah Richler
Sent: Tuesday, September 29, 2015 1:24 PM
To: James Pratt
Cc: Greta Levy; Valerie Dufour; Janet Solberg
Subject: Fwd: [Toronto Star] Facebook post re Jennifer Lawrence photos

Hello Illustrious Four
I'm off to the campaign office and have to rush.

An important development: Joanna Smith of the Ottawa bureau of the *Toronto Star* (see forwarded message below) has also been in touch vis-a-vis another Facebook post.

The fact that this and the *La Presse* items have happened over the same twelve hour period is interesting to me.

I have written a piece that I would like to submit to the *Toronto Star*, a paper read in my riding. Please note that if I do not speak for myself that Joanna will speak for me. As you did yesterday.

Read the piece. If I am to get it in — and I'll cc the publisher John Cruickshank and the editor-in-chief Michael Cooke, both acquaintances, so that if they do not run it, it's a stain on them — then I must do so by two p.m.

Please do not be timid. There is *nothing* here that affects the brand. Valerie, you will see that within the piece, I apologize again to the Quebeckers.

This is about getting in front of the story as I did with the drugs stuff. It's about us stepping up to the plate and saying enough's enough, we'll do this on our terms rather than having Smith and others frame the story (don't believe her little flattering tidbits of interest about the video, it's a ploy) and the dribble, dribble of a fight that we are facing in so many realms.

I'll be monitoring my cell.

Best,
Noah

. . .

"I do not Apologize."
For the *Toronto Star*, September 29, 2015.
By Noah Richler.

A couple of years ago, I entered into conversation with a number of NDP Members of Parliament about the possibility of running for the Party. I was wary. As a writer, I enjoyed a particular kind of authority from at least appearing to be objective, and this would be lost. I was worried that friends and associates would themselves be wary and talk to me in a different way and I didn't want that.

But, more worrying to my family certainly, my partner and I knew that to run for political office would be to risk immersion in an often tawdry world where not only are the gloves off but the punches come below the belt, from behind, and when you are sleeping. As a rule, dignity went out of politics long ago though fortunately there are, from time to time, politicians that rise above the seaminess of their milieu and remind us of just how elevated public service can be.

All of which is to say that I was prepared for the other reason my family thought I should not run, which is that inevitably there would be a moment at which journalists and rivals gleefully trawling my Facebook and Twitter posts of the last several years would confront me with them. Curiously—you tell me if it's a chance—within the same twelve hours my campaign team has learned of a *La Presse* article corralling what that newspaper is pretending are anti-Québécois posts, and this paper, the *Toronto Star*, has been enquiring after a Facebook comment I made in the wake of the over-the-top coverage of a Hollywood film star complaining about the release by a cellphone hacker of some photographs she had taken of herself naked.

This is the moment that my family and I were anticipating, but I can't say dreading. It is such an ordinary occurrence, and the ordinary response is for the subject to apologize and feign horror and shame in light of the person he or she was but is no longer and to recede, tail between the legs. Sometimes the political party will boot out the member. We've been through this a lot.

But this is not going to happen here. Because I own my posts, and I'll defend them.

And I will fight back against this paper, one that I have contributed to with great enjoyment over the years, plucking a Facebook comment out of the air and trying to frame an obvious comment about celebrity culture as anti-feminist.

Sorry? Absolutely not.

These journalists or party operatives or disenchanted "friends" (that ironic Facebook term) are, in truth, lazy.

How easy but also boring to have to trawl through all that social network nonsense! What amuses me is that if my pal from *La Presse* had really wanted to dig up a troubling view of mine, then he could more easily have turned to an edited, reviewed and published piece that I wrote for the *New Statesman* in which I suggest that an axis of Islamophobic Conservatives and Québécois extremists is what may do the NDP in. It would hardly have been plausible for me to describe that work as off-the-cuff or written emotively, *mea culpa*, etc.

And the Ottawa bureau of this newspaper might have turned to some of my numerous anti-Harper comments, a couple of which are, let us say, colourful.

But that dirt is not in fashion because harbouring enmity for Harper is not a story. Most of us do and still the work I'd be ashamed to do as a journalist continues. And one result of it will be that people like myself, in conversations with their partners as I myself was a couple of years ago, will not run for fear that a slip of the tongue or a risqué or witty or even intelligent remark, made while out of office and not even entertaining the prospect, will come back to embarrass them.

This has to stop. And it stops here.

Sorry. I'm not saying sorry.

. . .

Wrote Valerie Dufour, my buddy now:
"You criticized Katniss? Let us read!"

. . .

From: James Pratt

To: Noah Richler

Cc: Greta K. Levy, Valerie Dufour, Janet Solberg

Re: [Toronto Star] Facebook post re Jennifer Lawrence photos

Hey Noah,

I've got it with the war room. Are these posts still up? I think we may need to go through your feed.

This is not good but let me check with folks about how best to deal with it.

I'll be in touch.

James

. . .

My iPhone lit up—a 613 Ottawa number again.

"Noah," said Pratt. "We need you to stay home."

"What do you mean?" I said.

"You're not to take calls from anyone."

"You know," I said, "if I'd offered the *Star* editors a piece about how celebrity culture was sucking up attention on the social networks at the expense of people dying in Africa, they'd have sucked it up and been thrilled by the hits."

"Noah," said Pratt, "you don't get it. *You're on the wrong side of revenge porn.*"

. . .

"I don't know which party is the enemy," I said to Doug. "I'm not apologizing. This is the second time and it's silly."

If there was ever a moment in the campaign at which I was thinking of quitting, it was this one. And I knew Pratt knew it.

The party was keeping me on board, but the planks of the deck were straining as the crafting of another apology was underway.

At 3.54 p.m., Noah Richler wrote:

Hi James, Janet,

At moments like this, taking a stand leads to a new conversation—one about media ethics and witch (warlock) hunts during a campaign, and you might well find a lot of people rallying around that idea, as we all want good people to run.

Instead—and I am saying this as a team player—your office is running scared again. I am sorry we are such a timorous bunch. We are allowing "apologies" to be made as bogus admissions of guilt when they are in fact acts of convenience to you but extremely damaging to me, my reputation, my family and the dedication of the friends that have supported my campaign.

You are also—as the "War Room" (I hate military metaphors) has likely calculated better than I—greasing the way to losing one of your smarter contributors.

Perhaps, as Greta said to me sometime ago, intelligence and politics are not an easy mix.

I remain slack-jawed at the suggestion even that I am on "the wrong side of revenge pornography." You should be letting me take on any such accuser. But this is your game, not mine.

PS It would be foolish to have me skip the Quakers' environmental debate tonight especially as—serving us and this daft farrago—argument and insult are not allowed. Janet will explain.

At 4.01 p.m., James Pratt wrote:

New Edit:

Today, I was asked by a *Toronto Star* reporter to comment on a Facebook comment I posted in 2014. The comment was made in the wake of exhaustive coverage of a photo leak scandal involving female actors and models. Clearly, my comment was pointed at celebrity culture and the commercialized spectacle the situation had become.

Looking at the words in retrospect I can see that my words might be construed as indifference to women and their sexual exploitation, rather than frustration with the obsessive lens of the celebrity industry. This was never my intent.

. . .

I was twiddling my thumbs at home as Wendy explained to seniors at a residence I was scheduled to visit that I was "feeling unwell." Then Anna Vlachos, a City TV reporter, tweeted to see if I'd be attending the all-candidates debate at the First Unitarian Congregation that night, prompting Janet to ask if there were other posts that should worry the campaign. "There's one somewhere where I call Harper a shitty little man," I answered. "I may have taken it down though as a rule, I do this very little as it provides others a story of cover-up."

Obviously the situation was beginning to exasperate my campaign management team—as it was me, also, though Pratt had either ignored or not picked up on my having provided him the cue for a conversation about firing me. This I couldn't ignore: the party was doing more than putting up with me, it was providing support.

"Sorry," I added to my note to Janet. "I know you have other things to do, but I'm clearly being picked on here. And I also believe that standing up to this mild form of cyber-shaming is actually a winner."

. . .

The next morning, Joanna Smith filed a short, fairly innocuous *Toronto Star* item about my Jennifer Lawrence Facebook post, but the *La Presse* article was generating a fair amount of insult unimpeded by lousy grammar and spelling in both official languages. I was "a terrorist of thought" and, of course, I was the hateful racist son of my father Mordecai, whose writings against Quebec sovereignty had enraged the separatist old guard twenty-four years earlier.

> @T.: If want to expulse the Quebec from Canada, cause we aren't enough anglo for you, you can go fap yourself with Stephen Harper

> @P.: allez au diable avec votre religion multiculturaliste trudeauyiste. Les Québécois de souche n'ont opas des lecons à recevoir!

> @F.: What sort of influence a primitive racist hack like @noahrichler would exert in @NDP_HQ #NDP government?

But there was sweeter news. A former professor at the Montreal lyçée I'd attended had vouched for my character— what did that get him?—and, after a Montreal contact high up in the party wrote suggesting I be in touch with a major Bay Street player (and possible donor), the imperatives of the real were overtaking the distractions of the virtual. I emailed but, at the start, was not getting very far. Still, the online conversation was a lot more fun than the Twitter ones I'd been in.

. . .

From: Noah Richler
Sent: Sep 27, 2015, at 12:05
To: S.
Subject: Trying again

Hi S.

Noah Richler here. I was hoping we'd be able to meet and briefly chat so trying again.

Best,
Noah Richler

From: S.
Sent: Sep 27, 2015, at 4:20
To: Noah Richler
Subject: Re: Trying again

Hi Noah. I am out of the country and won't be able to attend. Good luck. S.

From: Noah Richler
Sent: Sep 27, 2015, at 8:15
To: S.
Subject: Re: re: Trying again

Hi S.

Just tell me if "good luck" means don't bother trying again. No one wants to be a nuisance!

And for your amusement, check out my campaign video, "The Escalator Works." It's gone viral. And that's the truth.

Best

Noah R.

From: S.

Sent: Sep 27, 2015, at 10:20

To: Noah Richler

Subject: Re: re: re: Trying again

Hi Noah. "Good luck" generally means "I probably won't be there for your journey. I may not even share your goals and aspirations, but I support your efforts and certainly wish you no misfortune." Having said all that, I genuinely admire persistence and would be happy to meet at my office.
S.

P.S. I watched Escalator and thought it both clever and likely effective.

· · ·

The offices of S., a senior managing director of a formidably powerful venture capitalist company, were on one of the highest floors of one of the highest towers on Bay Street and appointed in Old World style: lots of wood, French chairs with velvet seats, writing desks, books on shelves—and art, plenty of it, and good, too. I liked S. immediately. He was impeccably mannered, had taken time out from far more important (and lucrative) things to do, and it was immediately apparent that he had an ossiduous and interested mind. In his office, there were history books but also novels, both on his desk and at the round table where he motioned for me to sit. Photographs of some sort of NGO activity hung on the wall, along with a nineteenth-century shipbuilder's diagram.

"Thank you for seeing me," I said. "I've not come to ask for anything, or at least not for money. But I'm saying a lot of things on the campaign trail and I'd like to know whether you think these are true."

I explained my affection for Mulcair, and S. said that he had hosted lunches for him—the sorts of meetings, I figured, that Liberals and Conservatives were privy to all of the time but the NDP had to work for. S. did not appear to hold any of the prejudices that, at least in Ontario, were an obstacle for the party, the memory of Bob Rae and his NDP government's deficits not to be held against Mulcair; no, what mattered was said or done during the eleven weeks of the campaign. S. was heeding actions and the man.

I asked about the rationality of the NDP's pledges to raise corporate taxes by two points, and the party's plans to eliminate stock option tax credits.

"I think it's very difficult to argue that options aren't a form of compensation, or that they shouldn't be taxed at ordinary rates even though I'm a beneficiary" said S. When I brought up the NDP's plans for a corporate tax rate hike, he explained he would much rather see the elimination of specific tax breaks, debt forgiveness and other distortions and inefficiencies—such as, for instance, major loans to the automobile or aerospace industries. "But every one of those measures," said S., "is intrinsically tied to some sort of trade agreement or treaty, so I understand if the NDP is turning that way."

"So we're not in government," I said, "and I'll never be finance minister, but how about we raise the corporate tax two points and pledge to reduce it proportionately to the revenue we regain as these loans and distortions are eliminated?"

"That might work," he said.

"And what keeps companies in situ?" I asked.

"Good roads, good schools, good hospitals and police," said S.

We spoke for more than an hour. I thanked S. for his time, at which point he raised a hand and an assistant stepped into the room with a cheque that he filled out for fifteen hundred dollars, the legal maximum. S. handed it to me along with one of the books on the table I had asked about. The meeting had been invigorating, even without the wholly unexpected donation, and I walked out onto Bay Street with a renewed sense of purpose.

. . .

I'd barely made it to the Bay Street TTC station doors when Solberg called again.

"What this time?" I ask.

"The *Ottawa Citizen*," said Solberg. "You called Harper a pathological psychopath."

"Yes, I know."

"Don't speak to anyone."

"I'll see you at the office," I said.

. . .

Arrived at Bathurst Street, I handed Phil the fifteen-hundred-dollar cheque.

"Cash it," I said. "Now."

"NDP CANDIDATE RICHLER SORRY FOR ANTI-HARPER FACEBOOK TIRADE," ran the headline of Lee Berthiaume's story in the *Ottawa Citizen*. "NOAH RICHLER SORRY FOR CALLING HARPER A 'PATHOLOGICAL PSYCHOPATH,' NOT SORRY FOR MOCKING TRUDEAU'S ESCALATOR AD," said the rerun in the *National Post* and the rest of the Postmedia chain of newspapers.

Be careful what you wish for, indeed: the Facebook post was another of the three Sean and Young Ethan had identified in their August SWOT analysis—comments Sarah had complained about long before—and one I'd had in mind when I'd described, in the *Toronto Star* article the party had not let me pitch, "numerous anti-Harper comments, a couple of which are, let us say, colourful."

Now, a rite of twenty-first-century life, I was experiencing what the Welsh writer Jon Ronson has called the Internet's "great renaissance of public shaming." It was coming at me full on, I was in the stocks, and it was costing me—and the campaign. The article Jonathan Kay wrote out of his afternoon accompanying me on a canvass was positive, but qualified by the social media mess. Several columnists, including Kelly McParland and Chris Selley of the *National Post* and Eric Andrew-Gee of *The Globe and Mail*, were preparing their condemnations of candidates and their "gaffes"—lists in which I'd now be permanently included. Selley, who'd had it in for me before, would be particularly damning; the comments, he wrote, were "to political debate as a late-night 7-11 hot dog is to hunger." Gary Clement, the children's author and *National Post* political cartoonist, emailed to say that the full-page cartoon strip spread that had come out of our having spent a day canvassing together, was being killed. Bad luck that was, had the *Ottawa Citizen* story broken only a couple of hours later, then the page would have been off to the press and too late to reverse. And I was ordered not to participate in an evening of music and protest organized by Andrew Cash and the marvel-lously irascible radio polemicist, Torquil Campbell, lead singer of the pop band Stars. Quebec sovereigntists and assorted Liberals were still berating me on Twitter and Facebook, though—the analytics were what I was interested in—already, the conversation peaked. Lie low, Pratt had said, the furor will pass.

Looking again at the egregious *Ottawa Citizen* headline, I felt, for the first time during the social media storm, a tinge of regret. The words "Noah Richler Sorry for Calling Harper a 'Pathological Psychopath'" would be the first to appear after a Google search of my name for at least the foreseeable future (and probably cost me work), though it was not my slam of the prime minister that irked. No, not at all. What really bothered me was the redundancy of my bad phrasing. There was no getting around the fact of my awful syntactical overkill. Harper was pathological *or* he was a psychopath; he did not need to be both.

This was something I would have to live with for a very long time and I was gutted.

October 29, Ottawa, the Holiday Inn and Suites.

*Like we couldn't splurge a bit after our big day and fight it out
with the Liberals at the Marriott or the Château Laurier? This
does not bode well. Mulcair's trying to make a point and Trudeau
looks the hero simply by delivering yet more platitudes about the
need to get along. It's fascinating, really, that the qualities that
get a fella somewhere can be so jarring once he's arrived. Good
that we're in caucus because he's looking like Harper now—a man
with no friends, a man who can't trust. Maybe it's Gerald Butts
that's unsettling him—Butts is freaking everybody out, the
Liberals' Mr. Poker Face in the corner of the room, tapping into
his BlackBerry like a modern-day Madame Lafarge knitting
names into her scarf for the inevitable day, only months off surely,
when the government falls and it's off to the races again. Mulcair
is our Danton, he keeps talking about the historic victory but he's
being sabotaged daily by his own party. I mean who needs
enemies when there are Jacobins everywhere you turn demanding
their pound of flesh with no eye to the long game, and your best
friend is Naomi Klein, la Petite Robespierre, now in her seventh
consecutive day of rallying for the Leap Manifesto out of a tent
right in front of Parliament, the nerve of it—like our minority
government needs another division exposed. The press said
Trudeau would lead the coalition, but they hadn't banked on
Butts's savvy, the scrapper from Cape Breton knowing Mulcair*

and the Tories will look like the bickering old white men they are soon enough, the Liberals better off leaving the NDP to deal with the whackos in their party—pipelines but no rail, pie-in-the-sky promises to unions already giving us the squeeze and no fight against ISIL—*even before you get to the Leap loonies on the lawn. Adam Vaughan's been sucking up big time and his reward was Fisheries, serves him right. Dodged a net there, pal. Now we're coming to the biggies, you'd made your backroom pitch for Heritage but Pratt put an end to that.*

"Sorry, Richler, the Quebec caucus is dead set against it."

"Pourquoi?"

"'What is it about the blue and white?'"

"Jesus. We're in government, we're not on social media. I can explain—et en français, 'tabernac'."

"How should I put it?" said Pratt. "Let's see. You're on the wrong side of revenge—of, well, revenge politics, shall we say. But I can give you the address of the nearest HomeSense. You'll need a cushion on the backbench."

"So where have you put me?"

"Between Morgan Wheeldon and Alex Johnstone, why we let her run I have no idea. Call it Infamy Row."

"Where's Ashton?"

"As far away as possible."

"Megan?"

"Safe from you."

"Hollett?"

"Squirm, Richler. And don't fuck with me on expenses. One coffee is fine for breakfast. If it has to be a double, make it Tim Hortons and not an espresso, you ponce."

"Jesus, Jennifer had a serrano fig panini, you didn't complain."

"Count her followers. And Stroumboulopoulos retweets anything she posts. Who retweets you? Your fucking family."

Mulcair was dogged in the extreme—as if that was a shock—but his chief of staff, he was the kind of guy who'd stab you in the front.

"Hey, could be a good turn," said Ezra over lunch (that got you in trouble, but hell, he's nothing if not entertaining). "If the coalition lasts two years and you win your seat again, you can retire with a pension in the minimum six." You'd thought about it, done the math, because now it was looking as if a pension would be the only reward of a situation in which career go-getters were the ones gaining ground and no one was listening to your highfalutin ideas about the economy, the arts—or even the military, for that matter. You were a body—not even that. You were a puppet on a string with a hand raised up to say "Yay" or "Nay," depending on the order coming down from on high, not below. But still you rattled on about principles and good government, community and the fair chance, hoping one day—this day—your own bloody party would notice.

"Richler!" Pratt called.

It was like school, for Christ's sake.

"You're in luck. Tom wants to see you. Public Safety."

"You're kidding."

"Take it or leave it. Me, I wouldn't have given you anything."

Yes, yes, you're paying attention. That didn't happen either. But—you've heard me say it before—it could have done. (We're all in the right after the fact but who of us knew at the time, eh?)

"The Candidate on the campaign trail"
noahrichler.ndp.ca

CHAPTER FIVE

SIGNS

Normally, a piss a moment to be alone, I'd think, "When will we master the biotechnology that makes this bodily function and all the cumbersome infrastructure that supports it redundant?" and "Think of the savings!" or, "Jeez, would the biological revolution be the one that finally shuts Don Tapscott up?" But today, in the stall without a stack of lawn signs or a bike in it—free from volunteers and staff and candidate cards—the thought rushes over me.

A Liberal majority.

I walk back to my desk and the world seems oddly different. Like that time when I left the boardroom of Heller and Associates after my nomination run had been given the green light, only this time the sensation is strangely opposite. Janet, our well of caustic campaign commentary, is looking at me tenderly as a mother might. How is it that she already knows what I have come to realize so late in the day—or am I simply imagining she knows? She looks worried but I can't bring myself to acknowledge it.

I take the telephone Liz is thrusting at me with an outstretched arm. She's grinning, which means trouble.

"Hello?"

"What about the niqab?" says the woman on the telephone. She has a thick Russian or Eastern European accent.

"I'm fine with it," I say. "Women are required to reveal their faces to a judge at their official swearing-in. To ask a woman to remove it at a ceremony is to humiliate that person."

"It leads to failed states."

"Look, I don't like the *fact* of the niqab, I don't agree with women needing, being compelled or even choosing to cover their faces, but I am also confident in the changes in cultures that take place gradually and across generations here. As long as the person wearing the niqab is not infringing upon another's rights, or that person's rights are not being infringed by someone else, then we must respect that liberty (and any other) even when we dislike it. If it's not hurting anyone—"

"What about *homosecchs*? You like *homsecchsaewals*?"

"Well that's easy to answer."

"You call *homsecchsaewals* a marriage?"

"Yes, ma'am. Thank you for calling."

Janet hands me a Post-it note with the number of a reporter from the *Toronto Sun* who has called.

"What now?"

"You said Toronto taxicabs were disgusting," says Janet. She is speaking softly, like she is a doctor and I am the patient, the paper she's put before me a prescription.

#Toronto In another of our filthy, rank as piss taxicabs the city licences to keep me safe from Uber's recklessly clean and courteous cars

"Oh, yes, I did write that."

But Janet is smiling.

"It's okay," she says. "I asked her to read the tweet and she started to laugh and said forget about it."

Later, I'd endeavoured to contact the reporters to ask if my posts had been provided to them by a third party (apt phrasing for at least a couple more weeks), or if they themselves had "scoured" my pages. Not just *La Presse* but also the *Ottawa Citizen* had reported that my posts had been removed, though I'd not done so until two days after the articles were published. The *Citizen* also wrote that my posts had been "obtained" (read: "oppo" research received in a brown envelope or whatever is the e-equivalent). I'd reached one.

"I didn't scour," the journalist said.

. . .

On the upside, we were winning the signs war. We'd put up over a thousand—more than the party had ever managed to erect in Toronto—St. Paul's, and we were not yet done. But they were highly concentrated in NDP strongholds in the west of the riding. The condos were a challenge and so were the streets of the wealthy core. These were like the paper routes I dreaded as a kid—too much distance between houses, lots of people never home, and dispiriting after a while. It wasn't true that Toronto—St. Paul's was economically "diverse." It was a wealthy riding with a few steadily reduced pockets in which lower-middle-class and poor people lived. In the metropolis that is Toronto, you need to be upper middle class just to be lower middle class and, if you're worse off than that, well, there's Scarborough or Hamilton. For Toronto's ridings to be authentically diverse, at least in the economic sense that determines so much else, the sprawling city's electoral map would need to be redrawn as a pizza, every riding a slice. Each would contain the bready crust of exurbs and suburbs with their bedroom communities and sprawling mansions, then the all-dressed cornucopia of condominiums, town houses and community housing—the everything of downtown—and, at the centre, the dipping sauce of Bay Street. But ours was not that. Ours was a swath of the choice portion inside the rim: all prosciutto and arugula and goat's cheese, with just a sprinkling of exotic spices.

. . .

Some residents spoke so little English that the signs amounted to free lawn decorations, their real purpose impossible to explain: the rest of the street had them and they looked good so sure, why not? No, no, say the hand gestures, you don't have to phone, just come and put one up—which I'd text the office to do before the Conservatives or Liberals came by and the homeowner nodded his agreement to them as well or in my place. One house I visited, with just two residents able to vote, had all three of the major parties' signs posted in a neat row. A Chinese-Canadian senior told me the Conservatives said he was obliged to put up their sign—that it was the law—though it seemed to me more likely he was told he had the *right* to put up a sign and language got in the way. The Liberals took down my sign, said a few, one a donor and another a local Muslim filmmaker tweeting:

> @noahrichler your #NDP sign was taken from our house. You may want to look into why a few signs have gone missing in your riding . . . ?"

On my own walks, I'd noticed a couple of signs absent from positions I thought I knew well, and it was tempting to think the worse of it (all ridings get such reports), but I'd decided to be skeptical, figuring it might as easily have been neighbours or vandals. But I'd also had to block several very nasty people on my Twitter account, not exactly charmers, and made a note to talk to Phil. He said he'd come across one house with several of our team's large signs piled flat in his yard and, when questioned, the man told him they'd been dumped. "Can be kids doing that," said Phil. "It used to be if we caught them, boy, they'd remember."

I had the impression he missed those days.

. . .

"Don't say 'Justin'," says Janet. "Say 'Trudeau.'"

Janet has negotiated with HQ and I am able to participate in the panel on the environment at the First Unitarian Congregation of Toronto, in the heart of the riding. The mainstream and social media are still a-flurry with my indiscretions, and I am under strict instructions—a teenager with a curfew, an offender under a peace bond.

"And no reporters," says Janet. "You don't talk to *anybody* beforehand and you don't take questions from the audience if the subject comes up. Enough with social media, already."

We are late enough in the campaign that I am developing a real affection for a number of the people I'm working with. Janet, I decide, would be a good parent, the lenient sort that would have a hard time suppressing her own urge to misbehave.

"Agreed," I say. "No reporters!"

Kinsella, I'll have to tell him some time, was right—but tonight social media are the last things to worry about.

. . .

THE LIFE AND DEATH OF THE CANDIDATE

The Single Extant Canadian Work of William Shakespeare, Believed to Be an Early Draft of His Tragedy, The Life and Death of Julius Caesar

ACT I. SCENE II. A public place.

Flourish.

Enter THE CANDIDATE; THE CAMPAIGN MANAGER *and* DOUG BELL, *for the course;* CAROLYN BENNETT, *dressed in red, and* KEVIN FARMER *in green; a great crowd from Toronto—St. Paul's following, among them* THE POLITICAL WIFE, THE POLITICAL HUSBAND, THE ASSISTANT *and the* SOOTHSAYER, *an advocate for Leadnow.*

THE
CANDIDATE: Bennett!

BELL: Peace, ho! The Candidate speaks.

THE
CANDIDATE: Bennett!

BENNETT: Here, my lord.

THE
CANDIDATE: Stand you directly in the Campaign
            Manager's way,
            When she doth run her course? Campaign
            Manager!

THE CAMPAIGN
MANAGER: Candidate?

THE
CANDIDATE: Forget not, in your speed, Campaign Manager,
            To touch Bennett; for our elders say,
            The Liberals, touched in this holy chase,
            Shake off their sterile curse.

THE CAMPAIGN
MANAGER: I shall remember:
            When The Candidate says "do this," it is
            perform'd.

THE
CANDIDATE: Lead now; and leave no ceremony out.

Flourish

SOOTHSAYER: Candidate!

THE
CANDIDATE: Oh Christ, sorry, my line was *set on*!
            Who calls?

FARMER: Bid every noise be still: peace yet again!

THE
CANDIDATE: Who is it in the press that calls on me?
            I hear a tongue, shriller than all the music,
            Cry "The Candidate!" Speak; The Candidate
            is turn'd to hear.

SOOTHSAYER: Beware the ides of Ekos, Nanos, Forum and
Poll Tracker.

THE
CANDIDATE: What man is that?

ASSISTANT: A soothsayer bids you beware the polls. He's
unimpressed by your 23% in March.

THE
CANDIDATE: Then why does he not say so?
What's with listing poll trackers and where's
MacDougall?
Isn't she for the course? This is getting ridiculous.
Set him before me; let me see his face.

BELL: Fellow, come from the throng; look upon
The Candidate.

THE
CANDIDATE: What say'st thou to me now? Speak once again.

SOOTHSAYER: Beware the ides of March.

THE
CANDIDATE: He is a dreamer. Let us leave him: pass.

. . .

The rules of the evening's discussion are an adaptation of the
venerable Quaker practice of "scrupling" that encourages adver-
saries to "listen, share and search for ways to respond in

accordance with their own scruples and principles"—no challenges or confrontation allowed. MacDougall, the Conservative candidate, does not show. The audience is told she is hosting a fundraising event, only confirming my suspicions concerning the Conservatives' estimation of Toronto—St. Paul's as a field of money trees. It is also quite obvious that "The Intersection of Climate and Democracy," as the discussion is billed, is not exactly tops on the Conservative agenda. Nevertheless, I find myself missing MacDougall and the opportunity for a discussion of policy rather than having to listen to Bennett repeat tropes about Toronto—St. Paul's and Trudeau being a leader because he surrounds himself with good people. Now Bennett is talking about "the teachings of the First Peoples of Canada" and "an indigenous way of knowing that will protect Mother Earth," and I can hear Janet sighing from her seat in the front row.

Question time comes and Adam Deutsch, Green Party candidate Kevin Farmer's right-hand man, says again he'll probably vote for the NDP, which is nice. Then someone I have not seen before stands up with a slim binder in his hand and addresses not the candidates but the audience. It is actually fascinating; there is something approaching contempt in the way he has turned his gaze away from us and I know already I shall not forget the moment. He identifies himself as a member of Leadnow and explains the mandate of his organization and its polling of ridings that might see a split of the "progressive" vote, allowing a Conservative to come up the middle. Leadnow, he says, canvasses with a view to endorsing the Liberal or NDP candidate best poised to win, pushing the Anything But Conservative (ABC) vote in the direction most likely to achieve that end. I can hear Janet sighing again, and when it comes my turn, I tell him how misguided I believe the principles of the organization to be. My message the length of the campaign has been that a vote carries vital information in the short but also mid- and long term and, regardless of who wins, that it pushes a whole packet of conversations along. For instance, the idea of a parliamentary coalition that Stephen Harper and the Conservatives used, in 2008, to warn of an unholy alliance intent on overturning his government "without your say, without your consent, without your vote" had, by 2015, become a more rational and practical discussion about how a Liberal–NDP coalition might operate. And if, in the election just a few weeks away, the result was, once more, a party with but 35 percent of the vote handed 100 percent of the power, then it would become an even more vigorous and informed one about proportional representation. This is how votes influence a society over a period of time rather than on one particular day—but all this is undermined, and the information of a vote distorted, when a person votes "strategically." If people cast their votes with a view to just one issue, rather than a party's platform, then they are rescinding their right to complain about everything else the winning party has proposed, forfeiting their say in a plethora of issues for the sake of Leadnow's simple instruction.

The Leadnow speaker is unbothered and the scrupling rules prevent me from vigorously presenting my position. The man has made the pitch for his ABC strategy and announces it is the only purpose of his attending. I wonder whether or not I should be alarmed or offended that Leadnow is not actually polling in Toronto—St. Paul's. The soothsayer and his colleagues are looking more and more like the enemy, but it's hard to pay attention because the polls have been relentlessly negative from the start. I am looking for a miracle.

Janet greets me outside. "What's Bennett going to do next?" she says. "Come in with a headdress on?"

. . .

Things it is becoming harder and harder to talk about:
Balancing the budget
Pulling out of the fight against ISIL
Keeping plans to purchase the F-35
Hiring 2,500 more RCMP
Israel
Child care

. . .

Regular sleep is out the window. At today's 3 a.m. wakeup call, I dream that I am sorting bounced cheques and the bed combusts. Come seven, I have joined Sarah in the kitchen for the first of my two double espressos. The candidate's successful weight-loss program is the following: black coffee, revolting fast food you'd rather not finish and other meals on the fly, and the adrenalin-burning rush that ensues from a constant sensation of being half an hour late for you don't know what.

The radio is on. Sarah flips a pan-heated tortilla with a spicy avocado-and-tomato mix on my plate. Real food. Cooking is usually my call, but the campaign has retired me.

"See," I say. "Your life's not over. Just different roles."

"Have you called Rocco Galati yet?" asks Sarah.

"No," I say.

"Have you organized T-shirts?"

"No."

"Have you arranged for a closing night party yet?"

"No."

"Have you—"

"I told you. The answer to every question you ask me is 'No, I haven't done that yet.'"

Sarah flips from Jazz FM to Radio One despite Janet's instructions, and Éric Grenier, the CBC's "poll tracker," is cheerily imparting NDP-unfriendly news. We are continuing our slide in the polls, and I am doing my best not to compute. At the door I have been saying with a shrug, like I'm imparting a confidence from my own years in the trade, "Don't listen to journalists, don't listen to pollsters, it's a flawed science. They failed to predict the NDP victory in Alberta, Kathleen Wynne's in Ontario, the Orange Wave in Quebec—or David Cameron's Conservative victory in the U.K., for that matter. Listen to yourselves; the polls are wrong!" And the thing is, I believe this myself. Sort of have to.

The Liberal Party's child care ad is running again.

While two people claim to speak for the middle class, only the Leader of the Liberal Party of Canada, Justin Trudeau, will back up his words with actions. He will raise taxes on the wealthiest one percent, and cut them for the middle class. . . .

"Man," I say. "Why isn't the NDP advertising? We're the CBC's core audience, for Christ's sake."

. . . Thomas Mulcair will do neither, continuing to send Stephen Harper's child benefit cheques to millionaires. Mr. Trudeau will cancel them and send more money to families who really need it. That's real change.

"I don't know why we're not cancelling those cheques. It makes it really hard and I've lost one of my best lines," I complain.

"Which is?"

"Our plan is not about stuffing cash through the door for the parents to use. It's about the children."

Not once, during the whole campaign, will I hear an NDP advertisement. The Liberal one really grates.

. . .

Vaughan Road is my comfort zone, and as I journey along it in the later stages of the campaign I mumble quiet thank yous for the orange NDP signs with my name on them on almost every block. But, west of Oakwood, into little Jamaica, red is starting to pop up amid the orange. *The Liberals start weak and come on strong.* The front door of one house is wide open, hip hop blaring out into the fall air as three black men lounge on the front steps, a Bennett sign affixed to the porch. I pencil in a "4" on the sheet and turn up Northcliffe towards Eglinton. We are at the very north end of the street, a block south of where the Eglinton Cross-town LRT line is being built, its construction a source of local consternation. Hang on to your houses, I want to say, hang on to your bankrupted businesses—don't sell, because when the subway is finished, you'll be laughing all the way to the real estate bank. But sell now and you'll get nothing, your community will be ruined, and the developers will be laughing—at you. This may be better advice than any of the political stuff I'm pushing. The street here is lined with small one-storey strip malls of a kind that will have historical value soon enough—if they avoid demolition, that is. I pop into a dive bar in the middle of one, a couple of customers or maybe dealers hanging about outside, just room for a pool table and shot-taking inside, and a white guy is behind the bar who has probably been working there for forty years. He won't take a window sign, he says, "but I've got to congratulate you for coming in here. Never seen that."

Outside, past the co-op in which, on one of my first canvasses, I'd met the couple whose son had cystic fibrosis, I see the father sitting on a low wall and taking in the gentle afternoon sun.

"Hey," I say, the memory of the moment providing me a lift. "Remember me? I'm the NDP candidate!"

He nods. He's not smiling.

"What's your position on Syria?" he asks.

"It's a terrible situation, we should do what we can to—"

"How do we know they're not terrorists? Those refugees come here and they get everything. All my life I've been working and you're going to give *them* houses and money so they don't have to? They not welcome here. It's not *fair*."

. . .

It's been a while since anybody asked how Mulcair and the NDP would fare in a coalition. At the apartment door of a "1" I am offered reasons why.

"I've voted NDP all my life," the man says, "but now I have to vote Liberal."

"Why?"

"We have to get rid of Harper."

The man's daughter is standing beside him, and she says she lives in the neighbouring riding of Davenport and will be voting Liberal too.

"But you have an NDP MP already," I say. "Andrew Cash. And he's doing a really good job."

"I know," says the daughter. "But we can't take any chances."

"The Liberals are prepared to invest," says the father. "They're not hung up on balancing budgets. The Liberals are left of the NDP now."

"That's not true," I say. "You're being duped. The most progressive policy is to tax corporations more and the Liberals won't be doing that."

There's more I want to say—that we're not in a recession,

that we keep deficit spending in line so we're not paying a whack of interest down the line—but increasingly, I see the need to make the case for voting as you believe. The NDP, I say, is the only party insisting on the repeal of Bill C-51; the only one with explicit plans for carbon pricing or promising a specific system of proportional representation; the only party planning to raise the tax on corporations. A vote for the Liberal Party is a vote against the sum of these positions. In all of this, I am beginning to hate the polls—not for the data they gather but for when they do it and their sabotage of decisions I believe voters should arrive at themselves, rather than through the exertions of a public conversation that might as well be about best-seller lists or the latest cultural fad.

"Think of it like a case before the courts," I say. "The whole country is on jury duty and polls are pronouncing on matters *sub judice*. Pollsters should be banned from publishing anything influencing such an important decision in the three weeks before election day."

Not a bad idea, I think, but the discussion is with myself.

. . .

Farnham Avenue, closed door one of five:

The man's lips are quivering. I notice large paintings hanging on the walls of the living room behind him as he vents at the prospect of an NDP government and this presence of the party's candidate on his street. "*Do you know what would happen if taxes were raised on corporations? My pension would disappear! I'm from Alberta! I know the meaning of hard work! My grandfather fought on Corvettes in the Atlantic. He put his life on the line for this country!*"

"Then he understood the meaning of community," I say, and carelessly, "The election's not all about you."

"What did you say?"

"The NDP understands the first job of government is to extend a hand to those in need of support. You'd understand that. You're from Alberta and we have so much to thank you for: R.B. Bennett. Unemployment insurance. Old age pensions. The CCF."

Slam!

. . .

Arlington Avenue, closed door two of five:

"Oh, you're the NDP candidate?" An attractive woman, modern house, newly appointed. A child playing on the floor. Lots of toys. Tables with sharp corners, too. The trouble with architects.

"Wait there," the woman says. "My husband would like to speak to you."

The husband, perhaps thirty-five, comes to door. He's a doctor and there it is again, the quivering top lip. He grills me about cuts to health care and is citing figures at a level of detail I cannot hope to match. I try to get a word in but he won't stop speaking—about balancing the budget, about the NDP's misplaced priorities, their lies about numbers.

"All politics begins from principle," I start, but he raises his voice to the point that it is shrill and I can't find a way in.

"I'll be voting Liberal!" he says.

Slam!

. . .

Arlington Avenue *redux*, closed door three of five:

The Toronto Blue Jays are losing to the Baltimore Orioles, but it doesn't matter because they've already clinched the

American League East. Still it feels like not a good time to be making friends with a cheery door knock.

The man is a pensioner and a Canadian Armed Forces vet.

"I've been an NDP voter all my life," he says, "*and you're pulling our fighters out?*"

I'm all set to go with my potted speech about the futility of the war over Iraq—how we're supporting the venal dictator Bashar al-Assad; how we're de facto allies of Iran and Russia; how the Iraq borders the British drew up never made sense anyway; and how the NDP is the only party objecting to the unconscionable arms deal with Saudi Arabia, suspected by the British media of purchasing weapons ending up in the hands of ISIL, but I've barely time to draw an intake of breath.

"You should be ashamed," he says.

Slam!

. . .

Melita Court, closed door four of five:

"Oh, so you're the NDP candidate!"

A young black woman, maybe twenty-five, community housing, prints from the Caribbean, a crucifix—but by now the exclamation feels like a setup.

"Wait a moment," the woman says. "My father would like to speak to you."

That's the clincher: the first member of the household is used to the other's kitchen table rants and wants to see how the candidate copes. It takes a couple of minutes for the bed-ridden father, in his late sixties or seventies, maybe older, to shuffle to the door. His feet never quite leave the floor and the thick rubber-soled shoes squeak on the linoleum. The man is wearing a dressing gown—and there they are, the quivering lips.

I give him my moral moments spiel, talk about Tommy Douglas and pharmacare and the plight of seniors and throw in infrastructure, how hard it is to get around.

"Tom's not just talking about concrete but what is human," I say. "He's investing in *people*, in *social programs*. He knows that we're only as well off as—"

The man frowns.

"Ahbinheresinsiktyfreeanwokinsohahdhahderdanyouhahd derdendemrefugeedeygedindabenefitnodmeahnovodinuvodin libraluhear *no u novodin u* sonocomherelookadmewokinso hahdahdonlikeuheerahsay*go*!"

Slam!

. . .

Merton Street, closed door five of five:

More community housing and the familiar smell of cabbage on the top floors, bleach in the basement. Is bleach a heavier odour, I wonder? Surely there is a scientific explanation, or maybe it's sociological—janitors eating just as much cabbage but using more of the chemicals that come to them free with the job. You hold your nose, you knock. The door opens five inches. A tuft of long, uncombed white hair hangs to one side of the man's head.

"Save me!" he says.

Slam!

. . .

Long conversations, diminishing returns.

An elderly white Conservative voter sits on the railing of his deck, his wife in attendance. He is speaking thoughtfully, considering his sentences, reflecting on his points. He listens as if

your answers matter and so you like him. He is struggling with
the idea of whom to vote for but confides it won't be Harper. "A
lot of us never liked Harper even when we *were* voting for him,"
he says. He keeps you for ten, fifteen minutes. Peter Tabuns, the
NDP Toronto MPP and canvassing guru, would throw his
hands up in despair, leave you here and move on. But you are
appreciating the substance of what he is saying. It's why you
signed up. You feel, in your reluctance to leave, nostalgia for the
sort of banter that campaigning has left by the wayside, even as
you know nothing you say will sway him—not this time around,
anyway. Maybe some part of you is already campaigning for the
next time and wanting the man to have a good memory of the
pleasant, seemingly intelligent fella who came to the door and
made a case for a party and a vision he'd not, until now, entertained. Perhaps he will tell his wife, in the years to come, "That
NDP candidate, he'd be a good MP. Isn't it time someone
replaced Bennett?

"Love, remind me, why are we so afraid of the NDP?"

OCTOBER 1

CPC	NDP	LPC	BQ	GRN	OTH
32.3%	26.8%	30.4%	5.0%	4.8%	0.7%

. . .

*Some days, the last thing you will want to do is canvass, and then you'll
go out and canvass because that's what will make you feel better.*

It is the beginning of October and I hear Phil say, "All our
undecideds are Liberals," which is another way of saying there
may be no "undecided" votes left. Maybe that's why the meet
and greet events are thinning—more like greet and be done

withs, despite my stellar company. The jacket is off and the sleeves are rolled up, this not yet the trademark of a far more successful candidate, and I'm practiced in the balletic work of making everyone else feel they are not wasting their time. Enjoy the canapés. Be winning. Be the candidate.

Candidate, 'kandi,dāt,'kandidət, *noun: "one aspiring to office" (early 17th century: from Latin candidatus "white-robed," also denoting a candidate for office who traditionally wore a white toga). Subsequent early senses were "pure, innocent," "unbiased," and "free from malice," hence "frank" (late 17th cent) and "candour": the quality of being open and honest in expression; frankness.*

So let me be open, honest in expression and frank. It's been a long time since Rathnelly and the meet and greets have become events of endurance. Earlier in the week was the last of my September meet and greets, and at the penultimate one, in Forest Hill, the lox and bagels, not the NDP, were the attraction for the brunch crowd of predominantly young investors. At Marchmount Road, there were just four people in the kitchen. I have already cancelled the meet and greet slated for Cabbagetown, at which I'd hoped to raise some money because I'd lived in the district for seventeen years ("Neighbours for Noah")—that was a drag—and elected not to follow up on invitations for a couple more. Today's meet and greet, on the first night of October, was fixed some time ago. It is in an NDP-inimical part of the riding—among the enormous mansions of Wells Hill Avenue—and being hosted by a couple of generous and committed Jewish NDP activists honourably doing what they can in a part of the riding where their politics can hardly be mainstream. One has already taken me for a canvass along streets adjoining the road where she lives, knocking on doors and introducing me very personably. By the end of the block, she is like an old friend and I want to take her home with me and for us to watch movies and eat popcorn. It occurs to me, as I talk a calculated mile a minute, that I am becoming teary in moments of fatigue that are more frequent now. I tweet photographs of Toronto's gorgeous canopy of turning autumn leaves. I want to talk to people I haven't spoken to in ages. I am thinking of dead people. I want my father to have seen me doing this.

You will move through a carousel of moods.

Wells Hill Avenue faces the Loblaw's on St. Clair. Separated from the busy central thoroughfare by a small English green, it is, for all intents and purposes, a gated community. In perfect view of all the cars passing and entering the supermarket parking lot, and the steady stream of pedestrians using the TTC entrance right by it, is a great big red Liberal Carolyn Bennett sign mounted at the foot of a house that might as well be a castle. For the duration of the campaign, I have wanted to match it. On my way to the meet and greet I think "What the hell?" and try the house next door. The young father who answers is holding a small child and speaks, with an English accent, words I know to be an indication of what's to come: "NDP? Yeah, I was hoping you'd come round." Then he lets loose with a diatribe about Gaza and the NDP's censoring of Morgan Wheeldon, the Nova Scotia candidate who'd accused Israel of a little ethnic cleansing. I'm tempted to say, "Well, a Nova Scotian would understand. Did you know England's expulsion of the Acadians, back in 1755, is generally regarded as the first example of ethnic cleansing?" But I think better of it; some voters simply need to be let be. I knock one door further up and find myself having a much easier time, the fantasy of a NOAH RICHLER NDP sign next to Bennett's still alive. My dance partner is a dandyish retiree of the financial world with wire frame spectacles and brightly coloured striped socks. He is amused—his son comes home and is not—and I make a mental note to return with a copy of my first book because he's from out west and a reader. Maybe that will sway him. Yet, like so many things, I'll not get around to it and now it's time to move on to the appointed meet and greet. It is the weekend of Sukkot, the Hebrew harvest festival, and inside the house is a nicely laid out table of wine and Jewish foodstuffs. I am prepared for bad attendance, but this time some fifteen people arrive. After half an hour of niceties, I am shepherded from the hall into the living room to deliver my case for the NDP, everyone seated but me. Immediately, Mulcair's plans for a balanced budget arise and I talk about spending corporate taxes, not my children's money, and, contrary to popular mythology, the party's generally exemplary fiscal record. I talk about having visited Bay Street and my executive contact, "whose annual remuneration is likely that of a small Latin American country" (no laughs) and how he'd endorsed the NDP plan to cut stock option tax credits—which is when an elderly man with an Eastern European accent starts haranguing me.

"*Nonsense!* How am I going to keep my employees interested in startups if I can't give them stock options?"

I put up a fight but he doesn't stop, and finally it's the circle that tells him that's enough, and when, later, I make my exit, they are apologizing for him. "That's his nature," my hosts say, which I know to mean that he had the better of me and I've not won votes here. I cycle by the Carolyn Bennett sign, wonder in passing where she lives and worry I'm being shut out. It's depressing, and once back in my neighbourhood I make a pit stop to have a drink, wishing my local was in Toronto—St. Paul's and people were seeing me doing it. I have become my own toughest critic when it comes to the question of where a candidate lives, not due to issues of representation but because when you're campaigning at home, then the drink at the pub and the coffee in the morning or the walk of the dogs—it's all related and the job is easier.

The Mihevc fundraiser seems so long ago.

. . .

It can jaundice you, too much canvassing—are you seeing that? When, looking up a street interrupted here and there by cubic houses made of metal and glass or mock Tudor "dream homes" that look as if they were won in a lottery—houses indifferent to the architectural and the social rest—and I started to conclude, "no Dippers here," then I knew my game was up. Evidence? There was plenty. It had only been the rich, leaning out of over-sized custom front doors held just slightly ajar, who would berate me about government handouts or say, "The system is broken."

"People vote according to their pockets," I told Young Ethan as we worked some well-to-do part of the neighbourhood.

And why should that have been a surprise? Of course people do. The disenfranchised, the old and the marginalized depending on benefits were likely to vote our way, but weren't they voting with their hands in their pockets, too? I'd tried my arguments about the "'invisible' taxes" of Conservative intransigence and the benefits that would accrue to all in a more secure, just society—S.'s good roads, schools and hospitals—but the "middle class," that great big privileged tranche in which half of Canadians imagine they sit, and in which even more believe that they belong, appeared, in the conversations I was having, only progressive to the point ambitious social plans did not cost them. Then they were Liberal.

Or so I felt in the waning weeks of the campaign as a new spiel developed: "The Liberals are the Conservatives without Harper. We are the only party prepared to tax corporations more, and that's the difference," I'd say. "Trudeau *says* he'll tax the one per-cent but—you know the rich—they'll find a way around it."

Out went the early argument that the NDP was the only choice to defeat Harper, first in 103 ridings and second in 200 more, and in came—thank you, Wilhelm—an altered other:

"For the whole century and a half of Canada's existence, the country has been run by Conservative and Liberal governments. *Replacing Tweedledum with Tweedledee is no solution!*"

How else to fight Trudeau's announcement, crushing us now, that a Liberal government would deficit spend? I didn't have to agree with the Liberal plan—didn't then, don't now ("The prob-lem with Canada is that politicians are part-time Keynesians: they like the borrowing, they don't like the paying back part," said Andrew Thomson to the *Financial Times*)—but indisputably it had been a brilliant move, rendered more so by Mulcair and the NDP's failure to react to its overwhelming traction with voters. In Ontario, where former NDP premier Bob Rae's deficit spending constituted one of Canada's two traumatic political memories (the other, obsessing the West, was the 1980 National Energy Program of Pierre Trudeau's Liberal Party), there was never going to be any option but for Mulcair to emphasize the party's fiscal credentials—or, at least, initially that was true. But on the ground (I was hearing the same from Davenport and Eglinton—Lawrence), we were like paratroopers stranded inside enemy territory and deserted by indifferent generals. There was a yearning for Mulcair to show some sort of spontaneity—to say, for instance, "It's incumbent upon a government to be responsible with other people's money, but I am relieved and interested that Canadians are prepared to take on debts to alleviate and perhaps even to solve our economic woes. I've listened, and take note."

At the door, I'd defend as much as I was able against the Liberals' deft play:

"Balancing the books is not a partisan issue," I'd say. "It's about not taking the income of government—the taxes you pay—for granted. I'm uncomfortable spending money we don't have, our kids' money [*the dig*] not ours—and especially when there is no need. Did you know just last week StatsCan—I mean what's left of it [*deliver a collegiate chortle, intone the 'muzzling of scientists'*]—issued a report showing that of all the parties the NDP has balanced budgets the most over the last thirty years of provincial and federal governments? [*Phew, seem to have dodged bullet of NDP never having formed a federal government.*] And that we did so without cutting social programs [*so you say*], and furthermore when we did run deficits we did so as a lower portion of GDP than either the Liberals or Conservatives? [*Seem to have the momentum here.*] The Liberals, of course, have always been great *cutters* of social programs. People talk about Paul Martin having balanced the books, but we're still *reeling* from the cuts he made. We don't need to deficit spend because we'll be taxing corporations 2 percent more [*party talking point*] and shutting down stock option tax credit loopholes—and *we're the only party doing this.* Our job is to get the hundreds of billions of 'dead money' the corporations are hoarding, moving. And that's far more than a government can ever spend. And by the way [*deliver as another friendly confidence*], the NDP doesn't need lessons in deficit spending—we're the ones [*see how smart and capable we are*] who pushed Harper to do it in the last recession [*look for acknowledgment of reports that we are in another*]. We just don't think it's necessary right now.

"Perhaps there's something on your mind? Ideas, or worries, that I can take back with me?"

But the arguments were not working. The Liberal plan waved the carrot of work to Canadians who did not have it and told the vast numbers who did not need a break, "You're off the hook. Someone else will pay."

. . .

It's tough now. Like I'm out in the boonies and I've been sent up the wrong street; like I'm the DH in a ball game and my timing is off. No one is handing me anything back.

A couple of volunteers tell me they were barred from a condo tower.

"That's against the law," I say. (All canvassers have the right to enter apartment buildings and carry Elections Canada permissions to that end.) "Didn't you tell the super?"

Yes, they say—and, better, they got in through the back door and canvassed the building anyway.

. . .

I'm on the fifth floor of community housing in the northeast corner of the riding when I learn that Chris Alexander and Kellie Leitch, the minister for the status of women, have pledged funds and a "tip line"—a.k.a. a snitch line—to aid in the enforcement of the party's Zero Tolerance for Barbaric Cultural Practices Act. I am genuinely floored. I have to exit the building onto its public verandah and sit down on the ground to take the air. I'd grown up in Quebec—knew about folk using the language laws to rat out their neighbours to the Office québécois de la langue française— but still cannot believe that the ploy of a governing federal party has come to this. I am stunned at the lengths that Harper's desperate and cynical government is constantly superceding in order to create conditions of festering animosity and profit by them. But it is this—the existence of a prime minister and his disciples creating divisions between Canadians for political expediency's sake—that drew me into the melee in the first place. The measure has the mark of the Australian campaign strategist Lynton

Crosby, the so-called Wizard of Oz credited with cementing Conservative prime minister David Cameron's May 2015 U.K. parliamentary elections in similar fashion. Harper was said to have hired Crosby at the beginning of September in order to resuscitate the Conservatives' flailing campaign (though Mark Textor, the other half of the Australian's strategic consulting firm, Crosby Textor, would subsequently deny any involvement). Such was Crosby's reputation for effectively whipping up handy phobic sentiment, the Australian was believed to have been the mastermind behind the manipulation of the issue of the niqab that the new Canadian Zunera Ishaq was insisting she had a right to wear at the public citizenship ceremony, the defence of which wounded the NDP so after Mulcair stood by it in the September 24 French-language debate. When the news broke that Crosby's services had been engaged, I'd told friends it was a ploy that would not work, that Canadians would not fall for more of the invidiousness that had kept the Conservatives in power for so long. Now, sitting at the foot of the wall on the co-op verandah as if I'd taken a punch, I was not so sure. I contacted Jonathan and Doug, who quickly prepared a cartoon for a possible social media blast that read:

RAT OUT THE PRIME MINISTER
PHONE THE RCMP NOW AND REPORT
CHRIS ALEXANDER, LYNTON CROSBY
AND STEPHEN HARPER FOR:

BARBARIC CULTURAL PRACTICES
IF YOU HAVE TO SNITCH
SNITCH ON STEVE

But we decided not to dispatch it, keeping our energies in reserve for the videos. And, besides, blows weren't only coming from the CPC corner; I was beginning, finally, to be jealous of Bennett's glossier material—starting to notice just how much more effective our rivals' brochures were likely to be than ours. Their candidate cards looked better in the mail slots (fix them so the side with your picture is face out to passersby), looked better even when discarded on the path or littering an apartment block corridor. We were approaching the last two weeks of the campaign and, though it was not my business to keep track, I was sure there was enough money for a new colour brochure to be distributed. It was time for more campaign literature, I argued, and I wanted to know what we could afford.

The finance gang meets in the back room.

"What's in the account?" I ask.

"Hard to say."

There is a tabulation of outstanding and settled bills, and a confused recounting of the various ways money finds its way into the campaign's account—through the NDP site, via the central party, via a commercial credit card processor, as cheques or as cash. The discussion is protracted. It verges on the philosophical. After twenty minutes, the straightforward question still has no straightforward answer.

"Don't let anybody know about this," says Janet, watching over the meeting from the door and shaking her head in disbelief. "We're trying to convince the country we can form a government."

. . .

Even at the Wychwood farmers' market, the going is not so easy. October has brought a chill to the air, and more purpose. Not as much produce, save the glorious apples, and not so many people. There are fewer shoppers with smiles and they are ambling less. Almost no one is drifting our way willingly and stopping to chat. The only constant is that the farmers' market manager is persisting in giving our team a hard time: no signs, get off the paths, you're in the way of shoppers, etc. We know the charges.

"Why are you surprised?" asks American Sarah. She's been doing her homework and hands me the "Choose Your Canada" flyer that Bennett's pack of young Liberals, canvassing without harassment, is distributing further along the path. Bennett's flyer contains endorsements from a prominent clothes retailer, a Toronto District School Board trustee, the Liberal city councillor in the riding, and

COOKIE ROSCOE, WYCHWOOD BARNS FARMERS' MARKET MANAGER

I'm so grateful to have such an engaged politician in my riding. Carolyn's leadership inspires me every time I see her.

I find the impressive, expensive weight of the card it is printed on frustrating. We had the money, I'd argued at our finance gang's tête-à-tête—or, at least, we were reasonably able to expect it—but my gang is parsimonious by habit and won't run a deficit, damn it. We have produced, in the place of Bennett's nice glossy brochures, black-and-white photocopied letter-size paper sheets cut into thirds so poor in quality that, to my mind, they communicate only insufficient means and I'm not using them.

I see councillor Joe Mihevc and he tries to duck around me. Mihevc does a little dance that makes me think of Al Jaffee's *Mad* magazine illustrations of my youth, flashes me an uncomfortable grin and, as if in atonement, says he is canvassing for the NDP in University—Rosedale. The avowedly left-wing councillor had been incumbent since 1991, when his campaign was backed by the NDP. But no help had been forthcoming—no lists, no advice, no canvasses, no note of events, and certainly pictures of Mihevc and Bennett doing neighbourhood work together were easily found on social media. Between the local councillor, Cookie Roscoe and the CUPE head I'd seen chatting to Bennett in the market (and the insistence of one very prominent and influential local NDP activist saying he needed to avoid direct association because of social work he was doing with my Liberal opponent), I realize that what I am up against is the league and power of incumbency.

A young father approaches. He is on his own, pushing an empty pram.

"I think maybe you've lost something," I say. (It's a joke.)

"No," he says dourly. "He's with his mom."

I give a bit of a pitch, he says he knows who I am and wants to vote for me, but—I relieve him of the burden of telling me he's voting strategically and ask about a sign.

"We had one," he says.

"It was nicked?" I ask.

"No," he says a little sheepishly, "my wife made me remove it."

I nod. He moves on.

I do my best to convince another dad, who says he'd really like to put up a sign but he works for the CBC and is not allowed to show any affiliation.

"But your director of strategic planning and communications, Dan Lauzon, is working in the Liberal war room. Isn't that declaring an affiliation?"

"I'm not allowed to put up a sign. Sorry."

. . .

Fatigue is now a factor, and I am wary of incidents coming at me in threes.

Incident One:

Canvassing in the northeast, I take a moment in the late afternoon sun and put my iPhone on a bench. I do not realize I've left it there until I have cycled down to the University of Toronto to join Sarah for a book launch celebrating the publication of Massey Lecturer Margaret MacMillan's *History's People*. I make a spectacle of myself to guests staring out the window at the comedy of the fella in orange NDP colours who's patting his pockets and checking his bicycle panniers and then the ground around his feet for whatever it is that he's lost. Sarah is a sport, introduces me to a few businesspeople and academics from my riding and then, leaving her own pleasant garden party, uses a tracking app to pinpoint the corner where I left my iPhone. But it does so only approximately, Google Earth lagging behind the pace of Toronto condo development. We drive to the street in question and Sarah, in a smart dress and high heels, waits patiently as I walk up and down the block several times with her iPhone in my hand. I'm trying to make sense of the movement of the pulsing green dot and the correlation of the app's building shapes with the houses, offices and construction site to the north of me. Sarah follows me through a hole in the wire-mesh fence dividing the construction site from the parking lot of the community housing I'd canvassed earlier in the day, where I'm convinced I'll find my iPhone tossed in the detritus of wood and bricks underfoot. Sarah's had enough—she's in her Ferragamos—and goes back through the hole in the fence to the car and it occurs to me that I am losing perspective, if not my mind.

"It's a phone," says Sarah. She is angry, which is unusual. "Murders happen in places like this," she says. "Get a grip."

I spend the next morning obsessively watching the green dot on the Google Map of Sarah's iPhone leave the northeast and make its way down to a grittier part of Toronto Centre. Given to the apocalyptic, I am wondering how long it will be before the battery gives out, convinced some gang member is looking for the family-owned computer store that will wipe its contents.

Our landline rings and Sarah calls from the kitchen. A woman says her cleaning lady found my iPhone and could I come by to pick it up. When I meet her, she laughs and refuses a reward.

Incident Two:

On the Sunday morning, it is down to the Annex for a debate hosted by the Social Justice Committee at St. Patrick's Catholic Church on McCaul Street, where I am a late NDP stand-in debating Adam Vaughan and the Green candidate from the Toronto Centre riding. It is baffling to me that I am doing so but, a team player, I go—to the wrong address at first, though still in plenty of time for the meet in the church cafeteria and the showdown with Vaughan that would be routine had I been the Spadina—Fort York candidate. It is an off day and I don't perform well. Vaughan has statistics, and years of pugnacious city council experience, and the Green Party candidate for University—Rosedale, Nick Wright, speaks powerfully and on point. I am tired and in a bad mood, made worse because I am ashamed to be speaking below par. Vaughan is agile and unappealing but convincing, too, and I have nothing to match the claims he is making for housing policy in the city. He has me beat, there is no Conservative we might have picked on, and the event seems to have been lost until, at the end of it, I say I need to apologize because the panel and its chair are composed entirely of white men and no women and this anachronism makes me profoundly uneasy. There is nothing calculated about what I say; it is just the truth. My remarks earn the best round of applause of the day, and there is consolation in that. But I am ragged. My dreams are for cretins and, the night before, I'd been an understudy thrust on stage without a script but the stage manager said not to worry because I had no lines.

But in the evening, my spirits are lifted. It is the second of our pub nights, this time at the Wychwood Pub. The owner, Reza, is Persian, and I introduce him with enthusiasm to a volunteer from my bunch who knows his world, I figure they are kindred spirits, but don't get that far. The owner recognizes her and says she's not welcome; there's an outstanding bar bill and the bartender is not happy seeing her either. I calm the situation down and promise the owner that I'll settle the outstanding tab. An iffy start, but the night turns out to be terrific, one of my favourites, and what is making me proud is the diversity that was no one's intention but is simply a fact of the campaign: Quique had performed at the first pub night, and tonight, a musical duo with whom I'd worked at the Young Centre for the Arts—Waleed Abdulhamid, from Khartoum, Sudan (who'd also played at my nomination meeting) and John Millard, from London, Ontario—are performing on the same NDP Toronto—St. Paul's bill as Emily West, an affecting young singer-songwriter from Alberta, and Joanna Burt, a Métis opera student cast in a 2017 revival of Harry Somers's *Louis Riel* at the Canadian Opera Centre, whom I'd met canvassing and urged to participate. The reggae band Mike Garrick and the Posse were due to perform at the last pub night, scheduled for the week preceding E-Day, and we had canvassers from First Nations, as well as Canadians of African, Caribbean, Caucasian, Chinese and South Asian origin; we had young people and old; we had Christians, Jews and Muslims; and a panoply of LGBTQ diversity, too. It wasn't even an achievement; it was just the way it was.

OCTOBER 5

CPC	NDP	LPC	BQ	GRN	OTH
32.3%	25.0%	32.5%	4.9%	4.7%	0.7%

. . .

Mulcair must have listened to my or someone else's arguments, because he's called a rally for October 5 at the 99 Gallery on Sudbury Street at which a "major arts and culture announcement" is to be made. There's a disruption to the routine, would you believe. There's the usual claiming of front-row seats by candidates wanting to be in view, the platform of reporters and cameras, Sam Roberts's "We're All in This Together" blaring at top volume, but this time Andrew Cash brings on singer-songwriter Sarah Harmer and then Luke Doucet and Melissa McClelland of the husband-and-wife folk duo Whitehorse. They play marvellously and, after they do, a dozen or so Toronto producers and artists, including actor Gordon Pinsent, take to the stage to form the backdrop behind the party leader. Mulcair tells the assembled that an NDP government will restore $115 million to the CBC, introduce income-averaging for artists, provide money for digital content for the country's upcoming 150th anniversary and increase funding by $60 million for the Canada Council, the NFB and Telefilm.

But numerology is defeating us again. The $150 million Trudeau promised for the CBC; his "doubling" of the Canada Council budget, like the 50,000 Syrian refugees his party is pledging to admit, is an easy calculus without loose ends. Mulcair's $115 million is worse than $35 million less. Our number prompts, as 46,000 did in that other arena, the question, *why*—why not $110 or $120 or, indeed, Trudeau's $150 million? There is an answer, of course—the CBC has endured $115 million of cuts under the Conservatives—but the number is not inspiring. The Liberal numbers are more adhering and easily conveyed than the NDP's $60 million and the clarification it demands: did Mulcair mean $60 million for the Canada Council, NFB and

Telefilm *in toto*, or for each? Confusing—and what's confusing is not tweeted.

However, Mulcair and his staff have been right about something: from the platform at the front of the room, reporters servicing French- and English-Canadian media want to know about only one issue—and it has nothing to do with the arts. Question after question is put to Mulcair concerning the TPP, the Trans-Pacific Partnership free trade deal announced the day before and the terms of which the Conservatives were keeping secret. Mulcair answers the first few as he might have done in any scrum, but then he reprimands the pack for failing to address the announcement he'd just made. This he does without effect—until, eight or nine questions in, the audience vents its frustrations and starts catcalling, hollering for a question about the arts. Another comes about the TPP. And another. The game is for the television networks, not the room, and the media does not care. The media is paying no attention. Mulcair packs it in.

. . .

"Not that one," says Doug, walking up the few steps from the basement apartment to the street.

"No? You don't think he'll take a sign?"

"You've got to be kidding. He's a fucking stoner and we should be calling in Child Services. I can't believe he has a kid in there. But he said he'd vote for you."

. . .

Incident Three:

That evening, I am to appear on Rogers TV for an all-candidates debate. I'm driving alone and trying to make sense of a Google

Map that confuses my television station destination with an outlet for the company's retail operations situated in the nearby mall. The light changes to green and I turn left, but my head is down checking the map, I don't swing the unfamiliar car around tight enough, and I hit the curb before swinging back onto the road and not off the bridge.

The car went out of control, I think, imagining the sort of headline that has always seemed nonsensical to me. Cars are not animate so it's the driver, stupid, this one too preoccupied.

The Rogers TV station is its lacklustre self. A few minutes before the hour, a surly technician shows us the way to the studio from the holding tank where Bennett, her husband Peter O'Brian and the Green Party candidate Kevin Farmer are sitting on an ugly leather couch and the several candidates of the Scarborough—Guildwood riding are having it out on the TV monitor. MacDougall, the Conservative Party candidate, is a no-show again.

On the way to the show, Farmer pulls me aside.

"I'll drop out if it helps you," says Farmer. It's an offer that strikes me as charitable if a little disingenuous, as the ballots are already printed, but I also believe the arguments I've been making to householders telling me they will vote "strategically." So I thank Farmer and say no, not to think of it; I'd always urged people to vote for the platform they thought the best and if that one was Green, so be it. We take our places in the studio, and I'm the guy wanting my Canada back and Bennett is once again "reapplying for my job" and extolling the "St. Paul's model." The debate is, surprisingly, quite substantial. A good portion of it is centred on the economy, jobs, guaranteed livable incomes, getting "dead money" moving and whether deficits or balancing the books is the antidote to an economy that may or may not be in recession. But I am dour, would be lousy at poker and, to the degree that I am having a hard time being charming, it's Bennett's turn to perform better. Farmer speaks at length, and when Bill C-51 comes up I follow one of Bennett's answers with a question of my own, and the host chides me as a teacher would and tells me it's her job to ask the questions. Amateur hour, but what difference does it make? I am still feeling sore from the previous Sunday's relative defeat and so find a way to slag off Adam Vaughan, whom I say is taking credit for Toronto plans about housing long in the making. Unbeknownst to me, he and Olivia Chow are up next and in the waiting room.

"Hey!" says Vaughan, chirpily. "It's the *litterbug*."

"Excuse me?"

"Throwing trash in the video."

I mutter something under my breath about the litter landing on Trudeau's face being the Liberals' "Fairness for the Middle Class" pamphlet, so the trash is of their making. Bennett makes a show of being off to Edmonton for a First Nations meeting, busy at the job she is applying for (and the further one she is obviously negotiating), and Vaughan tells me he really did do everything he claims. Whatever. I step outside for a post mortem with Becky Fong in the parking lot and she couches her disappointment graciously. Farmer walks by and I offer him a ride back into the city.

"We need real democratic reform," says Farmer. "This campaign is really costing me, just by not working, as I imagine it is you too. But Caroline's on her MP's salary; she's being paid the whole time."

His observation makes enormous sense to me. I think of the Liberal candidate in Ottawa—Nepean, Catherine McKenna, having claimed that she'd knocked on 50,000 doors since her May 16, 2014, nomination, a rate of over 100 a day—an already impressive count that, if we are to believe the claim of a November tweet ("After knocking on 100,000 doors with my team, I'm hardcore"), would rise to an astonishing 700-plus doors during the remainder of the campaign, equivalent to one door a minute for twelve hours a day without breaks. The improbable pace is beside the point; already McKenna had been able to campaign for 457 days, and only select candidates are able to afford this. In Saskatchewan, the NDP candidate Sandra Arias has quit, citing a financial burden that she and her family can no longer carry. I decide that at remaining debates I'll bring it up—insist that if there is to be genuine electoral reform, then a stipend should be paid to all contestants gathering the requisite number of signatures so that not just the relatively entitled can afford to participate. The stipend would be paid out of the sitting MP's wages for the period of the campaign, divvied up accordingly.

· · ·

Less than two weeks to go, and too many conversations at the door are marred, now, by indifference and even boredom. People have made up their minds. The election campaign has been going on for too long and if, on the one hand, the extended campaign has served my team (and especially unknowing me) well, it is, on the other hand, going on three weeks too long for the NDP at large. My last meet and greet is on Kilbarry Road, opposite the madrasa of the wealthy that is Upper Canada College, and I arrive and find myself staring at rows of gleaming wine glasses and plates of hors d'oeuvres that my generous hosts have laid out for the occasion only to discover that apparently their neighbours have much better things to do—and there's not even a ball game on tonight. I feel really bad. I like my host. I've taken his money. I try to figure out the etymology of the word *pariah*. It's not a Latin word. It's not Hebraic. Must look it up.

"I'm sorry," says my host. "I must have invited two hundred people."

"No worries, really."

"I don't know what happened."

"What a lovely garden. Is it okay to step out?"

. . .

Nick, the sign blitz guy:

> *In addition to canvassing my polling subdivision, the campaign office asked if I would help out on a Saturday sign blitz on Manor Road—in the Yonge/Eglinton area—as there was no NDP sign presence on that street.*
>
> *None at all.*
>
> *After three hours of knocking on doors I was able to place two lawn signs: three hours of work for two signs!*
>
> *Back at the campaign office, Wendy greeted me. She smiled and said, "Thank you, Nick. We didn't want to send a rookie canvasser there because we were afraid the disappointment would be too great."*

OCTOBER 8

CPC	NDP	LPC	BQ	GRN	OTH
32.4%	23.6%	33.8%	4.7%	4.8%	0.8%

. . .

Another town hall, this one at the Marriott. The candidates are assembling and, as we wait, I take a moment for a little smartphone math.

Problem: *90 percent of a candidate's vote depends upon the performance of the leader in the last three weeks of the campaign. Calculate the prospects of an NDP win in Toronto—St. Paul's accordingly.*

Okay.

Given (1) in the 2011 federal election, the NDP's Jack Layton, who was tremendously popular, won 30.6 percent of the vote, and the Liberals' Michael Ignatieff, who was *not* popular, took only 18.9 percent, and

Given (2) my predecessor William Molls's portion of the 49,000 votes cast in Toronto—St. Paul's amounted to more than 11,000 votes equalling 22.6 percent of local ballots cast, and Carolyn Bennett still took upwards of 22,000 or 40.6 percent of the vote; and if

Given (3) Ignatieff's 18.9 bomb equalled a 5.1 percent drop in Liberal popularity, and 90 percent of Layton's 30.6 surge equalled, since the first day of the 2011 campaign, an 11.6 percent NDP rise, and

Given (4) that in the 2015 campaign we've seen, to date, a 7.9 pecent rise in the Liberals' popularity under Trudeau, and a 9.6 percent drop in the NDP's under Mulcair;

Then (5) what is the multiplier *e*, for E-Day, to be applied to approximately 79,000 eligible Toronto—St. Paul's voters in 2015, if, in 2011, *u* represents undecided votes, N represents bedrock category, 1 NDP votes and L bedrock Liberal votes, so that

$$\frac{N + u(0.9 \times 11.6)}{L + u(0.9 \times - 5.1)} = 1 ?$$

"Please give us something to work with," says the candidate sitting next to me.

And here we go again, the same routine wearing thin: Sam Roberts, the teleprompter, the leader in his statesman's grey suit—for fuck's sake, could he not ditch the jacket just once? Now Mulcair's coupling Trudeau with Harper as much as he is able: the Liberals and Conservatives are standing together to support Bill C-51, the Keystone XL pipeline, fifty billion dollars in tax cuts to corporations and the "secret" TPP trade agreement. Harper will be stopped—but by Trudeau, is finally the dread.

"I will never side with Stephen Harper to trade away good Canadian jobs to put Canadian family farms at risk," says Mulcair. Canadians, he says, "deserve to know why Justin Trudeau is not standing up to fight for auto jobs and for our supply management system."

There's nothing wrong with what Mulcair is saying, but he's off key, and his assault of the TPP is another symptom of the party not quite getting the city: Torontonians are worried about copyright and Internet privacy and national sovereignty; they're not worried about Quebec egg farms beyond the compensation they'll have to pay to that province.

"Only the NDP is saying it's time to make corporations pay their fair share," says Mulcair. "We're going to raise their taxes."

It's something to work with, but just a little—and late.

. . .

Coffee at Leah's and, across St. Clair, a couple of Liberal canvassers are striding confidently, the joy of the sunny day theirs. They are young, fit and, a gift of the age, beautiful. Their hair is long and thick, they're laughing and there's a healthy spring in their gait. They are girls with—was it Patricia Highsmith who said so?—"nothing written on their brow." This is their time: if not Muskoka, then this pleasant trotting about Toronto—St. Paul's and a high school credit for community service. The pair has about them the sense of a future they cannot possibly imagine will be anything but rosy. Raymond Carver's poem "Happiness" comes to mind; two young boys delivering the morning paper in his instance, two teenage girls in mine.

Happiness. It comes on
unexpectedly. And goes beyond, really,
any early morning talk about it.

You'd keep them at the door, these two. Let the light in. Some of my canvassers, by comparison, look like they crawled out from beneath a rock. They wear old T-shirts and ragamuffin outfits and shoes with thick soles for comfort. My best friend, the fella who got me into all of this, shows up looking like he slept on a bench—and not just for one night. I tease him about this and so does Phil, but still he does it. It's a bit of a WASP thing, like the kids at Oxford who'd boarded at Harrow and wore sweaters with gaping holes in the elbows because money was not a worry and they were to the manor born. Others are the geeks of a prior age, folk that arrived at their own identity weirdness too soon to have made dot-com fortunes. "The walking wounded," says Janet, after one such pair leaves the office. I wonder how many votes my bunch wins and how many they frighten right into the arms of the Liberals. If summer is theirs, then our season is February, November—overcast days with work to be done. But they are my gang, I'd have no other, and today what I'm seeing are the ties that bind across party divides; the belief this system works.

Later, someone will come out on top—the Conservatives, the Liberals or perhaps even the NDP: whoever's brand of "change" winning out before, inevitably, being worn down by the exigencies of office. The federal NDP would be no different, its record as yet unblemished simply because the party had not known power yet. Ensconced, it too would come by its stars and its scandals, its freedoms and constraints. But, for now—in this moment before the die is cast—there is nothing but best practices in the hurly-burly of the country's 1,792 campaigns.

Okay, not quite.

. . .

@Carolyn_Bennett 6.19 PM 10 Oct
Yet again @noahrichler folks r placing illegal signs on public property on Sat—City can't remove them til after wknd/longwknd #elxn42 #TSP

@noahrichler 7.14 PM 10 Oct
@Carolyn_Bennett You fret over signs (as #teamnoah's curiously disappear); I'm thanksgiving as good Canada wins out!

@Carolyn_Bennett 7.21 PM 10 Oct
@noahrichler We have #neverdoneitneverwill #lookelsewhere Rule is #nosignspublicproperty #StopIt Take those signs down now #elxn42

@noahrichler 7.26 PM 10 Oct
City quite right to remove signs erroneously placed; it's the #NDP2015 signs that #LPC removes from TSP lawns that offends

@Carolyn_Bennett 7.29 PM 10 Oct
As I've said @noahrichler #neverdonethatneverwill however my supporters wd love to remove your illegal signs on publicproperty&don't

@noahrichler 10.04 AM 12 Oct
A good citizen, checked & our signs in
public spaces permitted Sure you're
as good a citizen & will tweet same to followers

@noahrichler 10.05 AM 12 Oct
PS Happy Thanksgiving, a gorgeous couple
of days as we head into final week!

@MrTishman 10.24 AM 12 Oct
@noahricher @Carolyn_Bennett I suggest
U check again "election signs are not
permitted anywhere on public property"

#whatthefucklikeIdonthavebetterthingstodo.

@noahrichler 12.54 PM 12 Oct
@MrTishman @Carolyn_Bennett Not my
job to educate a politician unaware of
rules after 18 years. But here's a starter.

I'd attached a jpeg of the City of Toronto Election Sign
permit to the last tweet and the conversation ended, and Bennett
took to direct messaging:

Reason your signs r being removed by city is because they are on
illegal sites—paying the fine doesn't mean weren't speeding NDP
has always interpreted that "deposit 4" illegal signs was a "permit"
—it's not—every illegal sign costs U $25 when city removes it no
signs are allowed on public spaces!

"Okay, so help me out here," I say to Ron Grant, our signs

expert and the veteran of several campaigns. "If the City permit says that I am 'entitled to place election signs on selected public property locations,' then why do the Liberals persist in saying that 'no signs are allowed on public spaces'?"

"They always say that," says Ron. "The Liberals put me through this every time—and every time they're wrong."

Some of the locations Ron has used for signs really impress me: like the pair of large lawn signs staked in an "L" formation at the northeast corner of the busy junction at Bathurst and Dupont—impossible for cars in the constant stream of busy traffic not to see. *Good work*, I thought, but the next day my Twitter feed gave me pause.

@Lybasspring 2015-10-11 @ 10.04 a.m.
@Carolyn_Bennett @noahrichler
Lowballing political discussion.
Shame.

@noahrichler 2015-10-11 10.35 a.m.
You know, I agree. I'd say last night
Was the low moment of my TSP
experience and I apologize for my part in it.

—words, I had not realized, I did not need to tweet as I could have spoken them in the office with as much effect: Lyba Spring was one of our own volunteers.

. . .

I am not in charge: with just a week to go, the rest of the team is increasingly busy organizing for E-Day and has too much work to be bothered with me. Liz sends me out on foot again, this time with American Sarah. She's an unflappable, unfailingly positive woman who knows something about nursing the moody, as I may be now, and I am feeling all the subtle techniques of her having been personal assistant to whoever was the *divo* who employed her in Manhattan. Today, she is my babysitter and I can sense in her upbeat chatter that there was likely some sort of conference back at Bathurst—something along the lines of, "Get him to canvass more, at any rate we need him out of the office."

The elevator opens onto the third floor of the seniors' residence. The smell of disinfectant is overwhelming, though the nurse says she does not notice it anymore. A woman in a wheelchair is screaming, "*Hold the doors! Let me in!*" The nurse giving us the tour says to ignore her as the woman wails, "*Please! Get me out!*" We arrive at the floor's common area, where perhaps twenty residents are sitting against the walls or in wheelchairs. A large television monitor is mounted on the wall, though it's uncertain anyone is watching it. American Sarah prods me into action: Doris is West Indian and savvy and tells me she has no children when I ask if her family comes 'round. Fred's face is in his lunch. The brown turtleneck of a much younger man in a heavily motorized chair is speckled with dandruff and his ears could use a shave. We chat. He tells me he's a writer, I wonder if I'm looking at the future and I don't have the courage to ask what put him here. Now the Filipino nurse behind the desk is doing her version of a Māori *haka* and yelling with a big smile, "*NDP, that's for me!*" The woman in the wheelchair is still screaming, and Fred lifts his face from his food tray and starts to laugh. A South Asian woman with an arch-English accent tells me she's from South Africa.

"She's not," says the nurse, in earshot, and not as an aside. "She's from England and lived in Peterborough most of her life."

The woman looks up at me and smiles beatifically. She puts a hand on my forearm.

"I like Harper," she says softly. "I'll vote for you."

At what point, I cannot suppress the question, are these solicitations unethical? They're setting up a pre-election poll in the lobby and I am speaking to a woman whose memory may have a half-life of a couple of hours.

Outside, American Sarah asks, "Why do we think it's fair that old people who can't make sense of newspapers anymore are able to vote, but not teenagers or temporary foreign workers or Canadians living abroad?"

"Pass."

The seniors' houses and hospices are a circuit: Balmoral, Christie Gardens, Jackes, Mt. Pleasant, Russell Hill, Tichester, more.

At the Meighan Retirement Residence, I speak during the ball game. They're a good crowd and animated and have plenty of challenging questions—about the budget, the environment, ISIL and not seniors, which is interesting. I suppose it's natural that we begin life with overwhelming narcissism and lose it as we age, and I wonder when it is that our sense of ourselves and of others is most in harmony. It's a beautiful afternoon and so I step outside to sit on the bench in front of the residence for a moment and one of the women I'd been chatting with joins me. She's in a wheelchair, but appears quite able. I tell her she seems to be in a good home.

"*Life*," she says.

"Well, it's better than the alternative," I say gamely.

"No," she says. "It's not."

. . .

Another day, another home. At Pine Villa, a woman asks the same question repeatedly and other residents are yelling at her to shut up. Ten minutes into my chat, a retired police officer wearing a U.S. Navy Veteran ball cap ("Proudly Served") takes issue with—well, not so much the NDP's policy in the Middle East, as me. He's yelled down, too.

I press on. Somewhere, I am thinking, Trudeau has landed his motherfucking jet and is telling factory workers good times are about to begin, and eager student interns with the PMO in their sights are trolling my Facebook and Twitter posts one more time for tidbits their first sweep missed. In the shadows, the CPC is sending out crafty special advisors on refugees— you met one, he handed you a card—and here you are providing entertainment in the lounge where residents have been assembled for afternoon tea. The nurse on duty tells you Bennett did not perform that well and the Conservative candidate plain gave up. This is encouragement of a kind. You know these are the needy, unglamorous votes that other parties are, at best, only perfunctorily seeking. Not only Conservatives but also Liberals have learned from Margaret Thatcher's playbook that appealing to all is a losing game and a "waste" of resources: securing half of a select 80 percent—that tranche of Canadians identifying as "middle class"—will put you over. These folk ailing before you are not part of the "middle class" all the parties are on about; nor are they the youth vote the Liberals and Elections Canada are working hard to get out. No, they are folk at the margins and the NDP is their best chance. For some, their only chance. Trudeau, you don't doubt, has moved on to another youth rally by now. Maybe he's in Montreal with Mélanie Joly. Not a wrinkle between them, they might as well be MTV hosts, the votes of their massive teen audience not the last they'll cast, a wooden casket the next step, but the first of several generations, if not a lifetime of voting. That's clever.

Becky whispers not to forget Tommy Douglas, and from across the room, American Sarah gives you a nod. It's as good a moment as any to begin.

"*Can you speak up?*" yells one resident.

"The NDP is the party of Tommy Douglas and—"

"What did he say? *I can't hear.*"

The face of a doctor at the Montreal hospital where my father died flashes before me: he and I are sitting at a table, alone in the private room into which he has ushered me to talk about palliative care. Not a term I've yet had to use, I am dimly aware that I am oblivious to whatever it is he is saying. Later, I am astonished at how many other people, though not me, understood the significance of the timing of that conversation; how many knew what was bound to happen next. I had no idea.

"Of course you didn't," said Sarah. She'd been the first to look at my father and have to turn away and weep. "You were *in it*. You had to believe he would live."

Odd that I should be thinking about that scene now.

"THE NDP IS THE PARTY OF TOMMY DOUGLAS…"

October 10, 2015

🔒 video team

noahrichler 8.08 a.m.

Hi Video Team
We could put out the innocuous "muzzling of scientists" video today, that needs nothing, Harper on Monday as planned, and then the "Barbaric Practices" and "Strategic Voting" ones later next week; or put out the Harper vid today, on the long weekend, rather than Monday. There is, I believe, a case for this as I think we are about to have a Liberal landslide and the thing that is keeping us going is a modicum of originality and enjoyment that I don't want Central to kill.

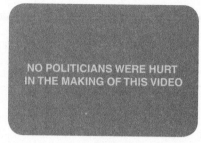

CBC LOGO WASHED OVER
WITH RISING ORANGE WAVE.

DISCLAIMER.

BEGIN "THE NATIONAL" PETER
MANSBRIDGE/STEPHEN HARPER CLIP.

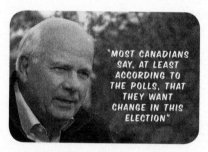

HARPER BEGINS ANSWER.

UNIDENTIFIED FIGURE REMOVES CANADA
PIN FROM HARPER'S LAPEL.

UNIDENTIFIED FIGURE BEHIND HARPER'S
SEAT GIVES IT A BIG KICK AND SENDS
HARPER OUT OF FRAME.

MANSBRIDGE LAUGHING AS THE
CANDIDATE TAKES INTERVIEWEE'S SEAT.

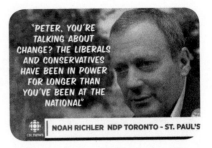

"PETER, YOU'RE TALKING ABOUT CHANGE? THE LIBERALS AND CONSERVATIVES HAVE BEEN IN POWER FOR LONGER THAN YOU'VE BEEN AT THE NATIONAL"

NOAH RICHLER NDP TORONTO - ST. PAUL'S

THE CANDIDATE ANSWERS QUESTIONS
IN PLACE OF HARPER.

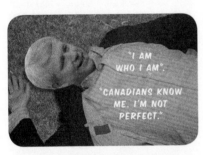

"I AM WHO I AM".

"CANADIANS KNOW ME. I'M NOT PERFECT."

HARPER SPEAKS FROM POSITION
LYING ON GROUND.

"OH, PLEASE."

"IF HE WERE MY INVESTMENT MANAGER, I'D FIRE HIM."

"HE'S PUT ALL OUR RESOURCES IN STOCK AND IT'S TANKED."

THE CANDIDATE DISMISSES HARPER AND
HIS ECONOMICS.

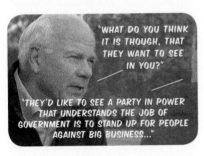

"WHAT DO YOU THINK IT IS THOUGH, THAT THEY WANT TO SEE IN YOU?"

"THEY'D LIKE TO SEE A PARTY IN POWER THAT UNDERSTANDS THE JOB OF GOVERNMENT IS TO STAND UP FOR PEOPLE AGAINST BIG BUSINESS..."

MANSBRIDGE AND THE
CANDIDATE CONTINUE.

"...AND NOT THE OTHER WAY ROUND. THEY WANT A PARTY THAT DOESN'T THINK THE ENVIRONMENTALLY CONCERNED ARE ECO-TERRORISTS, THAT FIRST NATIONS ARE TROUBLE...."

CANDIDATE ATTACHES HARPER'S CANADA
PIN TO HIS LAPEL.

HIDDEN HARPER RISES BEHIND MANSBRIDGE AND THREATENS CANDIDATE, THEN DISAPPEARS AS CANDIDATE CONTINUES TO SPEAK.

"...CAROLYN BENNETT VOTED FOR BILL C-51... AND STRONGLY SUPPORTS IT EVEN NOW. BUT YOU KNOW, SHE'S BEEN THE LIBERAL MP IN MY RIDING FOR 18 YEARS AND HER WEBSITE SAYS 'VOTE FOR REAL CHANGE.' I TAKE THAT TO MEAN VOTE FOR THE NDP. VOTE FOR TOM MULCAIR. VOTE FOR ME."

HARPER NODS HIS AGREEMENT FROM GROUND.

THE CANDIDATE LOOKS AT PROSTRATE HARPER AND THEN AT MANSBRIDGE, BAFFLED.

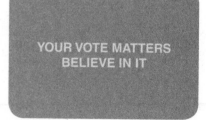

ALTERED CAPTION BEFORE CREDITS.

CHAPTER SIX

AT'S MY SEAT!" (NOT)

What does mood put into play? What does mood *invite*? Does mood determine fortune, or does a person's lot come down to chance?

In my late teens, unsure about university or the proper life course to follow, I'd made a chunk of money working a seismic job in Saskatchewan, Manitoba and Alberta. I decided to travel the world for a while, a less automatic decision then. In hostels and cheap hotels, there was the usual assortment of peculiar strangers: the Vietnam vet that leapt up from the bunk below mine and almost threw me to the floor because the clicking of my ballpoint pen (I was writing a letter) reminded him of grenades and triggers and brought on his PTSD; or the Canadian with the cinnamon-coloured pock-marked skin who was a disciple of Jim Jones and heading to Guyana, where, somebody told me, he really did "drink the Kool-Aid." On the road, I was learning the first lesson of travel, which is that you make your own chances as you go along. It is up to oneself to be sufficiently open to the world to let it in, or sufficiently guarded to keep it at bay. In the hostel in Rangoon, among the tattered paperbacks that travellers exchanged, was a copy of Joseph Heller's *Catch-22*, a novel that enthralled me. In its concluding chapter, the airman Yossarian takes a surrealistic walk through a grim, Dante-esque Rome, all the horrors that the war has put him through finding body in the shadows. It was an unforgettable literary experience and instructive to the eager young traveller, me. I realized that on days when I was in a bad mood, bad things were likely to happen; when I was in a good mood, good things did. "Cheap Charlie," the Vietnam vet, shrugged when the kid on the top bunk, wanting to calm him down, told him this. "Maybe, maybe not," said Charlie. "Everything happens all the time, it's just up to you to notice."

Be the butterfly. *Take a chance.*

. . .

It is the Thanksgiving weekend and the interval before the third period, the Liberals coming on strong and the NDP playing stoically but making the classic mistake of defending an early lead; scared of losing, forgetting how to win. Such was the cocoon my campaign lived inside that now, writing only months later, I do not remember having written we were about to lose, and badly. But this does not surprise me, because I know—any candidate knows—that it's not at all contradictory for me to have told my team a crushing Liberal victory was imminent while not heeding these words myself. How was I going to lead if I did not believe we could win? And it was also my duty to let the team understand how extraordinary their work was—how original, *how much fun.*

We hadn't been the only ones using videos to spread our message (and a little enjoyment). Scott Wyatt, an independent candidate for the B.C. riding of Mission—Matsqui—Fraser Canyon, had been first out the gates with a superbly entertaining video, "I'm Running for Parliament," in which the fella rides in on the back of a goose—a good Canadian—before slaying dinosaurs and aliens in the defence of his pro-Indigenous and socially progressive program. (The video was reported on internationally, all credit to him.) Other NDP candidates I did not meet were buoying their colleagues across the country with equally imaginative efforts. Matt Masters Burgener, running against the prime minister in the riding of Calgary Heritage, produced an artful video using a series of placards, revealed in order and then the reverse, to transform a dire political message into a hopeful one, a sweet turn that, like our Trudeau video, went viral. Jagmeet Singh, the provincial NDP MPP for the Ontario riding of Bramalea—Gore—Malton and provincial deputy leader, had also been an inspiration. The video of the handsome bearded Sikh cycling though his riding in shorts with a bright NDP orange turban and leading a posse of volunteers on bicycles during the 2011 campaign was a moving tribute to the late Jack Layton (an avid cyclist) that makes me happy when I think of it even now. The marvellous youth pack from Harbaljit Singh Kahlon's riding of Brampton East, wearing campaign T-shirts with a sweet caricature of the candidate, could only make onlookers smile. Their appearance together at an early NDP event is one of the best memories I have of any of the contrived meetings that are "rallies" and "town halls."

I do not doubt that other campaigns, across the barricades, found equivalent ways to motivate their own and perhaps to convert others, though in truth I have my doubts that any of the videos changed anyone's mind. Cognitive consonance and dissonance are not solely qualities of the Internet; they are merely amplified there. But I have a suspicion that in the NDP's grassroots derivation—for all its occasional failings (the parsimony, the aversion to the flashy, the inclusion of narrowly held views)—there is a freedom of expression that more than compensates for the ad agencies and focus groups and technologies barebones

campaigns cannot afford. I loved my team: its efficiencies, its failings, its idiosyncracies, its appetites. The Bathurst Street office
was not just a green room, it was the set of our very own made-
in-Canada hit show, and I am sure the feeling was the same in
the other 1,791 shows running concurrently across the land. Not
just the NDP but *all* of us were "in this together"—and what was
"this" but a dedication to the practice of the bigger idea?

Democracy: my bunch; the kids across St. Clair in their red
T-shirts—they, we, were doing it. "Democracy" is a big word,
lofty and sonorous, travestied and maligned a lot of the time too,
but that's what this was, in all the inveterate practices—the
knocking on doors, the "postal walks"—and in the new customs,
too. Of 1,792 candidates, 1,454 of us were bound to be "losers," but
who had time to think about that? There was work to do.

. . .

Doug and Nick had found good footage for the substantive
videos, transforming them into short, neat sermons for a better
Canada that please me still. I have more than twenty-five years'
studio experience and this crew was top-notch: capable of swift
and last-minute changes, no problem with instruction, inventive
with our limited means. Our net outlay for "The Escalator
Works," "That's My Seat!" and seven of the substantive videos
had been in the region of $115 ($100 for software and $15 for a red
Staples button). Nick's editing wizardry had been the glue.

The substantive videos had Bill C-51, the environment, the
muzzling of scientists, the integrity of Parliament, "barbaric cultural
practices," the new Conservative (and much ridiculed) category of
"Old Stock" Canadians, strategic voting and the demonization of
immigrants for subjects. We were sticking to our plan to release the
majority of these videos at regular intervals between the launches

of "The Escalator Works," on September 24, the revised version of "That's My Seat!" in the penultimate week and the remaining others in the election's waning days. None of the substantive videos had garnered more than several thousand views, though none were expected to have performed better than that. Each video ended with my asking the viewer to "vote for Tom Mulcair's NDP and, in Toronto—St. Paul's for me, Noah Richler," with the "Candidate" logo and then the message "Spread the Word" following, but the slogan was replaced with "Your Vote Matters" once the spectre of strategic voting was clouding the horizon irrefutably.

The further purpose of the videos with less viral potential was to keep the campaign feed live and varied and provide the Toronto—St. Paul's team a boost of morale despite their lesser traction. The video addressing the environment was pleasing for the quality of its images, even after the demand that we remove an offending frame of an oil sands project seen from the air was satisfied. The video attacking Bill C-51 containing the charge that Bennett "not only supported Bill C-51, she's still a strong and vocal supporter of the law even now" did so over images of police confronting a First Nations demonstration—this synchronicity a discreet, even under-handed jab at the contradiction of my Liberal rival's support of Aboriginal causes and the excessive security bill. The video con-demning the xenophobic intent of the "barbaric cultural practices" snitch line referred to "Stephen Harper, Chris Alexander and their hired hand, the Australian merchant of hatred and division, Lynton Crosby," but edits dictated from the street as I was canvassing led to a second "Barbaric Cultural Practices" video (that we'd impro-vised from existing tape) landing us in a spot of trouble. The latter version denounced Conservative MP Joyce Bateman's reading out a list of supposedly anti-Israel Liberal MPs to a Winnipeg South Centre audience "as if we were living in East Germany under Stasi operators," an image of Erich Honecker preceding one of

Harper under my voiceover saying, "Harper joins a rich tradition of shameful politicians using the cloak of prejudice as they pretend to look out for our safety." The photograph of the prime minister showed him frowning unpleasantly, as damaging to the idea of a sympathetic prime minister as the stock photograph of a bearded Mulcair angrily remonstrating in the House had been to the idea of a warm and cuddly NDP leader. Any choice of images can be so fantastically prejudicial as to constitute a cartoon, and our team indulged in a bit of this—the message was stronger for it—though the juxtaposition of Honecker's image with Harper's pushed the video beyond the bounds of acceptable taste (even during an election) and my campaign management team disabled it until the photograph of the East German leader was removed.

noahrichler

7.53 a.m.

Hi Janet. I am upset that you would go behind my back to Ethan to make an important decision without informing me, but I shall get over that. The important thing is that it was a good decision.

janetsolberg48

9.07 a.m.

Noah, I wanted to take it down quickly so that we could think about it some more. I did it in a mood of caution. The last thing you need or Tom needs is more media distractions.

OCTOBER 11

CPC	NDP	LPC	BQ	GRN	OTH
31.7%	23.4%	34.2%	5.0%	4.8%	1.0%

· · ·

Nerves were frayed ahead of the launch of the Harper video—the one that excited us most. We'd been cautious and tactical in our negotiations with the central office, conceding some ground to help ensure the release of "That's My Seat!" Twice, we'd amended the images. We removed the prostrate Harper from the background of my conversation with Peter Mansbridge and diminished the force of my kick sending the prime minister flying out of his seat—instead having Harper appear behind Mansbridge with the threatening words "I'm on to you, Richler," a clear reference to Bill C-51. But we'd needed no coaching when it came to ensuring that the video did not breach clause 29 of Canada's Copyright Act and constituted "fair dealing for the purpose of ... parody or satire." Lest anyone confuse our satirical piece with a genuine news broadcast, we'd altered the CBC logo at the beginning of the video just as the CBC's own long-running prime-time comedy show *This Hour Has 22 Minutes* does when it lampoons real products and institutions. (*The Mercer Report* would do its own spoof of the Trudeau advertisement later on.) I'd worked for the BBC, the CBC and newspapers and magazines in which the prospect of legal proceedings such as copyright or defamation suits needed to be taken very seriously and we were never about to proceed without a bona fide legal case and the NDP's clear and unambiguous go-ahead to run the video. This we acquired from the NDP's director of media, George Soule, on October 12. "That's My Seat!" was to be the apogee of the innovative side of our campaign and the last original push that we would realistically be able to make. We launched it on the thirteenth, the same day as the Arts Forum we'd hastily arranged at the Tarragon Theatre—six days before E-Day.

By this point in the campaign our primary objective had been reduced to showing a dignified face—that, whatever the electoral outcome, ours remained, as it always had been, a thoughtful, plausible alternative to the status quo. The Arts Forum, with the slogan "Send a Writer to Parliament," was a part of this last push. We'd learned from Mulcair's failed arts announcement that few even in the media attached much importance to a sector in which the party had shown next to no interest historically. But there would always be a next time, for someone else if not me, and the Arts Forum rounded out the set of conversations we'd treated in the videos and entertained at the door.

We were gathered in the same upstairs rehearsal room where my nomination as candidate had been approved, the panel for the evening preceded by the Métis opera singer Joanna Burt, who'd appeared at the Wychwood Pub evening the week before. Sandra Cunningham, the film producer on my team and erstwhile chair of the Canadian Media Production Association; Denise Donlon, formerly the president of Sony Music Canada and executive director of CBC Radio's English Language Services; Richard Rose, the artistic director of the Tarragon Theatre; and Matt Williams, the vice-president of the House of Anansi Press and president of the Canadian Publishing Association, discussed challenges to Canadian arts producers and my suggestion that allotments of money did not in themselves constitute arts "policy." Denise Donlon argued that when it comes to culture, "we punch above our weight," pointing out that most Canadians celebrated internationally are artists. It was time, she said, for the government to take steps for Canada to be thought of as an "arts nation," rather than simply for its resources or military and sports successes. Richard Rose wished for a prime minister able to talk about culture in a manner connecting Canadians across a plethora of issues. Sound points of view also emanated from the audience. Shannon Litzenberger said that a new federal government needed to understand—as Quebec's already did—that any decision it makes has a cultural aspect; to elevate the status of "culture" in government, cultural principles needed to be embedded in all departments. Jack Blum, the executive director of Reel Canada, an educational program touring Canadian films to schools, spoke of the importance of a cultural component in the syllabus of a film legacy of which students would otherwise be unaware. "We're desperate," he said, "for ways to celebrate our Canadian-ness." If a single concern dominated, it was that supporting artistic activity, whatever its nature, was not simply a matter of grants towards production, but of distribution and awareness across platforms and sectors of society.

And if there was hesitation in my presentation—I chaired the panel—it was an indication of how it was becoming that much harder to be blithe about the swelling Liberal tide. The rewards, now, were moral, these including a considered mention of the evening by Simon Houpt, senior media writer at *The Globe and Mail*. The notion that money was not in itself a policy, wrote Houpt, "could only seem radical within the narrow confines of an election campaign," but he was saying so in a respectful light: we had been taken seriously and an evening that was mostly symbolic in nature had not been wasted.

. . .

At the office, Doug was monitoring figures for the release of the Harper video on Facebook and YouTube and was ecstatic: its rate of viral spread was already exceeding that of "The Escalator Works," with more than sixty thousand views in less than twelve hours.

We were happy, despite the lesser number of gatekeepers pushing it. This was not entirely a surprise, as we probably exhausted a lot of journalists' and pundits' goodwill by sending out the substantive videos to the same bunch. Our bulletins, I expected, had come to resemble spam—how many of the NDP's own messages did I not bother opening, fed up with the battery of their number? The new, not the familiar, is what drives the viral.

And then, at four o'clock the next day, a courier arrived with a letter.

CBC ● Radio-Canada

Law Department
250 Front Street West
Toronto ON M5V 3G5

Sean Moreman
Senior Legal Counsel

Direct: 416 205-6494
Facsimile: 416 205-2723
sean.moreman@cbc.ca

<u>**"WITHOUT PREJUDICE"**</u>

October 13, 2015
New Democratic Party of Canada
300- 279 Laurier West
Ottawa, Ontario K1P 5J9

Via email: rebeccablaikie@ndp.ca
carlgrenier@me.com
anne.mcgrath@ndp.ca

To Whom It May Concern:

RE: **Canadian Broadcasting Corporation – Copyright Violation**

This letter is on behalf of the Canadian Broadcasting Corporation ("CBC") and concerns the unauthorized use by your organization of copyright-protected CBC material. We ask you to cease and desist from using such material immediately. Should you fail to do so, the CBC intends to take appropriate proceedings to determine the issue in a court of law.

The CBC material is being used in a video prepared and published for partisan purposes that serve to cast the CBC and its employees as participants in the political process rather than independent journalists covering it. This strikes at the core of the CBC's mandate and represents an infringement of the CBC's copyright that exceeds any fair dealing exemption and breaches the moral rights of the CBC employees involved, both performer and producer, by strategic editing and using their work in association with your institutions and their political causes.

For clarity, the video in question is posted on YouTube at the following link: https://www.youtube.com/watch?t=4&v=ayJA0IClab4

In the video, NDP candidate Noah Richler uses extensive portions of an interview conducted between Peter Mansbridge and Stephen Harper that was originally aired on CBC. Not only is the original interview the copyrighted work of CBC, but Mr. Richler has modified the video in such a way as to bring the work of Mr. Mansbridge into disrepute.

Breach of Copyright

In the CBC's view, the use of its material represents the copying of a substantial part of the broadcast in question. This is not simply a quantitative measure but also a qualitative one, and the inclusion of the host in the excerpts used represents an important qualitative element. Further, none of the specific exemptions for fair dealing under ss. 29, 29.1 and 29.2 of the *Copyright Act* (the "Act") applies in the circumstances.

In any event, the use made of CBC's material cannot be characterized as fair in view of the nature and purpose of the use and its impact on the CBC's position as Canada's public broadcaster and its need to be perceived as independent, non-partisan and trustworthy, particularly during the period leading up to an election. It is a critical source of news and information throughout the country, seeking to inform and enlighten, in accordance with is mandate under the *Broadcasting Act*. The jeopardy caused to this critical role is what has prompted the CBC to act and send this letter.

The effect of the mocking tone of the video diminishes the public's perception of the CBC as reliable and trustworthy source of news and information. This represents an effect that is well beyond any commercial impact and causes risk to the CBC's fundamental role in the broadcasting system and Canadian democratic life.

Breach of Moral Rights

Using the video in the manner that it has been edited violates the moral rights of the producer and performer of the affected CBC programs. The satirization of the original interview diminishes the importance of political reporting during an election period, and casts these individuals in a light that is damaging to their reputations for independent, non-partisan journalism. Their reputations have been prejudiced through this editing and the use of their work in association with the partisan causes and institutions your organizations represent.

As a result, we demand that this, and any other similar video that has not yet come to our attention, be removed from public view immediately.

We look forward to your confirmation of compliance.

Yours truly,

Sean A. Moreman, LL.B., LL.L.
Senior Legal Counsel

SM/

. . .

It was remarkable to me that the CBC and not the CPC was the institution complaining, though the call from the public broadcaster's law department to cease and desist was nothing if not anticipated—and exactly what I'd alerted the NDP it should be prepared to refute.

Point by point, the letter was easy to challenge. The allegation that the video "cast the CBC and its employees as participants in the political process rather than independent journalists covering it" was, frankly, outrageous and grasping, and also condescending to viewers. Beyond the circling of the wagons that had been the hallmark, for so long, of an institution conducting itself as if under siege (it had been), the letter suggested a disconnect with a type of televisual satire prevalent not only in contemporary broadcasting. It exists in the CBC's own programs—such as *The Mercer Report* and *This Hour Has 22 Minutes* (and the woefully unsuccessful *Punchline* website)—and is common on U.K. and American talk shows, including ones our editor Nick DenBoer had worked for (Conan O'Brien) and others he was subsequently sought out by (*VICE*). A manipulation of the real and the insertion of words into public figures' mouths are stock techniques of cartoons on the editorial pages of newspapers; of institutions as august as *The New Yorker*; of innumerable viral videos; bits of crowd-generated artistry; and an array of online magazines such as Canada's *Beaverton*. And, as described, we had also taken deliberate steps, such as the wash of orange in the opening frame (and also in the ultimate frames identifying each video as the work of the Toronto—St. Paul's riding "paid for and approved by the Official Agent"), to differentiate our product from CBC news broadcasts and identify the video as parody: preliminary grounds for "fair dealing" in Canada's Copyright Act, subject to the material satisfying the legislation's six-part test. (The six factors governing assessment of whether unauthorized use of material constitutes "fair dealing" take into account the purpose, character, amount and nature and effect of the re-use, as well as the "nature" of its subsequent dissemination and whether reasonable alternatives exist that, in lieu, would satisfy the consumer.)

The charge that we had used "extensive portions" of the Harper–Mansbridge interview representing the "copying of a substantial part" of the broadcast was easily denied on a simple mathematical basis: we had used, *in toto*, twenty-four seconds of the original interview's eighteen minutes, amounting to 2.2 percent and, while not stipulated in the Act, below the threshold of 2.5 percent that Canada's Copyright Board has deemed insubstantial vis-à-vis written works. Beyond purposes of parody or satire, the Copyright Act also specifically allows for the re-forming of unlicenced material towards an educational or non-commercial purpose, our video satisfying at least the latter requirement.

But, as in so many legal measures that are bound never to reach court, intimidation and not reason was apparently the purpose of the letter. The suggestion that "the mocking tone of the video diminishes the public's perception of the CBC as reliable [*sic*] and trustworthy source of news and information" with "an effect that is well beyond any commercial impact and causes risk to the CBC's fundamental role in the broadcasting system and Canadian democratic life" caused, in the first instance, hilarity—flattering as it may have been to think that the little roaring mouse of our video was detrimental to the CBC's reputation. What, to our minds, the pomp of the letter really showed was just how defensive was the conduct of the CBC, injured by years of budget cuts and then a suite of embarrassing episodes concerning several of its prime-time personalities, including Jian Ghomeshi, Amanda Lang and Evan Solomon. One of the last remaining personalities in the CBC stable to have retained their sort of heft was, of course, Mansbridge.

None of this escaped us, but, had we not received the message the first time, a slightly different letter was delivered to the Bathurst Street office from the CBC's external counsel, Brian MacLeod Rogers, alleging, more pithily, "the unauthorized use of work of Mr. Mansbridge and his producer," and advising, "I am instructed to commence legal proceedings against you tomorrow in the event that all public access to the advertisement has not been blocked as of tonight."

Janet, well used to the social network–based troubles of the campaign by now, was walking around in the office with a battle-weary, more than a worried, face. Calls from head office were inevitable and, in preparation, I contacted Julian Porter Q.C., one of Canada's pre-eminent and most accomplished libel lawyers and a friend, to seek his opinion.

"I can see why the CBC is upset," said Porter, "but you're completely within your rights. Fight this—and use my name if you want to."

Porter's vindication was buoying at a difficult time. We were already accustomed to the incapacity of Mulcair's inner circle to alter course in the face of anything untoward, and what I was bracing for was another encounter with a cowed NDP core with little sense that activities at the base might filter upwards with positive effect.

. . .

Greta Levy, consistently the most supportive of my central party contacts, was the first to call.

"Did they send you the letter?"

"Sorry, Greta, you thought you'd have a few days off," I said.

"My thinking is they're trying to scare us. Look at Michael Geist's writing—he's the authority on this—you'll see they don't have grounds to stand on."

"I couldn't agree more," said Levy, "but it all comes down to pissing off the CBC."

"Are they your friends?"

"Definitely not," said Levy, laughing, "and now even less so."

"Exactly," I said. "What have they done for us?"

I pointed out I'd been the one who'd informed George Soule, and repeated the arguments I'd already made for the video's satisfaction of the requirements of "fair dealing" as defined by the Copyright Act. "It's *parody*," I said. "Nobody in their right mind believes I booted Harper up the ass and certainly nobody believes that Mansbridge is sitting there straight-faced as Harper comes up behind him. Do we also want to point out that *This Hour Has 22 Minutes*, which is their show, does these sorts of parodies all the time?"

"Whom would you go to for a counter-argument?" asked Janet.

"I don't think they're interested in a legal argument at all," said Levy. "I think they just want it taken down because they find it embarrassing to be played with and that's it. I don't think, substantively, they have a case here."

"So it's all about Mansbridge."

"Yeah. Absolutely."

"So if we just say no, sorry, how long does it take them to speak to Facebook, how long does it take them to talk to YouTube, how long does it take for them to get an injunction? We're talking four days till the election—how long does it take them to put that together?"

"Well, certainly not until after E-Day. My issue with all this is whether this hurts us in the next four days. If people at the CBC are concerned enough to send a letter, does that mean that there's a likelihood this could impact the coverage they're giving us?"

We'd already learned of the CBC's releasing Dan Lauzon, its director of strategic communications and planning, to work in the Liberal war room on sabbatical—this not for the first time; he'd done the same for Liberal Party leader Michael Ignatieff back in 2011—and I suggested to Levy that the relationship did not speak of an organization that was "independent, non-partisan and trustworthy" and suggested a little needling apropos of this fact, but Levy would have none of it.

"This has been my bread and butter for the last three years," said Levy. "I know this stuff, I breathe it and sleep it and very much *nightmare* it, but it's irrelevant because it's picking fights with people who buy ink by the ink barrel. We don't have the power they do. You saw it very clearly at the arts announcement a week and a half ago. You'd think that the CBC, of all broadcasters, would have covered the arts announcement in depth, but they'll cover the news they want. The idea that you're going to somehow convince them of the folly of their ways—it's just not going to happen."

"So Greta," said Janet, "what it boils down to—I'm not being sarcastic here—is, 'We're right, there's nothing that we've done wrong here in Toronto—St. Paul's, but you're worried about the impact it will have on CBC coverage for Tom.' Is that what you're saying?"

"Yeah," said Levy.

"That's the whole thing."

"Yeah."

"And how do you think the video will affect it?" asked Janet. "How's their coverage been?"

"Do I want it to be any worse? Look, I'm with you on this. I don't like the idea of being bullied, I don't like the idea of a silly form letter not even tailored to your video—so much language in there that was laughable. I totally agree."

"What," said Janet, "if we don't respond right away and say we're thinking about it, we're getting a legal opinion?"

"Let them wait for a day," I said. "You don't have to answer this today—we're all busy, we're campaigning and nothing much is going to happen during the ball game—it's the Division final—and that's another reason not to answer their letter right away. If you wait till tomorrow morning, then you send a letter saying we're a little confused: we've used twenty-two seconds of Peter Mansbridge—that's 2.2 percent of his interview and well below the legal threshold—and it's clearly parody, which excepts it, and we endeavoured to make clear with the altering of the CBC logo right at the top, should anybody be in doubt. Please clarify your position, we're eager to be able to co-operate, we're just a bit baffled. That's two days gone and it's the weekend. As it is, the video will probably have plateaued in a day and had its effect."

"Are there other people you need to consult?" asked Janet.

"Always," said Levy. "How could you tell?"

. . .

An hour later, Pratt called—mock laughter as he spoke.

"We're on speaker phone?"

"Yes."

"Noah, I love you. I love you so much and I cannot wait for us to get drunk and go fight cops together when this is done, but you have to take your video down."

"Do you know who Julian Porter is?" I asked.

"*Nooooo*," said Pratt, like he wanted this to be easy and could see it would not be.

"He's the top libel lawyer in the country and he says, 'Fuck 'em, they have no grounds.'"

"I'm sure he's right," said Pratt, still laughing like he was my best buddy. "But it's a distraction from the campaign and my bosses are telling me to deliver this message."

"Who's going to give a shit?" said Janet. "What if we told the CBC we're pursuing a legal opinion and let it go for another day?"

Pratt sighed. "What does it gain?"

"Another forty to fifty thousand views, even if you delayed till tomorrow afternoon," I said. "If you don't respond, or respond slowly, that's the benefit—and more for you than to me."

"It's hard to imagine the CBC will be getting their knickers in a twist so much that it'll have an effect on Tom," said Janet. "You think they'll raise it in a question with him?"

"No," said Pratt. "But in the last days of the campaign there's very little room to craft a final message. I'm sympathetic, it's just nowhere in our frame."

"But James," I said, "I asked Julian about legal proceedings and he said it would take them months."

"Yeah, yeah, I know all that but there's no point in making enemies for this."

"But there's no way they're going to send an email or a circular to their own room to say, 'Pay less attention to the NDP,' they're just not going to do that."

"Noah, they wouldn't be that overt, but we're in a battle with these guys as it is and it's a distraction. The national director has had to deal with it, we have our lawyer having to review it, and now I'm involved."

"I've got you the best lawyer in the country, *pro bono*," I said.

"This isn't our fight."

"So just don't fight it."

Pratt laughed again.

"I'm serious. Don't fight it."

"James," said Janet, "the problem with you delivering this message—I can hear it in your voice—is that you don't give a fuck and you're doing what you've been told."

Well, this was something—Janet, the veteran of so many campaigns, the person who'd had to play defence on so many of our social network headaches, not backing down in the ninth.

"I appreciate you being a good soldier," she said, "but it doesn't make sense to us here. We're running it through our lawyers and we don't see any breach. The ball game is on and soon it's the weekend, so what the hell—"

"Why don't I write a letter," I said. "You can vet it and I'll send it."

The phone was quiet for a moment, Pratt outside or in a car somewhere. Then, the laughter gone, he said, "I'm ushering resources to all of the places I think we can win and we can hang on to. I'm laser-focused and I've stopped doing that because this is now an issue. Do you understand what I'm saying?"

Now it was my turn to be silent, and neither did Janet speak.

The silence went on—five, ten seconds.

"That was the sound of a rug being pulled," I said.

. . .

I left the office, no explanation necessary. The NDP brass had left us in the lurch for the sake of the bigger game—fair enough (it would have taken the miraculous for the riding to swing), but nevertheless, the abandonment sat uncomfortably in the gut. As a reporter at the *National Post*, I'd been co-defendant in a multi-million-dollar libel lawsuit, and at the BBC I'd needed to be mindful of "actionable" consequences of my work all the time. With both these institutions, just as I had done with the NDP central office regarding "That's My Seat!," I would "refer upwards" to discuss the possibility of a legal challenge and my defence, should occasion have required it. And, with both these other institutions, from the moment higher-ups provided consent, I knew I'd be defended to the wall—as, indeed, the *National Post* had done even though I was no longer an employee of theirs. It was a matter of integrity: word had been given. Yes, the NDP were lousy soldiers that brought to mind, through sheer force of the opposite, words spoken to me by the radio journalist I'd worked with in Haiti, in 1990, when the Tonton Macoutes were still lurking in the shadows of backstreets: "There's no one I'd rather go down the alley with," said my pal.

The NDP were nobody to go down the alley with.

I crossed St. Clair Avenue and went to the Wychwood Pub for a drink. The bar was packed for the ball game, but Reza was at the door and I could see in his face that he recognized I needed succour and without a word he ushered me through. On the screens overhead, the Toronto Blue Jays were staging a remarkable come-from-behind 6–3 victory to win the American League East over the Texas Rangers, who were suddenly bumbling the ball in all sorts of ways. I wrote the office to say that I was "watching another team make several unforced errors to lose the game."

Porter emailed, "Let people know about the issue, it's important." I'd kept Doug and Nick in the loop and they were offering to leak the video link to Gawker and across social media ("We were just trying to be funny. You be the judge"), but all I could think of were all the volunteers coming out to work for the campaign because Canada was the thing they believed in and they thought finally the NDP had a fair chance. I did not want a single member of my team to think I was grandstanding in any way, and so it was clear to me already that I'd comply. Doug and Young

Ethan were headed to the Sankofa bar, on the Little Jamaica stretch of Eglinton Avenue in the far northwest of the riding, for the last of the pub nights we were holding. I told them to bring their computers and that—

> The CBC is threatening to sue, no surprise, and the NDP is caving, perhaps that's not a surprise either. We're going to take the high road, but with a little pit stop. I have agreed to take the video down "tonight," as asked. We shall do so at 2359h but not before.

We were going to milk the video as much as possible in the hours that remained, stunned not that our ad was being challenged, but that it was the CBC and not the CPC doing as much. Doug and Ethan were already reposting it on YouTube and Facebook with the message,

> LAST CHANCE TO SEE! Hilarious @noahrichler video "That's My Seat" to come down at midnight tonight!

—and Ethan was under instruction to spend campaign dollars to boost the video "to the max" (which was costing us tens of dollars, not more). It was clear the party was in a calamitous, failing state and running about for swords to fall upon, long ago having reneged on any way of being bold. It had proved, in its disastrous adherence to balanced budgets, in its inadequate response to the Syrian refugee crisis and the arts announcement—in its sidelining of Linda McQuaig and in the "apologies" I'd been compelled to make—that it had little idea how to respond to its own people, let alone the machinations of other parties. There were far, far weightier and more pivotal moments in the NDP's undoing than my team's pulled video but, nevertheless, the incident was instructive.

At one minute to midnight we took the video down, as promised. Sankofa, we always knew, was going to be a fundraising bust, but building the money chest had never been the intention. The point had been to show a presence in a part of the riding that was traditionally Liberal and in which Bennett and her organizers hardly, if ever, showed, and now it was also to fete the staff. I'd canvassed the south side of the street with various members of the team several times (the north side was a part of Eglinton—Lawrence), bantering with small family business owners whose fierce loyalty to the Liberals was derived from Trudeau the father having been prime minister during the sixties, years in which many families in the area had arrived. This area made me happy—the tailors and haberdashers, the home food restaurants and the roti shops a brisk trade, the dozen or so barbershops filled even on a Sunday, whole families seated in chairs waiting. As barbers brought electric razors to their clients watching the white guy at the back in the mirror, I chatted from behind the chair, wanting the Little Jamaica voters to know that I respected the roots of their loyalty very much—but also that it was time for authentic change, now. I'd talk about Enoch Powell, the English Conservative MP and classical scholar who, on April 20, 1968, had warned of "rivers of blood" washing over the United Kingdom should immigration as it was continue—on the very same day that Pierre Elliott Trudeau became prime minister, still one of my favourite political coincidences. I'd ask how much this fact had to do with their emigration to Canada. I'd talk about Diefenbaker, who, not generally credited, had actually been the prime minister to open the gates when, in 1962, he'd removed race and country of origin as categories for the extant Canadian immigration points system. And then I'd ask if Bennett had been in lately.

"Who?"

"Bennett. Carolyn Bennett. She's been your MP for eighteen years."

It was a ploy and a play, the conversation more about sport than knocking my rivals—more about letting it be known the passing of decades demanded at least a review of long-held habits. I was enjoying the exchanges—the chats in the stores, the back and forth with men and women, a good many of them unemployed, hanging about the street benches (the woman who took one of my corrugated laminated cardboard store window signs, not flyers, and rolled it up and put it in her purse, no mean feat of strength). We weren't going to win, being there was the point, and by the time the Sankofa pub night came to pass, celebrating the campaign without the ignominy of the impending result was as much our raison d'être as anything. Denise Jones, a powerhouse producer of Caribbean entertainment and a firebrand I did not yet know, seized the microphone to deliver an impromptu, fiery tirade on the NDP's behalf and stuck around to entertain. A preacher spoke, a rapping poet, too. Mike Garrick and the Posse played out their reggae hearts.

OCTOBER 15

CPC	NDP	LPC	BQ	GRN	OTH
31.1%	23.6%	35.7%	4.7%	4.1%	0.8%

. . .

"You're not running to be leader," Sarah said on the long way home.

"I'm not trying to."

"That's not the way it looks."

She was delivering a variation on the familiar "that's not your job" message she was used to delivering when I try to fix the plumbing, or shift the carry-on of airline passengers with nothing under the seat in front of them and using half an overhead locker to store their coats while others have no place to put their bags.

"Stop trying to do someone else's job," said Sarah. "Stop trying to do Mulcair's."

. . .

Janet has told Phil, out of the office at the time, about the canning of the video and he calls the next morning. Phil's from a Catholic working-class family out of St. Catharine's, eight kids in the brood. He'd thought about joining the armed forces for a while, but events pushed him to politics and speechwriting. He likes the slight seclusion of the desk at the back and the shield it provides him from people when he needs it. Social media he cannot abide; he can handle email, though it's not a bad idea to give him a heads-up if you send one. And though he doesn't mind cellphones he's not the world's most communicative fella, so the call I get from him is affecting and a surprise.

"I've worked in central between elections," says Phil, "and part of your job when you're dealing with people in communities and ridings and you're confronted by questions like your video raises is to think it through, and what's going to happen if it's done—who will object, how will we benefit. Surely to Christ they knew the CBC was going to mouth off about it. They should have thought, 'Okay, so when they do, what are we going to do?'—and they should have told them to go pound salt. I'm sorry I wasn't there, Noah, I would have said, 'You know what? We knew this could happen. We told you, if it goes pie-shaped, your problem not ours, good luck.'"

"I talked about it with Janet," I said. "They're pretty stressed up there."

"Yeah, that's true, but I heard what Pratt said to you about ridings that can win and it was rude and inappropriate. But, anyways, people under stress sometimes forget their manners, so I suppose we have to forgive them. He knows his day is coming anyway."

We lapse into asides about the upcoming schools appearances—at Upper Canada College and, this morning, the Bishop Strachan School for girls. I can hear the concern in Phil's voice. It's for me. It is as close as the strongman will get to being emotional, and I appreciate that.

. . .

Everything seems slightly plaintive now. I am losing the stomach to fight, and I wander over to the glassed-in shelves in the foyer of the Bishop Strachan School, with its various plaques and the blue helmet of a UN peacekeeper. I am losing the will even to resent privilege, though I'm not sure how much sense that ever made, anyway—especially here. Our audience is endowed, certainly, but they are children. Marnie MacDougall actually deigns to appear this time, which is not a great surprise as she and Bennett were schoolchildren at Havergal College, one of Toronto's rival private schools for girls, and the turf is kindred.

. . .

"It's what I call the 'St. Paul's model,'" the Liberal candidate on a roll says for the umpteenth time. *Wait for it.* The first time, at Holy Blossom Temple, it was "my job," and you couldn't believe that she'd said it and that you'd missed the moment to crush her. And now here she is, about to throw out the same party platitudes in a big jumble, and you're beginning to wonder if she's losing it, that maybe she made a deal to run one last time, but you're mindful that interrupting may seem rude, so you don't.

Now the old head girl sounds like the Queen. Can't help it. Bennett's voice has jumped an octave as she declares, with a great big Royal O, that "*Every four years, One has to apply for One's job.*" No, it's *the* job, I want to say, but I let it go. The sea of girls' faces is adoring, and the chapel of BSS with its oak benches and panelled walls says this is Carolyn and Marnie's territory and not mine. Do they buy their wood polish wholesale? I wonder.

. . .

Politics, I am realizing late in the game, is a lot like writing. You toss ideas into the pond of our communal consciousness and they ripple outwards and have their own life. The winners brand those ideas for the good of themselves and the party. Losers take private comfort that the ideas were once theirs and watch as others take credit, because hanging on to them for advantage is selfish. If the public good is why you're in the game, then that's what you do, you toss your ideas in and see how they fare. The aim is to make things better for society, not you. If there is a moment during the waning campaign in which I am experiencing an epiphany, it is now.

"The national chief of the Assembly of First Nations should be made a de facto member of cabinet," I suggest, pointing out that technically a minister needs neither to be a sitting MP nor a senator to be appointed to that role, and that doing so would move the relationship of settler and Indigenous Canadians away from one of atonement and reconciliation, necessary as that is, towards more meaningful participation in a shared future.

In effect, I have taken Kevin Farmer's cue: it is my job to nominate ideas for others with the means to debate and implement, and a part of me, a growing part, has decided that saying this in front of Bennett is the best chance for the idea to be aired in cabinet, where it won't be me who's minister. I could sell the idea as a column, make three hundred dollars, but that would mean talking to the *Toronto Star* again. Fuck it.

Afterwards, Bennett approaches me excitedly. "I've always thought that the governor general should be Native," she says. "It's a ceremonial post!"

"But ceremony is what I'm trying to get beyond," I say, too late. The schoolgirls have her attention now, and I head for the door but am cut off by a geeky duo.

"What's the NDP's position on prostitution?" the taller girl asks.

She thinks she's being bold, and reminds me of Sandy Stranger, the savviest of Muriel Spark's Brodie's girls, before I put that iffy association to rest.

"Well," I say, "I can't tell you what Tom's is, but mine is that we should be doing everything we can to make the conditions of sex workers safe. Of course no one should be in the business against their will, but antiquated attitudes to sex work and pushing the trade into back alleys only does harm. And we must face up to the fact that some sex workers ply their trade out of choice."

"Thanks, that's what I wanted to hear!" says the girl, and the pair scurries off. Bennett, meanwhile, is surrounded by a fawning BSS scrum and I am reminded of more writerly wisdom gleaned from all the literary readings I've done at which perhaps half a dozen approach me with books to be signed, the line of a hundred at the famous writer's table impossible to ignore. The trick, I know by now, is not to sit down and *look* like a loser—idle, waiting, stuck—but to be free and standing and moving. If you see someone with your book, then approach them rather than the other way around. And if no one has bought your book, or you've already chatted to the two or three that have, then *get out of there.*

I head for the car park, a quick debrief, and the office.

. . .

We're into the last stretch of the campaign and Doug pulls up a video of Trudeau making an announcement in Vancouver against a backdrop of supporters from an array of ethnic communities.

"Do you notice how you never see older guys in his crowd?" I say. "Trudeau only appeals to women and young people."

. . .

Janet has that look again.

You need to think ahead when you're managing a team. You put a face on for the exigencies of the day, for the folk who depend on you—and brace for what comes next: the debate, the panel, the scandal yet to come or, this week, the election night party and the job of sending folk home happy. *The morning after.* A coffee at the local is no longer consumed with thoughts about strategy. A beautiful woman passes and your mind wanders for a moment along with her. Your life is drifting back to normal.

"So you're thinking about after," says Janet.

She will look at me from this point on with the dreadful mixture of affection and sorrow I am subject to now. Less my boss, more like an anxious relative.

"You're okay?" she asks.

"I'm fine."

. . .

Things we did end up doing:
    Funky town halls
    A cartoon crew
    Fundraisers

Meet and greets
Videos
The Bicycle Gang

OCTOBER 17

CPC	NDP	LPC	BQ	GRN	OTH
31.1%	22.2%	36.5%	4.8%	4.5%	0.9%

. . .

So here we are.

It had been a relief to discover how much I enjoyed canvassing. I'd been worried I would not, which would have made my turn as a political candidate hell. Even for a fella who knows Canada and the city of Toronto well, knocking on doors had been an unusual, thoughtful exercise—sometimes amusing, sometimes heartbreaking, but always illuminating. The memories accumulating were ones of diversity, of people wanting to talk, and of the complexity of lives conveyed in a matter of minutes.

The wealth of the riding in which I chose to run continues to astonish me; I should have gathered as much from the surprise the NDP expressed at my decision and surmised that Toronto—St. Paul's was going to be—what's the word—a challenge.

And here it is again, in the diagonal of the Kay Gardiner ravine beltline trail in the north central part of the riding. This is the route Liz has plotted for the Saturday canvass of our Bicycle Gang, fifteen of us in "Vote NDP Noah Richler" T-shirts and me at the head of the line with the megaphone that Nick has lent me. Along both sides of the ravine trail are immense, secret backyards. They are the size of small parks, and they are invisible, as is the nature of Toronto, to people travelling at street level. This clandestine part of the city will have no truck with the NDP, finding the party only obnoxious as, purposefully, we are being today.

But it is Forest Hill that is bothering me most—the unassailability of so many of its Jews' intractable positions on Israel and Palestine. How many, I wonder, have read the late, brilliant Barbadian-Canadian author Austin Clarke's "Toronto Trilogy" of novels, in which his 1960s Caribbean immigrant maid plays downstairs to a Jewish Forest Hill family's upstairs?

I'd wanted, at the start of it all, to film a bunch of teens skateboarding in Joe Fresh orange polo shirts (on sale, eight bucks a piece and my campaign's first purchase) and to post the video of my very own Orange Wave, but somebody, maybe it was Wendy, had worried what would happen if a kid took a fall, and it never happened.

So, instead, even better, we'd assembled our Bicycle Gang for a canvass and a bit of mischievous fun. It took a few blocks and my own tumble (too hard on the front brake with my one free hand) and then there we were, broadcasting our messages right out of the forties rather than our social-network-driven age.

"Hello, Forest Hill! This is Noah Richler, your NDP candidate. I'm here to tell you Stephen Harper is not your best friend!"

"I already voted," says an elderly woman angrily, "and not for you!"

"There's always a next time—"

A mother is chatting to her children.

"Only the NDP has a plan for a million child care spaces! Only the NDP is asking corporations to come to the table so that we can take care of the environment! This election, think about what's good for the next generation and vote NDP!"

And only the nannies are laughing.

"Vote NDP for a fifteen-dollar minimum wage—we'll set the example!"

It starts to hail.

"Avoid the long winter of our discontent! The Tories and the Liberals are the Tweedledum and Tweedledee of our political lives! There's only one vote for change, and that's for the NDP!"

The gang is cheered. Nothing if not a good day out.

. . .

With a week to go, I bring in Laverne, the woman from St. Vincent who comes once a week to help take care of the house. Laverne is formidable. She is my Supergun, my Devil's Brigade, my SCUD. At home, the television blaring, one hand on the iron, she bellows commands through her cellphone to an array of people who depend upon her advice: kids in her Caribbean-Canadian community not going to school. Single mothers. Wayward men. But also privileged whites needing to be told the obvious, needing to learn what to do with their insufferably spoiled child. "You tell him *no*," she hollers down the phone. "That's what you do." New Orleans after the hurricane is a morass of sinners; RAID on the bed is the solution to lice on Sarah's daughter's head. I realize, in the company of Laverne, how little I know of the communities I'm appealing to, communities I'm putting myself forward to represent—this in a good, immensely moving way. Whatever underpins the bridge of my attempts to reach out to families in less fortunate straits, whatever attempts to span the ford of race relations—my reading, my writing, my travels, my sensibility, my own encounters—Laverne shows to be scant. I watch as men and women recognize the Laverne in their lives and respect her. They smile, they laugh. Women hug her; a couple arguing in the corridor of their floor of community housing explains their predicament to her, in tears. "You go home now," Laverne says to the man. "You listen to her."

In the last week of the campaign, I'd been concentrating my canvassing efforts in the northwest and bringing Laverne with me. The Little Jamaicans hardly have a chance. On the narrow Oakwood sidewalk, a man tries to sidestep around Laverne, who has on the bright ruby cloth hat she wears for church. He almost gets past.

"*Hey*," she calls. "*You!*"

"Me?" says the man, meekly.

"Yes, *you*. You gonna vote?"

The man shrugs.

"*Yes*, you gonna vote! You gonna vote *NDP*."

The man shrugs again.

"How you gonna have change if you don't vote NDP? That's what you gonna do. What time you wan' me roun' here tomorrow? You gonna vote NDP. *I'm coming for you*."

"Okay," I say to Laverne, "we can go now."

But we don't. Further along the street another black man does a big half-loop to try to avoid Laverne, but she's blocking his path as a gunfighter might.

"You goin' to vote?" asks Laverne. It was more of a command than asking, really.

"No, I don' vote."

"Why? Why you don' vote? Are you stupid man? What you gonna say if you don' vote? You can' be complainin'."

"If I vot', I vot' *Liberal*."

"Why you gonna do that? Trudeau, he's too young, you can' see that? You gotta vot' *NDP*. You gotta vot' NDP an' den you see what they do."

"Because of hi' father I be here now."

"Are you crazy?! Hi' father *dead*. He not gonna help you now."

. . .

October 18 it is, and we have been clutching at good news where we can find it. The Assembly of First Nations has given the NDP's platform "full marks." *Canadian Art* has called Harper's record on the arts "abysmal" and the Liberals' "even worse," upholding NDP measures including the party's fifteen-dollar-a-day child care plans in its support of Mulcair. This almost makes up for the lack of mainstream media endorsements, and columns by *Toronto Star* writers—Haroon Siddiqui, in particular—that feel like betrayals, the editor emeritus having praised the NDP leader for all he has done, notably his brave stance on the niqab, and then backing the Liberals, the party with no position on Bill C-51. It's hard not to feel instructions from on high in the *Toronto Star* columnists' relentless unanimity. The NDP's botching of Mulcair's interview with *The Globe and Mail* columnist Jeffrey Simpson or (as reported by Jesse Brown on the website *Canadaland*) the latter's patrician snub of an actual conversation with the party leader, is also a sore point, but at this stage it hardly matters. We are at the Westin Harbour Castle for the final, E-Day rally. It is also the day of the Toronto Marathon, and maybe we can blame the thinning attendance on that unfortunate bit of timing rather than the fanfare and wan chorus that smacks of hubris now. *We're all in this together*, or at least we were in the beginning: in August, when we were leading in the polls and the city was mostly left to ourselves; or in the middle of it all, before the niqab sank us and we endured the ignominy of the Munk Debate. The gambit of Mulcair as statesman, the proven minister, has not worked. The "proven" is tired and not working and being rejected across the board, as evidenced by the weekend's choice bit of news—a photograph of the prime minister with Rob Ford and family that, rumour has it, led the Australian Lynton Crosby to quit the Conservatives' own disastrous campaign. Today, the force is not with us and the STOP HARPER signs the audience is holding for this last rally's reiteration of an old routine seem beside the point and look limp in supporters' hands. Now we are nearing the end, and across screens in the Westin Harbour Castle conference hall speaks a math of desperation and magical thinking. *The NDP won 103 seats in 2011 and came second in over 200 ridings! We only need 67 seats to form a government where the Liberals need to quadruple their seats.* The young Nova Scotian troubadour Joel Plaskett, a declared NDP supporter, plays "Hard Times Come Again No More," the Sam Roberts tune blares, *and now here he is . . . Canada's next prime minister . . . Tom Mulcair!!*

Mulcair steps up, the autocue rolls, but today the NDP leader ad-libs his lines.

"Pharmacare! Health care! Child care! . . . *MULCAIR!*"

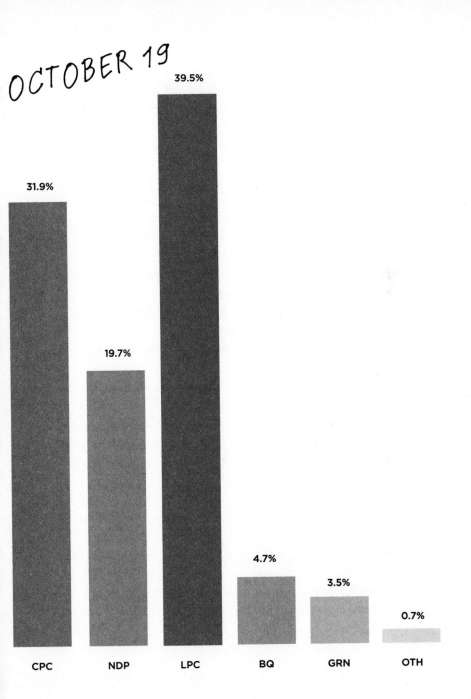

October 26, Toronto.

We were ten around the table in the private dining room in the back room of a glam bistro off King. Cash looked as spooked as an army veteran. MP for Davenport had been his dream job, he'd been good at it, and now it had slipped away. Scott seemed philosophical and curiously at ease. An MP from the GTA I'd not yet met was going on about how the Liberals had courted her and she'd said no. Chow was talking a lot, and kept referring to Toronto as the "epic centre" of something or other and I couldn't get beyond the malapropism to actually make head or tail of the point she was making. Nash, it was hard to know what to think of Nash, one of the first Dippers I'd met, who'd complained at the last of the rallies how it never got easier and she was still having to fight for her seat.

What makes the politician, I wondered? As the ten vented— as I was also doing (too much temper, too much outrage)—it was hard to believe, given only slightly different circumstances, that our lot might have been making decisions in government. Today, they—no, we, he corrected himself—appeared gormless, awkward and without the right stuff. We were losers. We didn't have it. How was it that so many had trusted us—had invested their time and money and labour in the chance this was not the case?

And yet this same bunch, minus the new contenders of which I was one, had done damn well in opposition. I was hard put to think of a party that had performed as admirably as the NDP since 2011, under the relentlessly hard-working, serious, committed leader who was Tom Mulcair.

Things I was told when I started:

This will end.

The days can be unbelievably long.

You will move through a carousel of moods.

Politics is everybody else believing they know better than you.

Politics is other people telling you what happened after the fact.

Some days, the last thing you will want to do is canvass, and then you'll go out and canvass because that's what will make you feel better.

Ninety percent of your vote will depend upon the performance of the leader in the last three weeks of the campaign.

The Liberals start slow and then come on strong.

If we'd said fifty thousand and not forty-six; if Zunera Ishaq had thought, "To hell with it, it's just a piece of clothing," or Mulcair had said, "I hear Canadians; if we need to borrow from our children, so be it." If Dan Gagnier had mattered more, if Dan Lauzon had mattered at all—

Politics is everybody else believing they know better than you.

Politics is other people telling you what happened after the fact.

If.

Then the media would be writing about the statesman Canada was always going to prefer, the mistake of Justin Trudeau, the disaster of Gerald Butts and the Liberal surfeit of pretty. The chattering classes would be saying celebrity did not wash here in Canada, place of order and good government, not the flashy. Oh no, not here. This, after all, was the country that did not find consensus in how to fight ISIL, Big Oil or a corrupt Senate, but in the outrage of the CPC denying Canadians their right to the census—their right to fill out a long form.

Maybe then, this same bunch now jockeying half-heartedly (there was really only one message to be had, and that was defeat) would have been in government—and capably, and with no more necessary qualification than Canadians having voted for them.

Ultimately, 1,792 was the number that mattered, and if just 40 people, give or take, had volunteered for each campaign, then 75,000 Canadians would actively have pitched in and done their bit for—well, love of country, and how could I think anything but good of that?

During E-Day preparations, I'd popped in to Wendy's seminar to thank some of those coming out to get out the vote and monitor the polls and vet the counting of the ballots. I'd recognized the French-Canadian teacher; the son of a friend; the daughter of another; the woman from Nova Scotia with the piano taking up more room than she did in her tiny apartment; the young Jewish woman who'd been at Bathurst most days; the bright young lesbian publishing students; the mushroom seller, a hipster in tweeds, who'd given the candidate a rough time on his very first day canvassing at the Wychwood farmers' market. It had struck me powerfully, even then, that I'd not met even a third of the people who had worked on the campaign—likely never would. But I was well aware, by then, they weren't in it for the candidate, they weren't in it for me, though maybe I'd given their hopes a face and a voice. I'd canvassed, I'd entertained, I'd sat with my orange bomber jacket on under the s'cach for Sukkot; I'd cycled and danced and clapped and led and imagined—and failed. But maybe somewhere along the line, I'd inspired someone else just as, at the beginning of this helter-skelter journey three years back, a couple of this group of ten had done for me.

I looked at the beaten, shell-shocked faces around the table and was proud.

CHAPTER SEVEN

WINNING

Bryan, the Liberal:

beclown (bɪˈklaʊn) verb. To make a complete idiot of oneself in public. To behave or speak in such a way, or to make
a comment or express an opinion that is so profoundly wit-
less, senseless and obtuse, that you have forever after defined
yourself as a person of comical value only. Never to be taken
seriously again. Of worth only as an object of ridicule and
derision.

*So, Canadians voted for Real Change. Now. Thanks for your
efforts, etc. Much appreciated. From a post-election vantage
point it all seems inevitable, but it was not. And—as is always
the case—"hope and hard work" had an assist from luck. Or a
terrible NDP campaign. Amounts to the same thing.*

On day one, when Mulcair refused to answer questions, I

knew they were in trouble. Man, they got off to a bad start—they put him up with Parliament Hill in the background, and played it safe. They thought they were the government in waiting.

The problem was, nobody else did, but that notion informed their shitty strategic thinking. Typical overreach. They believed their own spin, and that's always deadly. Deadly.

Case in point? The ads Richler put out—you know, the Dipper who ran in St. Paul's against Bennett. The first one was true to Dipper sensibilities, and the "they haven't had a new idea since we all had 8-tracks in our cars" tradition. And it was funny, too. I mean the Dippers are many things, but never funny. You can still watch it online, and you should.

The second ad is more interesting, though. You probably have not seen it and you can't watch it online.

Remember the two-men-by-the-lake thing that Mansbridge did with former PM Harper? He did a rip on that, kicked SH in the ass and took his place in the chair. The CBC complained and—can you believe it—the wise men in Orange caved and made their candidate take it down. And in doing so, the genius in Ottawa—should be my confrère—beclowned himself. Beclowned himself on the altar of Mansbridge!

They pulled the ads to avoid being shamed for their bad "strategic" decisions, and—I'm sure this played a part—they were worried Richler might turn his true Orange message and his last name into a leadership run. He was singing from the hymnbook, but not the new one HQ had written.

What a snapshot of an NDP campaign that could not figure out what they were selling! And if they don't know who they are, voters certainly couldn't—and they didn't.

We took all of the oxygen they were counting on. Having JT and sunny ways to contrast against at least four Mulcair personae—the prime ministerial question dodger, the angry guy,

*the crazy smiley-faced hyper child, the delusional prosecutor—
made it easy. They melted away.*

*Remember this, my friend. When your opponents have
poured gasoline on themselves and are about to light a match,
the most savage thing you can do is simply to watch.*

. . .

Megan Leslie fell, and in no time all of the Atlantic provinces
were coloured red. The tsunami had come and, reaching Quebec,
was leaving just a few isolated outcrops of blue and orange, Ruth
Ellen Brosseau one of the few NDP members left standing.
Politics is other people telling you what happened after the fact,
though Megan had not needed hindsight to get it right.

As Quebec turned, it occurred to me just how little of the
electoral conversation had been about the Sherbrooke
Declaration; how ineffective the sop, were it that, had been to
the province's so-called soft nationalists.

"This is bad," said Sarah.

Our constituencies were failing us, or we'd failed them, but
we'd seen it coming—enough to make sure there was a deejay,
a popcorn machine, boxes of pizza and an open bar, and to make
sure that a couple of other NDP candidates sure to lose were
able to feel good by being in the room with us, one of them with
the campaign management team that was his mother and aunt.
But, still, we'd not imagined this would happen. Maybe Janet
had—drinking, uncharacteristically, a second glass of red wine.

Not yet nine, I stepped outside to call Carolyn Bennett and
congratulate her. That's what a candidate does, no, or do we just
see national leaders do that on TV?

Not since the red of the British Empire had a map looked
quite like this.

By the time the red reached Toronto, I was thinking of Germany's 7-1 World Cup rout of Brazil. *This is losing.*

. . .

All results have causes. Nothing is ever "random."

It had been an election of participation; there was no denying it.

Four million new voters, and 8,224 among the approximately 77,000 eligible voters of Toronto—St. Paul's alone. (*Answer:* if 90 percent of your vote depends upon the performance of the leader in the last three weeks of the campaign and Mulcair won 10.9 percent fewer votes than Jack Layton, then a 7.91 percent drop of the Toronto—St. Paul's NDP vote—14.7 percent versus 22.6 in 2011—is actually a 1.9 percent improvement. Stats, eh?)

"I don't know where he found them," said Cash. "They weren't on our lists."

We were chatting over espresso, Cash and I, a few days after the devastation. There's a slightly out-of-body sensation to being walloped as we had been, and the two of us were like a couple of rehab vets languishing in the anonymity of a city knowing nothing of our pain.

We talked futures, the TPP, the arts.

"They made the better offer," Cash said.

. . .

Years before, writing about the Bilcon environmental dispute, I'd been racing about the Digby Neck trying to find someone to verify a quote reported to me second-hand. The aggregate company from New Jersey had been buying up land along the Neck with a view to quarrying the territory's basalt for American roads, and one of the company's enablers was the principal of a local high school, the student base of which—along with local resources and jobs and opportunities—was diminishing. The dispute was bitter and extensive and I'd been told the frustrated principal had scoffed at the project's naysayers and its dubious possibilities of work, saying the region "was full of idiots and old people." Driving along the 217, fuming at the insult of it all, this shit selling out the territory so that he could dine with the Big Boys, I suddenly realized how much a novelist would have enjoyed the man. *Loved* him. As a character, I mean. The novelist would have inhabited him, enjoyment the ticket if he were to truly understand someone wanting to leave the backwater and the idiots and old people behind him. I started laughing—never did find the confirming quote—because I realized, too, that I'd never be able to write such a rogue. My journalist's outrage and indignation would be useless to the task and would only have stood in the way of that enjoyment. The journalist takes things too personally, sees the world in the hopelessly limited terms of his own arrogant ego, imagining, necessarily, he knows better.

The election, I also took far too personally—as if not just the 75,852 eligible voters of Toronto—St. Paul's, but the 6.9 million Liberal voters who turned out on October 19 had rejected me. I felt retired. Done. Didn't think I'd even write anymore.

I wished that I'd been capable of more of that enjoyment and less outrage: at the sanctioning of Liberal friends revelling in the new government; at CBC presenters falling over themselves to bask in the reflected glory of the new prime minister; at the lingering ineptitude of the party I had chosen; at the curious hatred the mere fact of the NDP at times inspired; at Trudeau's Liberals putting into place so much of the platform that had been the NDP's to offer.

The last turn of events bothered me the most. The NDP had lost not only seats—not only the diversity that was theirs, before, to say, "We are you, Canada"—but the opportunity of a lifetime to introduce so many reversals, more than changes, ludicrously easy to effect: reintroducing the long-form census; meeting with the premiers; travelling to COP21, the twenty-first United Nations Climate Change Conference, with the premiers but also critics (where Trudeau, damn it, became the statesman Canada saw beside Merkel); introducing better benefits, child care and affordable housing. There would be credit for all this, but only once, and it would help to shore up the Liberal–CPC dance for another decade.

. . .

It was the lesson of the BSS morning writ large: politics—or at least good behaviour in politics—is about putting good ideas into the agora for the country at large to discuss. (Get back to writing, says Sarah.) To want the credit for oneself, or for one's party—well, that was not about introducing an argument or wanting to help and contribute to one's country. No, that was about being *a politician*. The *International New York Times* called to ask for a piece about the election and I flew the white flag. It wasn't hard. Then I called Chrystia Freeland and said I had good people working for me—Young Ethan, Josh—who had proven themselves deserving. Would she consider them?

"That's really good of you," said Freeland, "that the first thing you'd do is try and help your people find work."

But she didn't call back: they were Dippers looking for a job.

. . .

Sarah, the spouse:

Do I regret the adventure? Not one bit. We support one another in all we do, and when I finally came around to the idea of him tossing his hat into the political arena, then I was with him 100 percent. I was proud of him to be honest. Noah was great at connecting with people, if not winning their vote, and actively engaged with his constituents in conversation and debate. Yes, there were some tough moments, but they were moments we shared, not ones I felt alone in. And I have to say it was an awful lot of fun—but, as I feared, campaigning was all consuming and a true emotional roller coaster of a time. I really, really hope he never does it again. But if there's one thing I've learned: never say never.

. . .

The office was packed away. The computers and the telephones were unplugged, the polls behind what had been Phil's desk pulled down, the posters of Tom rolled up and the green folders and maps and data sheets packed into boxes. Julian had sent an email round to ask if anyone had a garage big enough to store 1,200 signs and I asked, "What for?"

"So we don't have to pay for them again."

"But they say 'Tom Mulcair's NDP' in the top right hand corner."

"You never heard of stickers?"

Said Sarah: "I think it's okay to show you Pratt's video now. We didn't want to before, because we knew you'd lose your shit."

She swiped at her iPad and opened up Facebook and then the NDP Canada page and brought up a campaign video in which Pratt—wearing sunglasses, the paunch pushing the buttons of his untucked short-sleeved grey shirt—plays the swaggering tough guy. The House of Commons is behind him and he is walking across the green summer lawn of Parliament Hill and towards the camera, swinging his arms and then thrusting the back of his hand, four fingers splayed, as he makes the case for Tom Mulcair, "a guy who quit as government minister on a position of principle, because he wouldn't stand by and let the government turn a provincial park into a bunch of condos, a guy who was courted by both the federal Liberals and the Conservatives but, instead, decided to run for the NDP at a time when we were *the fourth party in a province where we had never won*—because Tom Mulcair is a guy who stands up for what he believes in."

"Beyond belief," said Doug.

"Are you Facebook friends with Pratt?" asked Sarah.

"I don't know," I said. "Maybe."

"Take a look at this from the man who accused you of 'revenge porn.'"

Then Sarah pulled up the NDP director of organization's Facebook page and clicked on photographs of Pratt giving the finger to whoever was taking the picture of him alone or with party staffers or doing the same in older shots from university days; then others of him boozing stupidly and a couple of him appearing to be cuffed by a police officer. On Twitter, Pratt had posted a picture of a gun aimed at an unfortunate arachnid with the caption, "How to kill a spider."

Now it was my turn: "Wow," I said.

Really. "Wow" was all I could say. I was laughing but also reeling from the display of an operative fancying himself a performer in *House of Cards*. What drives these people, I asked myself? I'd had an early impression of their kind at the Scotiabank Giller Prize years before, when I'd seen the provincial Liberal Party operative with the red bow tie and unpleasant mug look furtive as he swiped the card-key and entered the hotel room just down the corridor. Like a drug deal was going down; like he'd *wanted* to look like a thief, or maybe just a backroom big shot in his politician's *Boys' Own* world—he'd leave his hard-working wife soon enough. How is it, I wondered, that a TV aesthetic of bullish behind-the-scenes power is so influential that folk signing up to further democracy and supposedly "open" practices make it their profession to hoodwink the public? At what point does a spin doctor decide, "The public is a meal ticket and an impediment, not a cause—the path to office is for me to wield power *secretly*"? At what point does the political strategist or field director conclude, "Honesty is not the path; the best way to serve the public is to *manipulate* it, sell them something"? Is James Carville, Lynton Crosby, Alastair Campbell or Kevin Spacey to blame?

. . .

Ideas for an NDP government to pursue:
    A commons law
    An education act
    Aboriginal studies as a mandatory high school matriculation requirement
    Free Internet access
    A minister for old people
    Pharmacare

. . .

More radical ideas for an NDP government to pursue:
    The pursuit and representation not of unions, but of *disorganized* labour
    A living wage
    Compulsory national service in communities, NGOs and the military, with the possibility of paying for university studies as one of its benefits

The creation of a permanent Canadian Peace Operations Regiment

The creation of a University of Peace Studies

Saying Canada is a soft power and an honest broker and the habit doesn't have to be just military: saying that we are going to be the party that takes labour laws it has taken two centuries to arrive at and push them at the supranational level, fighting monopolies and cartels and corporations evading these laws

. . .

Ideas that didn't matter:

Bill C-51

Bill C-24

The politician with experience

. . .

Ideas that won't happen:

The House of Commons as a travelling show, rotating in major cities around the country for one of each year's sessions

Rebuilding the Houses of Parliament as three concentric rings: the 338 MPs around the first (and the Speaker seated in the middle); Elders, whether Senators or Native, around the second; and the people looking in from the third

Paying residents of northern communities and remote places a decent living wage for simply being where they are, because the truth of Canada is that we're still a country colonizing itself and we might as well 'fess up to the fact and make a virtue of it

. . .

"You know they were ready to go through the whole heroin thing if the Facebook stuff didn't work," said Doug.

"That's why I got it out of the way."

"Nobody would have remembered," said Doug.

Forgetting counts for a lot in politics. We forget about others and the part we ourselves have played to appoint some above the rest. How many Canadians were forgetting their role in ten years of a Canada that was so suddenly being wiped from the chalkboard of our experience?

It was astonishing how instantly forgettable Harper had been—how the "legacy" (that's how politicians speak) had no substance. The oil and gas lobby was responding to Alberta NDP premier Rachel Notley and her carbon tax plans; Kellie Leitch, on the brink of tears, would distance herself from the "snitch line" she and Alexander had proposed; and Tony Clement, the minister who'd seen to the execution of the long-form census, would disassociate himself from the man who'd been his master. "I think I'd have done it differently, looking back on it," said Clement, far from the only Conservative to build a makeshift sod hut in the chasm left by the resigned leader not even his own party seemed to like anymore. "A respectful tone and civil tone and working across the floor with other parties," said the interim CPC leader Rona Ambrose, "is something our members would welcome, that our caucus would welcome, and that Canadians would welcome as well."

It was as if all the Conservative nastiness and hatred and alienation of big chunks of the franchise, the blockading of the media and the vilification of opponents, the plans for a snitch line had never happened—not even in CPC minds. The errant Senate, Omar Khadr: so much of the last ten years already belonged to another time.

It was like—it was like *waking up from a bad dream.*

. . .

This will end. Time passed and I was good for not much. Heller
was emailing, still looking for a place to store our campaign's
eleven-hundred-plus signs. He'd already moved on to next time.
Then, on November 4, Phil called. He mentioned that Stephen
LeDrew and Ann Rohmer, the hosts of CP24's *Live at Noon*,
were wondering if I'd join former Liberal MPP George
Smitherman and John Capobianco, the CPC candidate who'd
lost in the 2006 federal election to the then Liberal leader,
Michael Ignatieff, in the Etobicoke—Lakeshore riding, to provide commentary and debate on the three hours of Justin Trudeau
and the Liberal cabinet's swearing-in at Rideau Hall.

"No cab fare," said Phil.

"Sure, I'll do it," I said.

I liked Phil, knew I would miss him and wanted to speak
for the party without Ottawa on my back. I put on my orange
Fluevogs and a blue summer sports jacket and jeans, and
headed down to the old CHUM-City building at Queen and
John. Smitherman was himself and domineering and pushing
Liberal credit for everything, Capobianco was affable, Ann
Rohmer a little tense and LeDrew droll and a good host. As
Trudeau and his cortège of ministers-in-waiting slowly
walked past cheering onlookers to Rideau Hall, I pointed out
that the father–son PM example, a first in Canadian history,
had a precedent with William Pitt the Elder and Pitt the
Younger, the latter twenty years Justin Trudeau's junior, in
early-nineteenth-century Britain. Who would care about
that? Smitherman muttered. Who cares about history? I
answered. The throng of smiling Liberals continued their
sunny walk and I wondered if Sophie Grégoire-Trudeau was
pissed off that Mélanie Joly, soon to be appointed minister of

heritage, was also wearing a white autumn coat—but this was Canadian politics, not the Academy Awards, and I kept the musing to myself. Smitherman feigned astonishment that former Toronto police chief Bill Blair, the "star" Liberal candidate who had defeated the incumbent NDP MP Dan Harris in Scarborough—Southwest, was not to be seen in the ebullient gang.

"Hold on," I said, "I think I see Blair being kettled at the back!"

"I should point out that the views you are hearing are those of the contributors and not the network," said Rohmer.

The cabinet-in-waiting entered the Rideau Hall ballroom, Phil Richards's portrait of the Queen hanging where there used to be Jean-Paul Lemieux's *Charlottetown Revisited.*

"I have to say, as a Republican, that I miss the Jean-Paul Lemieux that was there before this portrait of the Queen."

"The views you are hearing are those of the contributors and not the network," said Rohmer.

Capobianco leaned my way and whispered, "I've been doing this show for years and that's the first time I've heard her say that—and twice. Well done."

I was aware of a small electric current of pleasure running though my veins. The Liberals, I pointed out, had not appointed a single African-Canadian to cabinet, so that a generations-old loyalty had been "abjectly denied." I was enjoying putting the boot in. And I was hoping that someone in Little Jamaica was listening. Smitherman excused himself and, for the first time since October 19, I thought, *I could do this again.* I was almost ashamed. I was having a good time.

. . .

Drove home from Montreal and sent a postcard:

November 2, 2015

Officer H.

This may be a first for you, but I wanted to thank you for ticketing me for speeding (offence 19087662). Not that I want to part with the money, or lose the points, or was travelling much faster than the average car, but in truth I was obviously depressed, and a bit angry (I'd run for the NDP and you know what happened there) and I was probably too stressed to have been responsibly behind the wheel. No personal mood warrants putting anyone's life in danger. Once again—

Thank you!

Noah Richler

Up, down, up, down.

You move through a carousel of moods and get stuck in some.

. . .

"Dreamed I was in bed with Trudeau last night," I told Sarah.

"Oh?" says Sarah. "Tell me more."

"No hanky-panky, we were fully clothed, just he and I having a little pillow talk. I called out to you to make coffee—you were in the kitchen—but you went to bed in one of the girls' rooms and so I told him to go to the kitchen and make a coffee himself. When I came down, the espresso machine was all in bits on the table. He'd taken it apart and was pouring dirty water through the grinder."

"He's making a mess of your mornings, that's what your dream is saying."

. . .

London, England, 1997. I have been in psychotherapy for a year, and am in the session I did not yet realize would be my last.

"Your dreams used to be so interesting," she says.

. . .

Squash, again, and Doug and I are Statler and Waldorf back on the *Muppet Show* balcony, dreaming up slogans in advance of the next time around: "We're Still Here," "We're Watching You," "Community Is Not Big Business." Behind the desk of the Hart House gym are three students in red gym T-shirts. One of them takes my pass without looking my way. Doug asks for a squash ball, we've forgotten ours, and the young woman bouncing on a Pilates ball hands it to him. She's not looking our way either.

"They're Trudeau's generation, not ours," says Doug.

"We had our time," I say.

"What about party leader?"

"Oh come on, I'm white, fifty-five, and male."

"So?"

"So maybe I can help the right person."

We wait for the third student to press the buzzer to let us in to the locker room, which she almost manages to do without looking our way. Except that when she hands me a towel she has to lift her gaze to see if I have taken it.

"Hey," she says. "You were the NDP candidate in my riding. I voted for you!"

"Thanks," I say sheepishly.

"Great campaign. Loved your videos."

"We did our best," I say. "And this fella, he got me into it."

She smiles.

"Will you run again?"

ACKNOWLEDGMENTS

I owe a big, first debt of gratitude to Scott Sellers for seeking me out and pressing all the buttons to make *The Candidate* happen, and pushing it out so ably in the marketplace. Thanks, as well, to Kristin Cochrane, my editor Jordan Ginsberg, designer Scott Richardson, and to Susan Burns and Tara Tovell, also on the Doubleday Canada team. Jonathan Rotsztain and Marc de Mouy were as generous with their graphics and photographs during the writing of this book as they were during the campaign; and thank you Doug Bell, Ralph Benmergui, Sean Caragata, Michael Geist, Julian Porter, Siobhan Roberts and Shawn Van Sluys for giving the manuscript or portions of it an early read and subsequent advice, any errors of course my own. Thanks, too, to Philip Carter, James Cudmore, Elizabeth Glor-Bell, Wendy Hughes, Julian Heller, Bryan Leblanc, Penny Marno, Tom Mulcair, Janet Solberg and Peter Sussman for providing monologues in good faith to a book I would not allow them to read in advance. I must also thank Daryn Caister, Kevin Farmer, Shannon Litzenberger, Christian Peterson, S., Erinn Somerville and several of the staff at Elections Canada, all of whom helped with my researches in various ways.

Thank you to the staff, campaign and E-Day volunteers, and hosts and donors not just of my own run—but also to the impassioned, crazy lot across the spectrum and the country—that give in all sorts of ways when elections come around, and to Canadians for being interested, in 2015, in record numbers. There'd have been no candidates without you.

And, above all, thank you, Sarah.

INDEX

Abdulhamid, Waleed, 99, 289
Adams, Eve, 41–42, 45, 101, 132, 158
advertising. *See also* video advertisements
    lack of NDP, 268–69
    by Liberals, 268
    quality of printed material, 284, 285
    signs, 259, 260–61, 269, 277, 278, 286, 295,
        299–301
    video launch, 211–12
    videos, 293, 307–10, 312–13
Afghan Luke (film), 194
Akin, David, 214
Alexander, Chris, 177, 315
    in NR's imagined scenario, 3, 5
    snitch line announcement, 282, 361
    and Syrian refugee issue, 174–75
Alexie, Robert Arthur, 38
Amarshi, Hussain, 222
Ambrose, Rona, 361
Amed, Daniyal Ulysses, 161
American Sarah, 132–33, 302, 303, 304
Anderson, Nichole, 115–19, 175
Andrew-Gee, Andrew, 249
Angus, Charlie, 150
Arias, Sandra, 294
Arts Forum, 317–18
Ashley, Bernard Ross, 60
Ashton, Niki
    in NR's imagined scenario, 252
Atwood, Margaret, 20–21
Auf der Maur, Nick, 69

Barton, Rosemary
    and Alexander refugee interview, 174
    in NR's imagined scenarios, 5, 163, 164
Bateman, Joyce, 315

Beaverton (online magazine), 322
Bell, Doug, 119, 200, 201, 213, 241, 361
    advice to NR, 54–55, 76, 155, 159
    canvassing with NR, 291
    donation to NR, 100
    and escalator video launch, 214
    friendship with NR, 21–23
    and making of videos, 192, 194, 196, 202, 212
    and Mansbridge-Harper video, 319, 330
    in mock Shakespearean play, 262–64
    pub nights, 330–31
    and snitch line ad, 283
    squash playing with NR, 365
    and video creation, 314
    and video release, 331
Bennett, Carolyn, 96, 182, 286
    abilities of, 53
    advertising material, 284, 285
    all-candidates debate, 292–93
    appearance in riding, 332–33
    assessing as opponent, 112
    and Bill C-51, 188, 221, 315
    at Bishop Strachan debate, 335–36, 337
    Christmas truce chat, 187
    climate and democracy debate, 265, 266
    economy issues, 172–73
    financial resources, 114
    and Holy Temple debate, 156, 157, 158, 159
    and lawn signs, 278, 299–301
    length of incumbency, 36
    in mock Shakespearean play, 262–64
    NR calls to congratulate, 353
    NR meets canvassing, 133–34
    in NR's imagined scenario, 5–6
    as NR target, 124
    parliament voting record, 52

369 —

reputation in Toronto—St. Paul's, 40
as subject of video advertisement, 195
success in riding, 296
suitability of NR as opponent of, 38
video about, 215
Bergeron, Alain, 116, 118
Berthiaume, Lee, 248
Bicycle Gang, 340–41
Bielby, Justice Myra, 9
Bilcon, 67, 154, 155, 354
Bill C-51, 135, 293, 360
Bennett's vote on, 188
controversy over, 19–20
and Galati, 62
Liberal position on, 45, 51, 52, 101, 130,
158, 221, 297, 343
NDP position on, 271
NR on, 60
as topic for video ad, 195, 211, 221, 310,
314, 315, 317
as topic in Munk Debate, 227
Blair, Bill, 45, 101, 158, 363
Bloc Québécois, 14
Blum, Jack, 318–19
Borg, Charmaine, 33
Boutilier, Alex, 56, 62, 87
Brewster, Murray, 192
Brison, Scott, 10
Broadbent, Ed, 171
Brosseau, Ruth Ellen, 33, 192, 353
Brown, Jesse, 343
Bryan (Liberal), 35152
Bryant, Michael, 160
Burgener, Matt Masters, 313
Burt, Joanna, 289, 318
Butts, Gerald, 119, 348
in NR's imagined scenario, 251

Cameron, David, 283
Campbell, Torquil, 249
Canadaland (website), 343
Canadian Broadcasting Corporation
issue about NR video material, 320–29

Canadian Security Intelligence Service, 19
Capobianco, John, 362
Caragata, Sean, 61, 112, 153, 154, 188, 248
Carney, Mark, 147
Carter, Jimmy, 164
Carter, Phil, 104, 107, 202, 203, 275
advice to NR, 109, 150
dislike of social media, 334
NR affection for, 362
NR desire to reassure, 149
opinion on NDP budget policy, 170–72
position in campaign office, 108
thoughts on co-managing NR
campaign, 105–6
and video advertising, 209
and video withdrawal, 334–35
Carver, Raymond, 297–98
Cash, Andrew, 62, 85, 270
at arts and culture rally, 290
as immigration critic, 178, 179
at Labour Day parade, 182
at Mihvec fundraiser, 87, 89, 90
and music and protest evening, 249
in NR imagined scenario, 346
post-election, 354
Ready for Change rally, 150, 151
Catch-22 (Heller), 312
Charlie Hebdo attack, 18
"Checkers, Fred," 38, 191
Children of the Broken Treaty (Angus), 150
Chow, Olivia, 28, 31, 37, 38, 132, 220, 293
in NR imagined scenario, 346
Cirillo, Nathan, 17, 20
Clarke, Austin, 340
Clement, Gary, 148, 249
Clement, Tony, 361
Clinton, Bill, 164
coalition, 266, 270
Cole, Susan, 134–35
Collett, Jason, 87
Cooke, Michael, 237
in NR's imagined scenario, 4
Coyne, Andrew, 41, 214

INDEX

and CBC threat to sue, 320–29
concerns about his past, 16
concerns about Mulcair, 280
concerns about racial diversity, 40–41
desire for arts and sports policy, 218, 220, 222–24
desire to run in West Nova, 24, 25, 27–28, 30–31, 33
dream about J. Trudeau, 364
early political activities and explorations, 11–12, 14–16, 69–70
education, 72–73
and escalator video, 202
fundraising efforts, 85–93, 96–97
imagined scenarios, 4–5, 163–64
kills Bennett video, 201
Labour Day parade, 181–82
Lifeline Syria demonstration, 178–81
loss of iPhone, 287–88
and media, 165, 228–35, 236–43, 244, 248–50, 258–59, 261
meeting with Heller, 41–43
and niqab issue, 258
nomination bid approved, 59
nomination meeting, 98–102
observations on Munk Debate, 226–27
opinion of media, 75
opinion of NDP, 182–83
opinion of politics, 75
personnel in campaign office of, 110–11
on possible Liberal-NDP coalition, 266
preferred portfolio, 116
psychotherapy experience, 95–96
Quebec postings controversy, 228–34
Rathnelly meet and greet, 175
Ready for Change rally, 150–52
sense of humour, 103
and S. Lewis, 79–82
and social media posts, 35, 68, 188–89, 191, 214, 225, 228–34, 243, 248–49
stock option tax credit issue, 247
support for Mulcair, 173, 247
thoughts on J. Trudeau, 185–86

and *Toronto Star* interview, 50–57, 62, 65
and J. Trudeau escalator ad, 166–68
and vetting process, 26, 29–30, 34–35, 37, 38, 44, 49–50
and video advertisements, 183–84, 187–88, 192, 194–97, 201–2, 208–11, 320–29
on voters' choice of political parties, 94–95
Roberts, Sam, 151, 296
Rogers, Brian MacLeod, 324
Rohmer, Ann, 362
Ronson, Jon, 249
Roscoe, Cookie, 285, 286
Rose, Richard, 318
Rotsztain, Jonathan, 112, 197, 209, 283
Run Over: A Boy, His Mother and an Accident (Bell), 21

Sankofa bar, 332
    pub night, 333
Satz, Michael, 132
Saul, John Ralston, 20
Sauvé, Jeanne, 72
Scheinert, Josh, 153–55, 159, 356
Schwartz, Gerald, 198, 201
Scott, Craig, 10, 16, 25, 27, 28, 36–37, 62
    and NR nomination meeting, 100, 153
    background, 15
    meets with NR, 14–16
    in NR imagined scenario, 346
Selley, Chris, 249
Sheikh, Nazneen, 207
Sherman, Barry, 113
Shook, Michelle, 90
Shopping for Votes (Delacourt), 111–12
Siddiqui, Haroon, 343
Simpson, Jeffrey, 343
Singh, Jagmeet, 313
Sitsabaiesan, Rathika, 203
Smith, George, 218
Smith, Joanna, 236, 237–38, 244
Smitherman, George, 362, 363
snitch line issue, 282–83
social media